Hellenic Studies 96

A Monument More Lasting
than Bronze

Recent Titles in the Hellenic Studies Series

chs.harvard.edu/publications

A MONUMENT MORE LASTING
THAN BRONZE

CLASSICS IN THE UNIVERSITY OF MALAWI, 1982–2019

Edited by
Paul McKechnie, Steve Nyamilandu,
and Samson Kambalu

CENTER FOR HELLENIC STUDIES
Trustees for Harvard University
Washington, DC
Distributed by Harvard University Press
Cambridge, Massachusetts, and London, England
2024

A Monument More Lasting than Bronze: Classics in the University of Malawi, 1982–2019
    Edited by Paul McKechnie, Steve Nyamilandu, and Samson Kambalu
Copyright © 2024 Center for Hellenic Studies, Trustees for Harvard University
All Rights Reserved.
Published by Center for Hellenic Studies, Trustees for Harvard University,
    Washington, D.C.
Distributed by Harvard University Press, Cambridge, Massachusetts
    and London, England
Printed by Gasch Printing, Odenton, MD
Cover Design: Joni Godlove
Production: Kristin Murphy Romano

ISBN: 978-0-674-27850-9

Library of Congress Control Number (LCCN): 2023933679

Contents

Contents

Preface

PAUL MCKECHNIE, STEVE NYAMILANDU, AND SAMSON KAMBALU

SOMETHING HAS BEEN HAPPENING in Africa. The title of this book may seem to be missing a question mark: will the monument last? Incredulity has greeted the classical part of it in some places, as Cybelle Greenlaw narrates in her chapter of this book; and even in Africa, our educational endeavors may be associated with music in the public mind.

Early in the 1980s, Hastings Kamuzu Banda, as Life President of the Republic of Malawi, mandated the teaching of Classics in the University of Malawi, having first built a boarding school in his home village—a showpiece to his own people and to the world of foreigners—a school where Latin and Greek became compulsory studies for every student. Classics is still taught in both institutions.

Paul McKechnie taught Latin and Greek at Kamuzu Academy, as Head of the Classics Department, from 1987 to 1991. Steve Nyamilandu heads the Classics Department at Chancellor College, University of Malawi. Samson Kambalu, an Oxford-based artist, Fellow of Magdalen College and Professor in Fine Art at Ruskin, grew up in Malawi and attended Kamuzu Academy from 1989 to 1995.

In this book, we editors, and the other authors, disclaim any intention of constructing a connected narrative. This is not an institutional history of a small unit in Chancellor College, University of Malawi. The stakes in a simple departmental history would not be so high. We do not deny, however, that (in part) our book is an examination—to add to the many others which exist—of what classical studies are for.

The Introduction lists us and explains the kinds of belonging which bind us to Malawi and the University of Malawi. We are not uninvolved; but we write *sine ira et studio*. This book is offered as a critical reflection on the past and the present.

We combine a fragmented narrative with insights and analysis. The interface between political power and the world of learning created Classics at Chancellor College, and made it inescapably a naughty department—in the minds of some—as it is to this day. It has played a bit part, at most, in the drama of the University of Malawi as a place of radical political dissent. We reflect on the pedagogical mision of Classics: on educational structures, on the experience of teaching and learning, and on the everyday reality of an African university across the past forty years. Most of the names in this book are real, though one or two have been changed to protect the innocent.

We wish to thank Harvard University Press for permission to reprint the Loeb edition text of Horace *Odes* 3.30, and Niall Rudd's translation. We wish to thank Prof. Samson Sajidu, sometime-acting Principal of Chancellor College, and now (2023) Vice-Chancellor of the University of Malawi. We wish to thank Dr. Robin Darwall-Smith, Archivist of University College Oxford, for his advice about the statue of Queen Anne. We wish to thank Prof. Klaus Fiedler of Mzuzu University for Kachere publications—an invaluable collection of specialised writing on Malawian history and culture. We wish to thank Father Claude Boucher of Mua Mission in Dedza for his indispensable research and cataloguing of *Gule Wamkulu*. We wish to thank Susan Kambalu for copyediting and advice, and Francis Mulauzi, Marcus Beale, and Dr. Blackwell Manda for photographs. Other thanks are embedded in the chapters concerned.

Introduction
Monument and Symbol

PAUL MCKECHNIE[1]

The Changeable Power of Monuments

QUEEN ANNE STANDS OVER the front gate of University College, Oxford, and seems to shake her fist in defiance of her enemies—above all, Louis XIV, *le roi soleil.*

Figure 1. Statue of Queen Anne (1709), University College, Oxford.
Photograph by Samson Kambalu.

[1] With contributions from Steve Nyamilandu and Samson Kambalu.

Figure 2. Statue of Cecil Rhodes (1911), Rhodes Building, Oriel College, Oxford. Photograph by Samson Kambalu.

There is no doubt that the absence now of the sceptre she held in her right hand in early photographs impacts the gestalt effect. The statue has been there since 1709, the year when victory at Malplaquet cost the British and their Savoyard allies 20,000 casualties.

How to construe her pose now? Aggression? Petulance?

This patriotic work today fails—I hesitate to use that word—to attract significant notice. In 2021, when I corresponded with the Archivist of University College, Dr. Robin Darwall-Smith, about an image to reproduce in this book, he told me that "we don't have a 'good' image of Anne to share with you."

The inference is inescapable: as loud as Queen and College shout their dynamism and equivocal triumph from 1709, the symbol they created has lost its power.

We speak the language of symbols, but falteringly. When people from the past address us, we may fail to comprehend—or we may understand them all too well.

So with the iconography of Cecil Rhodes. A short way along the same street—High Street—stands the 1911 Rhodes Building: its frontage a hymn in stone, in praise of Oriel College's own Cecil Rhodes (who matriculated in 1873). He stands between serpentine columns on a pedestal inscribed with his name, RHODES; in his hand, a slouch hat, suited to the Prime Minister of the Cape Colony.

Figure 3. Rhodes Building, Oriel College, Oxford. Marcus Beale Architects.
Photograph by Marcus Peel, reproduced by permission.

This powerful monument puts Queen Anne even further into the shade. The Rhodes Building enunciates an early twentieth-century arrogance of empire—and if that were not enough, Oxford is also home to the Rhodes Trust and Rhodes House: the heart of the structure Rhodes created to deploy his wealth to support Oxford students from around the world. The gains—first realized from the De Beers company and Rhodes's near-monopoly in diamond mining and trading—are still, a century later, channeling African wealth into Oxford.

On 9 March 2015, in Cape Town, South Africa, Chumani Maxwele[2]

> travelled by minibus taxi out to Khayelitsha, picked up one of the buckets of shit that sat reeking on the kerbside, and brought it back to the campus of the University of Cape Town (UCT), where, in 2011, he had gained a scholarship to study political science. He took it to a bronze statue of the 19th-century British colonialist Cecil John Rhodes that held pride of place on campus, just downhill from the convoca-tion hall. Rhodes had been one of the main architects of South Africa's segregation. "Where are our heroes and ancestors?" Maxwele shouted to a gathering, curious crowd.

[2] Fairbanks 2015.

Figure 4. Statue of Cecil Rhodes removed at University of Cape Town, 9 April 2015.
Photograph by Tony Carr. Creative Commons License: CC-BY SA 2.0.

Then he opened the bucket and hurled its contents into Rhodes's face.

Maxwele's action caused "Rhodes Must Fall" to gel as a protest movement—one which blossomed across South Africa through the rest of 2015 and beyond. The statue at UCT was removed on 9 April. Judicious editorializing from Andrew Harding on the BBC followed:[3]

> Now, unsurprisingly, we are seeing anger growing. Some will argue that it is dangerous, misguided, fuelled by new populist firebrands. But many, for better or worse, will take a different lesson from what Mr Maxwele did with that statue: that patience has its place, but sometimes anger is necessary. Even constructive.

In 2020, responding to the echo (heard in Oxford since 2016) of Rhodes Must Fall, the Governing Body of Oriel issued a statement expressing their wish to remove the statue of Rhodes and the plaque in King Edward Street marking where Rhodes used to live.[4] But that statement was countermanded eleven months later, in May 2021, by a new statement referring to "... regulatory and financial challenges, including the expected time frame for removal, which could run into years with no certainty of outcome, together with the total cost

---

[3] Harding 2015.
[4] Oriel College 2020.

of removal."[5] At the time of writing this, Oriel means to keep its Rhodes monument—while expressing an intention to devote additional resources to "educational equality, diversity and inclusion."[6] It remains unknown whether, in the future, this "intention" will prove to be firmer than the "wish" the College had in 2020 to remove the statue.

In a 2016 article, Amit Chaudhuri recalled his 1990 impression of the Rhodes statue at Oriel as "night watchman-like" and "unobtrusively, and insidiously, guarding an always-shut door below him."[7] However, following 9/11 and the bombings in London of 7 July 2005, he argues, there was a "closing of the ranks by the rich in Britain," so that

> beneficiaries of the legacy of empire began to resurrect that legacy as a powerful and legitimate form of capital. At the forefront of this recuperation was a new kind of aspirational history-writing—not a history written by and for rulers, but by a new kind of revisionist historian, such as Niall Ferguson or Andrew Roberts, who sought to legitimise the previously unmentionable, and in so doing to transform their approval of the imperial past into a form of present-day cultural capital, and forge their own careers in the process.[8]

In short, Cecil Rhodes's power multiplied as sympathy for the version of history expounded by the "neo-imperial school"[9] has taken hold in Britain.

Gary Younge's solution, aired in *The Guardian* in June 2021, is for every statue to come down: "... let's get rid of them all!"[10] But this is a counsel of desperation. We know it cannot work, not only because it has been tried before, at the time of the Protestant Reformation—witness empty niches in churches all over England. More importantly, it cannot work because the power a monument can draw upon and amplify, ebbs and flows. Queen Anne is dead, and where commemorating her is concerned, the tide has gone out. Cecil Rhodes still has the power to provoke anger, or, conversely, nostalgia.

In the American context, the murder of nine people by Dylann Roof at Emanuel AME Church in Charleston, South Carolina (the "Charleston massacre") on 17 June 2015.[11]

---

[5] Baker 2021.
[6] Baker 2021.
[7] Chaudhuri 2016.
[8] Chaudhuri 2016.
[9] A phrase borrowed from Eric Hobsbawm (2007:50) to refer to Niall Ferguson and others of similar outlook.
[10] Younge 2021.
[11] Southern Poverty Law Center 2019.

sparked a nationwide movement to remove Confederate monuments, flags and other symbols from the public square, and to rename schools, parks, roads and other public works that pay homage to the Confederacy.

Roof's display of Confederate symbols, along with the shocking impact of the massacre of African Americans—some prominent persons, inside a famous church—lent urgency to the campaign. The symbols Roof's criminality drew upon had a power similar to or greater than the power the icons of Rhodes's were exercising. Since then, a coordinated campaign against Confederate symbols has had considerable success: the Southern Poverty Law Center's 2019 survey found "114 Confederate symbols removed since the Charleston massacre, including 48 monuments and three flags, and name changes for 35 schools and one college, and 10 roads,"[12]with another 160 Confederate symbols removed in 2020.[13] But this still represents only a minority of the Confederate monuments which exist across the former Confederate states and beyond.

The American political scene differs from Britain, where (as Chaudhuri observed) a relatively narrow base of support for imperial monumentality exists in "beneficiaries of the legacy of empire" and historians set on building their careers on a particular kind of revisionism.[14] In America, by contrast, on 29 June 2020, the House of Representatives voted to remove statues of white supremacists and Confederate leaders from the US Capitol—Congress's own premises; eventual passage of this measure depends on the uncertain prospect of securing sixty votes for it in the Senate, and, for the time being, the statues remain where they are.[15] A majority of Republican members of House and the Senate, whether as a matter of principle or as a signal to the voters who sent them to Washington, favors retention of these monuments.

Malawi can scarcely compete with the US or the UK in the number and prominence of its monuments, but public discussion can arise over appropriateness. A proposal by the Indian High Commission to erect a bust of Mahatma Gandhi at Ginnery Corner in Blantyre provoked a petition in 2018[16] and further protests in 2019.[17] In 2021, the High Court ruled against Blantyre City Council, which had agreed to the erection of the monument. Justice Mike Tembo agreed that the public display of the bust was a different matter from the naming of a

---

[12] Southern Poverty Law Center 2019.
[13] Southern Poverty Law Center 2021.
[14] Chaudhuri 2016.
[15] Holpuch 2021.
[16] Chikoko 2018.
[17] Mlanjira 2019.

road—it would have been sited at the junction of the existing Mahatma Gandhi Road and Masauko Chipembere Highway. Justice Tembo added that the bust[18]

> would not sit well with the dignity of the claimants and those like them who know what racist statements the one honoured by the statue said about black people and what views he held about black people.

Late in 2020, the bust was unveiled—in a far less public space, at the Indian High Commission in Lilongwe.

The power of, or the power behind, statues is reflected once more in Samson Kambalu's *Antelope*—his statue-group selected to occupy the fourth plinth in Trafalgar Square in London from 2022 to 2024. This work represents the Rev. John Chilembwe, founder of the Providence Industrial Mission in Chiradzulu, who, in 1915, led an armed rebellion against the colonial government in Nyasaland. In a scene inspired by the last known photograph of Chilembwe, he and white missionary colleague John Chorley—both dressed in a sober clerical style—wear hats in defiance of the colonial rule that Black people must remove their hats in the presence of white people. Kambalu's success in the Fourth Plinth competition has been welcomed in Malawi,[19] and he himself met President Lazarus Chakwera during the president's visit to London in July 2021.

The Scotland-Malawi Partnership (SMP), a "civil society network coordinating, supporting and representing the people-to-people links between [Scotland and Malawi]," campaigned for votes for *Antelope*; after the result was announced, David Hope-Jones, Chief Executive of SMP, said:

> It is a powerful, practical and constructive expression of all we have been talking about around Black Lives Matter, for an inspiring Malawian artist to be commissioned to make an inspiring statue of an inspiring Malawian freedom fighter which will sit alongside, and size up to, the many expressions of imperial power in the heart of London.

> We understand the desire held by many to tear down statues which are no longer in keeping with our values today but we think it is perhaps most important that we build new statues, literal or figurative, to ensure the roles played by key black figures is not forgotten.[20]

[18] Namangale 2021.
[19] Sundu 2021.
[20] https://www.scotland-malawipartnership.org/about-us/introduction (31 July 2021); on the Antelope campaign, see Scotland-Malawi Partnership 2021..

A Brazen Path to Monumentality

As Hope-Jones writes, statues may be figurative as well as literal. In another era, Horace—poet to the court of the emperor Augustus—expected no literal statue. Ending *Odes* Book Three in 23 BCE, however, he claimed literary immortality:[21]

> Exegi monumentum aere perennius
> regalique situ pyramidum altius,
> quod non imber edax, non Aquilo impotens
> possit diruere aut innumerabilis
> annorum series et fuga temporum.
> non omnis moriar, multaque pars mei
> vitabit Libitinam: usque ego postera
> crescam laude recens, dum Capitolium
> scandet cum tacita virgine pontifex.
> dicar, qua violens obstrepit Aufidus
> et qua pauper aquae Daunus agrestium
> regnavit populorum, ex humili potens
> princeps Aeolium carmen ad Italos
> deduxisse modos. sume superbiam
> quaesitam meritis et mihi Delphica
> lauro cinge volens, Melpomene, comam.

I have finished a monument more lasting than bronze, more lofty than the regal structure of the pyramids, one which neither corroding rain nor the ungovernable North Wind can ever destroy, nor the countless series of the years, nor the flight of time. I shall not wholly die, and a large part of me will elude the Goddess of Death. I shall continue to grow, fresh with the praise of posterity, as long as the priest climbs the Capitol with the silent virgin. I shall be spoken of where the violent Aufidus thunders and where Daunus, short of water, ruled over a country people, as one who, rising from a lowly state to a position of power, was the first to bring Aeolian verse to the tunes of Italy. Take the pride, Melpomene, that you have so well earned, and, if you would be so kind, surround my hair with Delphic bay.

---

[21] Horace *Odes* 3.30, trans. Niall Rudd. Loeb Classical Library 33. Horace *Odes and Epodes* (Cambridge, MA, 2004). Translation reproduced by permission of Harvard University Press.

Figure 5. Dedication plaque, Great Hall, Chancellor College, University of Malawi, Zomba. Photograph by M. D. Usher.

Figure 6. Detail of dedication plaque, Great Hall, Chancellor College, University of Malawi, Zomba. Photograph by M. D. Usher.

A youthful indiscretion forgotten (in 42, he had fought on the wrong side in the Battle of Philippi), Horace in the early thirties BCE had gained the favour of the emperor's trusted friend Maecenas. A decade and a half later—now having received from his patron a country estate, as well as an entrée into the highest circles in Rome—Horace could look back, aged in his early forties, on a poetic achievement he could have confidence in. Hence the claim in *Odes* 3.30 to have *finished* his "monument more lasting than bronze."

He links his work with the abiding efficacy of ritual—the priest climbing the Capitol with the silent virgin—and to enduring reputation in his home territory of Apulia, where the river Aufidus (Ofanto) runs. The eternity of Rome and Italy, then, he implies, is the power animating his monument. He belongs to "a country people"; but from humble beginnings, he has become great, thanks to the Aeolian verse—that dynamic poetic strain—which he was first to bring to Italy.

Horace and the Great Hall at Chancellor College, University of Malawi

In 1982, nine years after Chancellor College moved to Zomba from its interim premises in Blantyre, the Great Hall was added. A plaque memorializes the opening ceremony, when (on 11 December of that year) the Life President of the Republic of Malawi, Ngwazi Dr. H. Kamuzu Banda, declared the complex open. The English text on the plaque is in prominent, raised letters, but beneath it, in small sunken italic letters, stands in Latin:

Exegi monumentum aere perennius–HORACE B.C. 65–8

This first line will be recognized from above and gives this book its title. Steve Nyamilandu informs me that R. M. Ogilvie (about whom, more below) suggested the line to President Banda as suitable for use in this context.

In 2018, *Odes* 3 was one of the texts I charged a third-year undergraduate Roman Literature class in Chancellor College to study in English. In class, I quoted the first line of 3.30 in Latin as well as English and wrote it on the board, then asked (one of those questions teachers ask) if it was familiar to anyone. No one instantly recollected the small lettering at the bottom of the foundation plaque of the Great Hall. But after some discussion of bronze and Roman monumentality, I turned back to the foundation plaque and its unveiling by the College's founder, President Banda. What, I asked my students, did they think the "monument more lasting than bronze" was, which he had asserted (following Horace, of whom he had been reminded by Ogilvie) that he had finished?

Not only the Great Hall, was their answer: the monument (they inferred) was Chancellor College as a whole. It is, as they would say, "The College that God Loved the Most." Or such was the slogan on the t-shirt one could buy from the Students Union of Chancellor College in 2018.

I would have been unfair to fault my students on their answer: President Banda's portrait in oils is displayed to this day in the staircase of the College Library, as his loss of the Presidency in the 1994 election did not lead to *damnatio memoriae* at the College he named after himself.

Figure 7. Oil painting (1978) by Witness Kay Chiromo (1951–1994) of President Hastings Kamuzu Banda dressed as Chancellor of the University of Malawi, staircase, Chancellor College Library. Photograph by Francis Mulauzi.

And yet, Chancellor College in 1982, though now adorned with a Great Hall and the Little Hall behind it, was not "more lofty than the regal structure of the pyramids." The College was not, therefore, the only monument which President Banda claimed (implicitly) to have finished. The key lies in the second half of the poem: Banda, like Horace, belonged to "a country people"; he rose "from a lowly state to a position of power," and—as contributors to this volume will show—he made a claim to be (metaphorically) "the first to bring Aeolian verse to the tunes of Italy."

It is fair to assume that the citation from Horace, though recommended by Ogilvie, was inscribed on the Great Hall plaque by Banda with full intent—and that what "Aeolian verse" meant to him in Malawian terms can be parsed. Horace was a Latin speaker, who claimed that he brought Greek lyric poetry, in the Latin form he shaped it into, to his rustic home in Italy. Therefore, "Aeolian verse" must stand for something foreign brought home by a Malawian. If read in purely musical terms, one might take a claim like this as applicable to the writers of hymns in the first missionary generation, influenced by Scottish hymn-singing, plus Moody and Sankey, say, between 1875 and 1900. But nothing so archaic (in 1982's terms) as lyric, in its literal sense, could have been in mind. And, as for first discoverers of classical studies, Emily Greenwood, in this book, deals with who, before and other than Banda, has a claim to be recognised for bringing them into Nyasaland.

Poetry ought, however, to be taken on its own terms—even when merely alluded to—and not read through too literal a filter. No doubt Banda did wish to cast himself as Horace and Malawi as Apulia, Horace's district of origin. The monument he claimed to have finished, then, would (in its full realization) not be simply the Great Hall, or simply Chancellor College: it would be a tradition innovative in the local context, drawing on (what Banda took to be) an exemplary foreign font of thought and creativity—a resonant statement of intent for education in independent Malawi.

The purpose of this book, therefore, is to reflect on Classics as a particular and characteristic feature of the way educational development has advanced in independent Malawi. Contributors will examine the actualized metaphor which crowns President Banda's appropriation of *Odes* 3.30: his having brought "Aeolian verse to the tunes of Italy"—or, to state it prosaically, his wish to bring the study of Greek and Latin Classics to Malawi, and, in particular, to Chancellor College, the federal University of Malawi's arts and sciences institution (in American terms, its liberal arts college). Michael Chappell, for example, discusses in this book how he himself adapts a classical curriculum to the needs of his Malawian students; and M. D. Usher draws Malawi into a reflection on Pier Paolo Pasolini's encounter with newly independent Africa.

Chancellor College: Contested Territory

In October 1982, two months before the Great Hall dedication ceremony, President Banda visited Chancellor College to mark the occasion of the opening of the new academic year. In his speech to the College, he delivered a reproach which is remembered and resented to this day: "How can you people call yourselves a real university if you don't have a Department of Classics?"

This chastisement did not come at random or without warning. In 1978, a resolution had passed the Malawi Congress Party (MCP) Congress, calling for the establishment of a Department of Classics at the University of Malawi.[22] This was, evidently, the Party articulating the Life President's wishes.

The thinking behind the creation and development of the University, however, had come from diverse sources, and not only from the dream Banda had while imprisoned by the British in Gwelo.[23] David Kerr and Jack Mapanje

---

[22] Jenner 2001:161–162.
[23] Kerr and Mapanje 2002:78.

describe a "compromise between British liberal humanism ... and the other, more radically socialist, Afrocentric ideals of the nationalists" in the hopes entertained for the (future) university, in the last days of colonial Nyasaland.[24] Their account goes some way to explain why, within the institution founded after independence, there still was, a decade and a half into its existence, a powerful sense of its own direction—at least among some of its staff—and of the freedom which it ought to assert. The internal power-structure of the University was diffuse: and so, in the late seventies, compliance with the wishes of Life President and Party was not a foregone conclusion.

However that may be, not long after the Party conference resolution, the Vice-Chancellor, David Kimble, commissioned Robert Maxwell Ogilvie, Professor of Humanity (i.e. Professor of Latin) at St. Andrews, to visit Malawi and report on the feasibility of establishing a Department of Classics at Chancellor College. Ogilvie's report—written after his visit to Zomba in June and July 1979 (and detailed further below by Steve Nyamilandu and M. D. Usher)—recommended creating a department of three teaching staff, who would teach a classical curriculum of a conventional kind, centered on Latin language and literature.[25] The recommendations Ogilvie made were educationally conservative, and relatively modest: their resource implications and their likely impact on the character of Chancellor College and the education it provided were far from excessive.[26]

Against this background it may appear surprising, given the unambiguous political guidance supplied by the Party Congress resolution, that action by the College and University did not follow promptly. The Ogilvie report was "quietly shelved," as Ted Jenner writes.[27]

The background to the subsequent three years of inaction, which provoked the Life President to ask "How can you people call yourselves a real university ..." in 1982, is complex. The founding of a national University had been under discussion in the midst of the crisis which followed Independence (6 July 1964): it was a high priority and a personally cherished project, as far as Prime Minister Banda was concerned. It was the second item on the agenda of the cabinet meeting of 26 August 1964. Discussion showed differences in preferred approach. Informed that a European academic had already been offered the post of Vice-Chancellor,

[24] Kerr and Mapanje 2002:76.
[25] Jenner 2001:162.
[26] Kerr and Mapanje (2002:80) describe the University being forced to establish its Classics Department "at a time of acute financial crisis in the early 1980s." The financial exigency was real, but the potential cost of the Ogilvie proposal was not large in the context of the University budget as a whole.
[27] Jenner 2001:162.

Kanyama Chiume (Minister for External Affairs[28]) advocated appointing a Malawian understudy who would take over in due time. Banda replied that high-caliber expatriate staff might be expected to attract outside investment to the University. Colin Baker proposes that this line of argument may have been "designed further to draw out the ministers" into the confrontation that seemed, by then, inevitable.[29]

After that meeting ended inconclusively, the ministers, two days later, drew up and communicated to Banda a list of demands ("the Kuchawe manifesto"), in which they advocated for not moving the capital to Lilongwe and for siting the University at Soche Hill College in Blantyre, instead of Zomba.[30] This lengthy manifesto then proceeded to deal with other matters, including relations with the People's Republic of China.

In 1965 the University admitted its first students—in Blantyre, not Zomba, consistent with the concession Banda had been prepared to make when the Kuchawe manifesto was handed to him. The University from 1965 to 1966 taught Chemistry, Physics, Biology, French, Mathematics, English, Geography, and History—with Education, Agriculture, Economics, Philosophy, Psychology, and Sociology listed to be added from 1966.[31]

Chancellor College felt the political heat from time to time in its Blantyre years,[32] and control by the government was tight: Chifipa Gondwe, returning to Malawi in 1972 with a French PhD in Political Science, was indeed appointed—but allocated to teach basic International Relations in the Department of Government: "We couldn't mention Political Science," as he said to Kapote Mwakasungura and Douglas Miller, authors of *Malawi's Lost Years*.[33] In their account of this phase, Kerr and Mapanje write of the University's academic freedom being crushed—and of the paradoxical effect of autocracy, such that the "very skills of creativity, innovation, and independent thinking that

---

[28] Baker 2001:80.

[29] Baker 2001:109.

[30] Baker 2001:128–129.

[31] Sasnett and Sepmeyer 1967:904.

[32] Louis Nthenda (Nthenda 2020) quotes a letter from a Chancellor College Assistant Lecturer (whom he does not name there, but who was Simon Cameron Downie—who, Nthenda notes, was PI-ed soon afterward). In the letter, Downie writes of eight students being ordered by President Banda to return to their villages. Vice-Chancellor Ian Michael, Downie says, called "the surviving students" to a meeting and "explained that the eight were not expelled by the University and he had told Kamuzu only the Government would be held responsible for the removal, not this University." Downie adds, "…since the end of last term we have lost 18 out of 186, mostly for political reasons."

[33] Mwakasungura and Miller 2016:64.

universities nurture were the very qualities that led intellectuals to question the basis of the regime's legitimacy."[34]

After the move to Zomba in 1973, senior staff of the College were taken into detention in unprecedented numbers,[35] until the arrest of Albert Muwalo Nqumayo (Secretary-General of the Party) and Focus Martin Gwede (Head of the Special Branch) in September 1976.[36] The fall of Muwalo and Gwede was a political reversal, which was followed by the release of a large number of Chancellor College detainees, including Chifipa Gondwe.[37] But it proved to be no more than a pause in ethnically-motivated arrests of academics.

Ethnicity was not the only factor in play, however. Not all academics were consistent in avoiding politically unacceptable talk and action: Chancellor College, despite continuous surveillance by the Party and intermittent action by the Special Branch, was never far from the boiling point. When, in 1981, Zimani David Kadzamira became Principal, the political meaning of the appointment was clear: Kadzamira doubtless owed his elevation to his sister, the Official Hostess, Cecilia Tamanda Kadzamira; but at the top level of government, he must also have been considered capable of keeping a lid on the seething pot. His loyalty to his patrons and to the status quo had been amply demonstrated. In the days of Muwalo and Gwede, he and a certain coterie (Kings Phiri reminisces) would find an excuse to gather whenever a key northern academic was arrested: they would "come together and drink, play chess and rejoice, literally rejoice, that another ha[d] gone down"—whether at the Zomba Gymkhana Club, or even in the Senior Common Room at the College itself.[38]

With the Kadzamira principalship came both the Life President's public rebuke, "How can you people call yourselves a university ... ," and action on the Ogilvie report. It seems that no elaborate plan was formed, but responsibility for doing something devolved on the Dean of Humanities. In his time of need, a

---

[34] Kerr and Mapanje 2002:78–79. Academic freedom remained a concern in 2012, as Esela Munthali's chapter in this book observes; she writes of recent collective action directed to securing it.

[35] Mwakasungura and Miller 2016:64. Kings Phiri adds (same page): "They ... would arrest the colleagues at night ... It was only the students they came for during the day." By October 1976, Kings Phiri and one other were the only two staff of Chancellor College from northern Malawi who had not yet been detained (Mwakasungura and Miller 2016:76).

[36] Carver 1990:33. Both were tried in the Southern Region Traditional Court, found guilty of treason, and sentenced to death—Gwede's sentence was commuted to life imprisonment (he was released in 1993). The Africa Watch report (Carver 1990) describes unsatisfactory features of the trial, then editorializes (36): "There is no suggestion that Muwalo died for conscientiously-held beliefs. As secretary-general of the party he was undoubtedly responsible for some monstrous crimes—but it was not proven that he was responsible for the one for which he was convicted."

[37] Mwakasungura and Miller 2016:143.

[38] Mwakasungura and Miller 2016:76.

job application dropped unsought on his desk—from Rhodes Scholar Caroline Alexander. It was "manna from heaven," as he said to her.[39]

The Heart Wants What It Wants[40]

Banda's reasons for wanting a Department of Classics, and for pressing for it in 1982, can, in part, be traced. As noted above, a university was a priority for him in 1964—not far down the list from his determination to outmaneuver his rivals and have a cabinet which would be amenable to his wishes. In 1965, however, the spread of subjects taught was nothing unusual: it was largely what would have been expected at any comparable institution. In 1967, Bunda College of Agriculture (in Lilongwe District), which had admitted its first students in 1966,[41] and the Polytechnic (in Blantyre, and founded in 1965)[42] were added to Chancellor College to form a federal structure for the University of Malawi.[43] Both Bunda and the Polytechnic had been built largely on American aid funds— American attitudes to Malawi and interventions there feature in Cybelle Greenlaw's chapter in this book.

Classics, therefore, was neither a foundational teaching subject in the University of Malawi, nor added in the first tranche of serious change. Banda himself, however, had been a Classics student at the Universities of Indiana and Chicago, before he embarked on his medical studies. Emily Greenwood writes of this below, and the H. K. Banda archive, which she draws on in her study, is held in the University of Indiana in Bloomington.

Speculation is possible over what kind of exercise in elite-formation he had in mind when he mandated the University of Malawi to teach Classics. It is clear, on the broader scale, that his medium-term expectation was that independent Malawi would operate as a peasant economy whose backbone would be rural production—of maize and tobacco as cash crops—but still with a substantial subsistence-farming sector. As Kerr and Mapanje argue, the immediate post-colonial style of managing the economy in Malawi was "a strange mixture of capitalism and state control ... a system of patronage and asset entitlement that guaranteed the support of a loyal bourgeoisie and a kulak class of entrepreneurial farmers."[44]

[39] Alexander 1991:58.
[40] Emily Dickinson *Letter 262* (Dickinson 1958).
[41] Kanyama-Phiri 2016:56.
[42] Read 1967:53, 63.
[43] University of Malawi 2017.
[44] Kerr and Mapanje 2002:77.

Education was made neither compulsory nor free at any level: universal primary education was not implemented until 1995, after Bakili Muluzi took over as President. The hypothesis that, in mandating the existence of a Classics Department, President Banda wished to create a channel for educated Malawians to buttress their social advantages must be treated with caution. In the 1950s and early 1960s, the high schools which existed in Malawi could be counted on the fingers of one hand, and the "mission boys" from whom the members of the independence cabinet were drawn were the kind of men whose independent thought and political energy President Banda wanted to curb rather than to encourage. And yet the move in the direction of Classics is explicable in the broader context of the history of Malawian education—and the explanation can be traced back to the legacy of Robert Laws's thinking and the Livingstonia Mission.

When Laws's retirement came, in 1927, after five decades of missionary endeavor, he relinquished control of the structures he had built up—and, in particular, the Overtoun Institution, the school at Livingstonia where he had pioneered advanced education in the Nyasaland Protectorate. Kenneth R. Ross and Klaus Fiedler, in their *Malawi Church History* (2020), list the "outstandingly well-educated leaders" who were produced there in the 1920s.[45] In this late-career phase, Laws hoped that the future would bring a University of Livingstonia, with the Overtoun Institution at its heart. But others saw drawbacks, arguing that Overtoun graduates supplied the need that Europeans in Nyasaland and further afield had for educated labor—but that their advanced qualifications did little for the community they were drawn from in northern Nyasaland.[46] W. P. Young, Laws's successor, redirected the educational program at Livingstonia away from advanced studies, which in Laws's day had included Theology and Greek language, towards producing primary school teachers. By doing so, he brought Livingstonia closer to the thinking and practice of the Dutch Reformed Church Mission—to the south of Livingstonia's area of influence.[47]

In some respects, Laws's and Banda's aims (forty or fifty years later) were not so different. In both cases, the aim in the long run was to use Classics to undermine traditional authority and to open Malawi for purposes which they found to be transcendent—or at least ultimate. Laws wanted to form a learned clergy on the Scottish model, to advance Christianity in Nyasaland and beyond—and a by-product would be a cadre of indigenous men qualified to work for the colonial government or for modern-sector employers. Banda's motives, however, were more mixed. Kerr and Mapanje infer that he hoped his classically-educated elite would gain "Victorian virtues of restraint, stoicism, and loyalty, which he

[45] Ross and Fiedler 2020:210–211.
[46] Ross and Fiedler 2020:212.
[47] Ross and Fiedler 2020:213–214.

found so singularly absent from [Malawian] university graduates [*sc.* in the late seventies]."[48] To the degree to which they are right about this, Classics was to be introduced as an antidote to the lingering influence of the ministers dismissed in 1964 (and then variously exiled or imprisoned)—the cabinet crisis casting a long shadow. But it may be more realistic to think that Banda's wish was to use the Classics as an instrument to serve his autocratic purposes: the ultimate principle being (as O'Brien puts it to Winston Smith in *Nineteen Eighty-Four*) only that "always there will be the intoxication of power, constantly increasing and constantly growing subtler."[49]

Kamuzu Academy

In 1977, the year before the Party Congress called for a Classics Department, President Banda began to plan Kamuzu Academy: a boarding school with many excellent facilities, in his home village in Kasungu District.[50] Two boys and a girl would be selected per year from each district in Malawi (there were then twenty-four) for a six-year high-school program centered on Latin and Greek. In other respects, the curriculum was similar to what was offered in government secondary schools, except that Chichewa and Agriculture were not taught. The fees were the same as those charged in government secondary schools, but the real cost of what was provided was vastly higher.

Kamuzu Academy admitted its first students in 1981. Before it opened its doors, however, it caused a new ripple in the pool of Malawian politics. Banda personally had too little cash in the bank to meet the cost of this asset: he relied on the Press Corporation to pay the bills. Jan Kees van Donge, in his 2002 article, explains the history and ownership structure of this corporation, which, in the 1970s, had expanded on the back of the tobacco boom.[51] But the world economy went from boom to bust in 1979—the bust which is remembered in Britain for James Callaghan's Winter of Discontent. Press, and the banks in which it had holdings, faced liquidity problems. In 1980, Aleke Kadonaphani Banda, Managing Director of Press Trust, went to the Life President and told him it was necessary to reduce the amount of money he was drawing from Press to

---

[48] Kerr and Mapanje 2002:80.

[49] Orwell 1949: Part 3, Chapter 3.

[50] In a fax dated 23 August 1996, Cecilia Tamanda Kadzamira informed Donald Brody that the Board of Governors for Kamuzu Academy had been established in July 1977. (H. K. Banda Archive, Box 1, Folder 15.) I wish to thank Prof. Emily Greenwood for drawing my attention to this. John Dubbey, Vice-Chancellor of the University of Malawi from 1987 to 1991, says in his book that Ian Michael (first Vice-Chancellor) told him that "Dr Banda had been contemplating the new academy even in his time [1964 to 1973]" (Dubbey 1994:152).

[51] Van Donge 2002:656–657.

meet his expenditures—including on Kamuzu Academy. This was a courageous stance for a man who had been dismissed from the Cabinet in 1973, and, far from securing the Life President's cooperation, Aleke Banda was detained and imprisoned for twelve years.[52]

The foundation of Kamuzu Academy was a curious move.[53] At the heart of President Banda's motivation must have been his failure, despite energetic and prolonged attacks in the 1970s by Muwalo and Gwede, to bring an end to the atmosphere of barely suppressed political dissidence at Chancellor College. "Quietly shelving" the Ogilvie report may seem to be the most passive kind of resistance imaginable—but there can be no doubt that its implications were understood in the ruling circle at Sanjika Palace. Banda's attempt at making a political and educational end run by building the Academy was, therefore, a response to something he saw as an intractable problem:[54] Kerr and Mapanje write of Kamuzu Academy as "a concrete expression of Banda's disillusionment with the university."[55] John Lloyd Lwanda comments that the real reason behind the "whites only" staff policy at Kamuzu Academy was "to exclude Malawi intellectuals whom he saw as a threat to his ideas of 1920s and 1930s education."[56]

The year before Caroline Alexander's arrival in Zomba, therefore, teenagers were learning Latin from the Scottish Classics Group's *Ecce Romani* textbook series—three hundred kilometers to the north, in Kasungu District.

At this point I must acknowledge my share of responsibility, because I was one of the white teachers, from 1987 to 1991. My hope, indeed, was to nurture Malawian intellectuals—not to exclude Malawian intellectuals. But I was wrong in those years to have a sense of being able to stand outside Malawian politics. Samson Kambalu, in this book, cites Aristotle on a tyrant's preference for having foreigners rather than citizens as guests and companions, "feeling that citizens are hostile but strangers make no claim against him."[57] Kamuzu Academy, where teaching was in the hands of foreigners, was insulated from the ordinary operation of Malawian politics: in my years there, Party officials almost never intervened in anything. Once, something was stolen in the boys' hostel, and

---

[52] Van Donge 2002:658.
[53] I wish to thank Prof. Emily Greenwood for discussing this issue with me.
[54] And an expensive response: see Emily Greenwood's chapter on the cost to the Ministry of Education of Kamuzu Academy, although it was given out that it was a private school funded by President Banda personally—there was no public admission about how Press Corporation's money was being used. By contrast, the University of Malawi cost much less, at about 22% of the government's educational budget (Lwanda 1993:178): as Lwanda comments, "his economic repression of the university in favor of the Academy is evidence of his dislike of any thinking educated elite" (Lwanda 1993:183).
[55] Kerr and Mapanje 2002:80.
[56] Lwanda 1993:182.
[57] Aristotle *Politics* 1314a.

someone, or more than one, alleged through a Party channel that the thief was a certain boy. The police came and arrested him. This occasioned surprise in the small world of the Academy teachers. When the boy's case came up at the Traditional Court, the Senior Master, who was in overall charge of the boys' hostel, went and testified: he said he had investigated the theft as carefully as he could and had not found any evidence to indicate that the accused was the thief. The chief acquitted the accused (and acquittals were unusual in the Traditional Courts—if the police believed one was guilty, one was nearly always found guilty). Taking a stand against what Party and police wanted was unusual and can be considered a political act—but, as well as his senior job and the general advantage of white privilege, the Senior Master had on his side the well-understood (though unofficial) fact that Kamuzu Academy was His Excellency's private garden and the Central Region MCP was expected to keep its hands off it.

As well as being a private garden, the Academy was a national showpiece. During my years there, diplomatic visits were made by Joaquim Chissano, President of Mozambique, and by Ali Hassan Mwinyi, President of Tanzania. In July 1988, President Chissano came as part of his four-day visit to Malawi, which was distinguished (on 7 July in Blantyre) by saying he was convinced that Malawi was no longer supporting RENAMO (the South-African-sponsored anti-government guerrilla movement in Mozambique) and speaking of Kamuzu Banda as "my father"—a warm reference in anyone's diplomatic language. At the arrival of his motorcade, Malawian students and white teachers together sang the national anthem, "Viva, Viva a FRELIMO" in Portuguese. On his tour of the school, Chissano visited my classroom and commented to students on how similar the Greek letters on the board were to the Russian letters he had been used to in his Moscow days. The following year, President Mwinyi was welcomed in the same way—and the Chairman of the Governors, in his speech, invited him to send one of his children to Kamuzu Academy. Later, Salama Mwinyi duly came to the school.

All this illustrates that, in the 1980s, Kamuzu Academy was as political as anything in Malawi.[58] A report on the front page of the *Daily Times* in August 1983 quoted President Banda as saying he had been told that many students at the Academy did not like Greek, Latin, and Ancient History:[59] he responded by stressing that such students should not study there. What he had heard ran against what I was to experience when starting four years later: there was little

---

[58] I wish to thank my co-editor Prof. Samson Kambalu for discussing this issue with me.
[59] "Academy is for Classics Pupils" 1983.

grumbling about Greek and Latin (and exam results were sound[60])—though almost all students saw other studies as more relevant to their own futures.

Alexander's Ideal State

In 1991, nine years after Caroline Alexander brought Latin to Chancellor College—and six years after the completion of her sojourn in Zomba—she published in the *New Yorker* a narrative of how she came to Chancellor College and commenced teaching Latin and Classical Civilization. Her article, "An Ideal State," reflects on President Banda's enthusiasm for introducing these studies to Chancellor College, but she eschews almost all temptation to speculate on the internal politics of Chancellor College. Her determination to create "a viable, functioning—as opposed to a token—Classics Department"[61] I can attest, from the harvest of books, journals, and other educational materials which still lined the shelves of the three offices in use by Classics lecturers when I was last there in 2018.[62] Alexander's efforts to corral support from international networks were met with considerable success.[63]

In addition to books, Alexander secured valuable sponsorship and scholarship assistance, thanks to the goodwill of the Greek Honorary Consul in Blantyre;[64] and from her American compatriots, she obtained a Fulbright Teaching Fellowship to fund the staff member who would replace her when she departed in 1985.[65] Support from within the College was slower to come, except in that the Rev. Rodney Squire Hunter of Zomba Theological College—from 1961 to 1965 Librarian of Pusey House, and Chaplain of Wadham College,

---

[60] My source for this is my recollection of the results sheets; but see also Dubbey 1994:156, "surprisingly good."

[61] Alexander 1991:88.

[62] Prof. M. D. Usher reminds me that he, himself, too has donated many boxes of books. I have not tried to ascertain who gave the most books, or the most useful. The late Prof. Martin Bernal of Cornell University presented the first two volumes of *Black Athena* to Chancellor College—where they were used as the foundational text in an undergraduate course called "Classical North Africa and the Black Athena Controversy" taught by Michael Chappell. Bernal himself told me that his first job—after he left school in 1955 and before he went to university in 1957—had been as a tea assistant on an estate owned by a relative in Nyasaland. Before travelling there, he went to the School of Oriental and African Studies in London and asked about learning Chinyanja: he was put in touch with Orton Chirwa, who became his teacher. Chirwa would be Minister of Justice and Attorney General in the Independence cabinet in 1964; see further in Samson Kambalu's chapter in this book.

[63] Alexander comments on how "anything at all beyond the most basic operating costs" had to be asked for from sources outside the University (1991:83–84), but adds that this was true for all departments.

[64] Alexander 1991:84–85.

[65] Alexander 1991:88.

Oxford—was hired from 1982 on a part-time basis to teach beginners' Latin.[66] At the time of Alexander's departure, the College advertised two further appointments in Classics, in addition to her own replacement;[67] Classics, as a department, came into existence after she was gone. By attracting investment in the University, she had, in fact, achieved what Banda had envisaged that high-caliber academic faculty and staff should do, in the discussion at the cabinet meeting of 26 August 1964.

Her contribution was not only Latin and Classical Civilization: Alexander took care to accept every invitation to participate in what other Humanities departments were doing:[68] Sophocles's *Antigone* for English Department students; less comfortably, Catullus for intermediate Latin students; and Euripides's *Medea*—a text which provoked the pseudonymous Mr. Mwale, Alexander's favorite foil in "An Ideal State," to aver that "We in Malawi would never permit such an ... um ... *wanton* performance."[69] In her article, the shockability of Malawian students[70] collides awkwardly with Alexander's sense of the "inability of Westerners to cope with ... unfamiliar forces"—namely, "the mystical, irrational, at times dark forces of Africa."[71]

Her sense of President Banda as a Platonic figure—as someone to whom the separation of the population into three categories in the *Republic* must appeal,[72] and whose Malawi Young Pioneers might correspond to the "well-bred watchdogs" Plato expected to draw from the auxiliaries, or the people with silver mixed into their souls[73]—comes through more powerfully than the notes of skepticism in "An Ideal State." When she mentions the time when four students were taken into detention, she does regard them as politically harmless and speculates that they were targeted because of "a dangerously anomalous manner—a distinctive appearance or way of speaking that marked them as too intelligent, inquiring, or non-deferential for their own good." Her analysis is superficially plausible but shows no sensitivity to the decade and a half of unjustifiable detentions of

---

[66] Not yet fifty in 1982, Rodney Hunter (1933–2006) impressed Alexander as being an elderly man ("exactly how elderly I never ascertained"). Summarizing the situation in 1991, she noted that he, "the apparently immortal Reverend Hunter" (then 58), was still on the staff at Chancellor College (1991:71, 88). He left in 1996 and afterwards served as a parish priest in Nkhota Kota District (Jenner 2001:166).

[67] Alexander 1991:88.

[68] Alexander 1991:72.

[69] Alexander 1991:72–74.

[70] For instance, over the small genitals of Greek male nude statues (Alexander 1991:76), I showed the Riace bronzes on screen in class in 2018, unintentionally provoking a *frisson* not unlike the one Alexander describes.

[71] Alexander 1991:75.

[72] Alexander 1991:64.

[73] Alexander 1991:66.

Chancellor College staff and students which had come before. When Alexander comments on the fear of being seen as unusual, saying that "this tendency is inherent in Chewa culture—as it is in other traditional societies,"[74] she comes uncomfortably close to facile acceptance of systematic oppression. Her title ("An Ideal State") comes without a question mark.

Alexander, on 7 June 1995, met and interviewed Banda in Blantyre: a meeting arranged by Gustave G. Kaliwo, the lawyer who acted at that time for the former Life President. This was an outstanding vote of confidence in her, and the interview was published in *Granta*, as part of a fuller retrospective by Alexander on Malawi.[75] Her parallel between Malawi and Plato's *Republic* features again, together with her conception of the Young Pioneers as Plato's Guardians and the subsistence farmers as Plato's bronze class. But the atmosphere of the piece changes when she ends by citing the 1994 Report of the Commission of Inquiry into the incident of 18 May 1983 near Mwanza, in which Dick Matenje (Minister without Portfolio and Secretary-General of the MCP), Aaron Gadama (Minister for the Central Region), Twaibu Sangala (Minister of Health) and David Chiwanga MP (Chikwawa East) died:[76]

> This Inquiry should also serve as a warning to all governments that however strong and unchallenged their authority may seem at a given moment in time, life is dynamic and things change, and that one day the meekest of the meek will be in a position to rise and question their deed, and that the truth cannot be suppressed completely and forever.

This Monument

The agenda in this book is not simply to deliver a history of the Department of Classics in Chancellor College. That Department, and the studies which are carried on in it, are still a living part of Chancellor College Humanities. At the time of writing this Introduction (July 2021), the number of majors expected to complete their degrees this year is, at six, the highest in years—a modest number, and numbers at this level reflect the ups and downs classical studies have been subject to in Zomba. Accordingly, the book's purpose, drawing on a representative selection of expert voices, is to provide a critical account of the past and present of Zomba Classics in the context of the African academy.

---

[74] Alexander 1991:66.
[75] Alexander 1995.
[76] Mtegha 1995. Publication of this report was followed by Banda and four others, all on trial for murder in 1995.

An account of the discipline within which our endeavors are located is called for, commencing with the 1979 report.

The preconceptions and the temperament which R. M. Ogilvie brought to giving advice on a Classics Department for Chancellor College were more conservative than might have been expected from a St. Andrews professor in the 1970s. Ogilvie, born in 1932 and educated at Rugby and Balliol, died suddenly in St. Andrews on 7 November 1981; in his British Academy obituary in 1982, Russell Meiggs comments that Ogilvie firmly remained on the right, contrary to "the general tendency of his generation."[77] When he comes to discuss his comments on the place Thucydides and Plato held in English education in the nineteenth century, Meiggs points to the influence on Ogilvie of both Thomas Arnold (Headmaster of Rugby School, 1828–1841) and Benjamin Jowett (Master of Balliol College, Oxford, 1870–1893): "there was something of both men in him."[78]

Nineteenth century thinking, then, informed Ogilvie's conception of classical studies as an educational enterprise. In the chapter of Ogilvie's *Latin and Greek* (1964) where his debt to Arnold's and Jowett's thinking is made explicit, Ogilvie reflects on empire quite as trenchantly as on education. His baseline is the supposition that "the English acquired their empire, like the Romans, reluctantly and fortuitously"[79]—a sentiment which sounds even less plausible today than it must have sounded in 1964. Though seeing both Thucydides and Plato as influential, he states straightforward views on the difference between the Athenians and the British as imperialists:[80]

> despite the fundamental difference that the Athenians were ruling fellow-Greeks of equal intelligence and culture, whereas the English governed heterogeneous and, in many respects, inferior races, the attitude of both states could be summed up in the words of Thucydides (1.76) ... The fatal weakness of the British empire was exposed by those very problems to which the Athenian empire provided no parallels. The Athenians did not have to surmount the obstacles of race, religion and colour.

Ogilvie's inexcusable reference to "inferior races" hits harder today, probably, than it struck the readers Ogilvie assumed he was writing for in 1964. Samson Kambalu's phrase for it, in discussion with me *per litteras*, is "thoroughly

[77] Meiggs 1982:628.
[78] Meiggs 1982:631.
[79] Ogilvie 1964:120.
[80] Ogilvie 1964:121.

depraved": and he adds that it points to the "underlying imperialist aims of Classics in Malawi."

In 1969, as well as going to Yale as a Visiting Professor, Ogilvie went to South Africa as Hofmeyr Fellow—a Fellowship created in memory of Jan Hendrik Hofmeyr (classicist, Rhodes Scholar, Balliol man, and later United Party cabinet minister). In addition to the Hofmeyr Fellowship, Ogilvie held a Visiting Lectureship at the University of the Witwatersrand and gave lectures at all the South African universities. In his British Academy obituary, Russell Meiggs comments that "It was typical that he also made a point of trying to understand the mentality of the Afrikaners by meeting as many as he could."[81]

This was the degree of experience in Africa that Ogilvie, who had known in 1964 that the jig was up for the British empire, brought with him to the task of designing a scheme for classical education in an African university. His recommendation not to attempt Greek teaching may have been conditioned by what he took to be practical, in a country where numbers completing a high-school education were still small—but it is also unlikely that he considered that understanding the necessity for an imperial power to "secure control ... up to the natural perimeter" (exemplified in Thucydides's Melian narrative) would become a high priority in Malawian national life.[82]

As noted above, however, the Ogilvie scheme was killed by reluctance and foot-dragging in Zomba. And when goaded into action by a new Principal and by the electric shock delivered in the presidential speech, what Chancellor College got instead was Caroline Alexander—fresh from Rhodes House, but not an imperial nostalgist in the Ogilvie mode. Hers was in some respects a forward-looking outlook. At first without classical colleagues, she taught an eclectic version of Classics. Later, she would earn a classical PhD from Columbia University, and after a varied career as a non-fiction author, she became, in 2015, the first woman to publish a translation of the *Iliad*.

Meanwhile, reflections on Classics and its place within education and society have become a more absorbing topic for academic scribblers than ever. This book is only tangentially a contribution to that literature: it is directed more towards being an account of the situatedness of Classics in Malawi than a theorized examination of its educational or moral value. But we, the authors, are inevitably mindful of the meaning of what we have been doing, or still are, as Classics teachers, and the ramifying discourse on that subject exerts an inevitable fascination.

---

[81] Meiggs 1982:632.
[82] Ogilvie 1964:118–119.

Mary Beard, in *Confronting the Classics* (2013), acknowledged the (widespread and well-attested) decline in the teaching of ancient languages and laid out competing interpretations: on the one hand, the view of Classics as a "Dead White European Male" subject which used to be "a convenient alibi for a whole range of cultural and political sins, from imperialism and Eurocentrism to social snobbery and the most mind-numbing form of pedagogy";[83] on the other hand, the view of the decline as caused by Ivy League academics who "have wandered down some self-regarding postmodernist cul-de-sac."[84] Beard herself evinces sympathy for the first view, while the second (advocated by Victor Davis Hanson and John Heath in *Who Killed Homer* [1998]), she is clearly against. In a follow-up book, *Bonfire of the Humanities* (2001), Hanson and Heath included sections by Bruce S. Thornton that broaden the argument to apply it to Humanities study as a whole—or rather, to position Classics as a paradigm case, standing for whatever may be worthwhile in the Humanities as a whole.

In 2019, however, in their book, the Postclassicisms Collective[85] enunciated a distinctive definition of "classicism":[86]

> a construction of Greek and Roman antiquity as at once an ideal and an origin, at once beyond time and located in time, a value-laden narrative that stands both as paradigmatic for mainstream society as a whole (i.e., "the classical tradition" is imagined as continuous and integral to the genealogy of a present that is often framed, implicitly or explicitly, as European and Western) and as the structuring principle of the academic discipline known most commonly in the Anglo-American world as classics.

The Postclassicists refer helpfully to a dialogue—between the study of a body of ancient material and "the intellectual and sociocultural framework(s) of our own era"; they ground their discussion in the issue of value, glossed as "the investment that we, as moderns, make in the culture of the past: the reasons, that is, why we are drawn to it."[87]

Their apprehension of a sort of primacy of the aesthetic sense is one which I am not disposed to argue against. But the feeling behind *Postclassicisms* is

---

[83] Beard 2013:15.
[84] Beard 2013:15–16.
[85] Alastair Blanshard (University of Queensland); Simon Goldhill (King's College, Cambridge); Constanze Güthenke (Corpus Christi College, Oxford); Brooke Holmes (Princeton University); Miriam Leonard (University College, London); Glenn Most (Scuola Normale Superiore di Pisa and University of Chicago); James Porter (University of California, Berkeley); Phiroze Vasunia (University College, London); Tim Whitmarsh (St. John's College, Cambridge).
[86] Postclassicisms Collective 2019:3.
[87] Postclassicisms Collective 2019:4.

different from any of the reasons why I, myself, was drawn as a young man to become a Classics student. I would now describe myself at that age as having been driven by a kind of historicist outlook, though without the dramas which attended the life of Friedrich Schlegel (1772–1829), the "first discoverer" (as it were) of historicism—and a classicist who became a leading figure in Jena Romanticism, not to mention his also being an atheist who turned to Roman Catholicism.[88] He started out in Göttingen as a student of the Law, whereas when I learnt (from a roommate) what studying the Law would involve, it made me certain that I would have to do Part II Classics. Instinctive reactions can differ, though. When a former student of mine from Chancellor College recently wrote to me about having begun studying for a Diploma in Law, I told him this story. His response was, "To me, Law is Part II Classics."

As time has gone on, I have become a social constructionist, and I find that my outlook on life chimes better with that of Peter Berger—sociologist and sometime Protestant theologian—than ever it did with Schlegel's. At the bottom of the history that I write is the wish to examine how ancient people constructed their understandings of the world around them—and how those understandings could and did change. Not all of us Monumentalists (see below) share this stance: readers who want to diagnose each case have the evidence in their hands.

The Postclassicists see their project as the more urgent because "the study of ancient Greece and Rome is no longer integral to the major paths of cultural formation in North America and Western Europe."[89] Hence, their plan to examine why the Postclassicists are as attached to the classical past as they are and, simultaneously, to examine their justifications for studying it. The nature of their book, accordingly, is introspective—as this book is as well, but on different terms.

In the *Times Literary Supplement*,[90] Johanna Hanink gave *Postclassicisms* a reserved welcome, showing disappointment at how narrow a range of contributors to the Great Conversation merits discussion. "*Postclassicisms* conspicuously shies away from addressing race," she observes, "despite its several claims that the project is grounded in political 'urgency'."[91] Hanink describes a different set of concerns behind her own journey into Classics—as far, perhaps, from mine as from the concerns which animate the Postclassicists: she is a product of a New England education in which she learnt of Phyllis Wheatley, an enslaved woman who knew Greek and Latin, and who became the first Black woman in America

---

[88] Speight 2021.
[89] Postclassicisms Collective 2019:7.
[90] Hanink 2020.
[91] Hanink 2020.

to publish a book of poetry.[92] Plenty in the Postclassicists' definition of classicism remains open to discussion.

Our discipline has come a long way, then, from where Ogilvie located it for us in 1979—and further still from his pipedreams of 1964. It has, for the most part, resisted pleas for simplification along the lines of Jeremy Toner's 2002 argument for disaggregating Roman history from the edifice—an edifice in which he observed the same kinds of cultural and political sins identified by Mary Beard. In *Rethinking Roman History*, therefore, he advocates separating Roman history from classical learning, in order to move it forward without a "set of intellectual baggage which prevents it from reaching a wider audience."[93] Institutional contexts differ, and I, myself, (except during irregular sojourns in Zomba) teach in a Department of History and Archaeology; but, in general, Roman history continues to be associated with the rest of the Classics, regardless of whether one side of that equation should be counted as "intellectual baggage." The Postclassicists' advocacy of "other classicisms" in the "world literatures" manner envisaged by Hutcheson Macaulay Posnett seems less likely to inform future institutional structures.[94]

This book, therefore, has both a descriptive side and an argumentative side. Not (as noted above) a departmental history, it does draw on the study of the Department contained in Steve Nyamilandu's 2016 St. Andrews and University of Malawi PhD thesis. It is not a monument erected in memory of Hastings Kamuzu Banda, whom readers will find subjected to critical examination, together with his legacy; it is a book which has room for the personal along with the scholarly.

The Monumentalists: A Third-Person View

If the Postclassicists merit their appellation, no doubt those who have written this book might best be called Monumentalists. Three of them are Malawian (Nyamilandu, Kambalu, Munthali), the rest not. However, each has a connection with Chancellor College or with Malawi more broadly. To this degree, this is an insider account. They rely on their critical faculties to counterbalance the affection they hold for the College, for the African academy in general, for the people of Malawi, for the Classics, or for all of them.

---

[92] Hanink 2020.
[93] Toner 2002:8.
[94] Postclassicisms Collective 2019:196.

Paul McKechnie

Paul McKechnie, first-named editor of this book and writer of this Introduction, is Associate Professor (CoRE) in Ancient Cultures at Macquarie University, Sydney, Australia. He lived in Malawi from 1987 to 1991, when he was Head of the Department of Classics at Kamuzu Academy. He first visited Chancellor College in 1989, during the Headship of Dr. Maryse Waegeman (author of *Amulet and Alphabet: Magical Amulets in the First Book of Cyranides*),[95] and in 1990 he served as external examiner for the Department of Classics. In the interests of full disclosure: a Kamuzu Academy master was in effect President Banda's employee. In addition to this, McKechnie was introduced to Banda on an official occasion and shook his hand. Later, after the free republic was restored, he taught in the Department of Classics at Chancellor College as a Visiting Lecturer in Classics in 2004 and as Visiting Professor of Classics 2018.

Steve Nyamilandu

Steve Nyamilandu was born to the family of the late McRester Evans Trinta Nyamilandu (a teacher trainer) and Patricia Nyamilandu (née Saini), a trained elementary school teacher turned homemaker. Steve's late elder brother, Alexandre (an ex-student of Paul McKechnie at Kamuzu Academy) inspired him to like Latin through reading-aloud sessions of *Ecce Romani* books borrowed from Kamuzu Academy's library. Fortunately, Dedza Secondary School, where Nyamilandu was selected and admitted, offered Latin. From Dedza, Nyamilandu proceeded to Chancellor College in 1989 to enroll in a BEd (Humanities), which he completed in 1993.

Nyamilandu taught Latin at Blantyre Secondary School for a term before he was recruited by the University of Malawi (UNIMA) in February 1994 in the Department of Classics. After joining UNIMA, Nyamilandu earned additional degrees: BA (Hons.) in Classics from the University of South Africa; MA (Language Education—Latin) from UNIMA (the thesis title was: "Using the Communicative Approach in Latin Reading at Junior Level in Malawi") and a second MA, this time in Ancient Languages and Cultures, from the University of South Africa (thesis title: "Myth and the Treatment of Non-Human Animals in Classical and African Cultures: A Comparative Study").

Nyamilandu completed his PhD in 2016 under a joint Scotland-Malawi PhD program, supervised jointly by his home university (under Prof. Emerita Moira Primula Chimombo) and by Prof. Roger David Rees of the School of Classics at the University of St. Andrews, as part of the cotutelle arrangement between the

---

[95] Waegeman 1987.

two universities. Nyamilandu's study included two spells in St. Andrews, where *inter alia* he was able to research the important contribution to Malawian Classics made by the late R. M. (Robin) Ogilvie. The title of his PhD is "Contextualising Classics Teaching in Malawi: A Comparative Study." Nyamilandu is interested in pedagogical and curriculum strategies for teaching Classics as a way of decolonizing Classics. He continues to expand his research by interrogating how cultures of the Greco-Roman world have shaped the history of ideas in the modern world. In his leisure time, Steve Nyamilandu fixes old cars—and that keeps him out of trouble.

Nyamilandu is the author of two chapters in the present volume. The first, Chapter Two, is "Classical Studies in Malawi: its Health, Purpose and Reputation." Here, the history of Classics teaching in Malawi is discussed, both broadly and with a particular focus on UNIMA. The work complements similar works on Classics in Malawi written from an expatriate viewpoint by various scholars, including Caroline Alexander, Paul McKechnie, Josef De Kuyper, Ted Jenner, M. D. Usher, and Emily Greenwood. The chapter is unique in that the issues raised are much more in-depth and current. But, as well as being written from a Malawian point of view, the chapter presents information from Nyamilandu's surveys conducted on Malawian Classics students regarding their attitudes towards Classics—including their views on the relevance of classical studies to their culture and their reasons for liking the Classics courses that they did. The chapter puts on record the times, experiences, and contributions of different staff who have served the Department in varying capacities from the beginning to the present. The reader is invited to reflect on the experiences of teaching and learning Classics in an African context.

In Chapter Four, "A Mini-SWOT Analysis of the Classics Program, Chancellor College," Nyamilandu borrows from the business world the concepts of SWOT (Strengths, Weaknesses, Opportunities, and Threats) analysis in order to gauge the lived experiences of the University of Malawi Classics Department. As a comparative aside, the chapter gives a summary of analysis of similar issues from select international university Classics programs which have been compared with UNIMA Classics—for the purposes of reflecting on features that may relate to best practice and may be worth emulating. Next, both positive and negative attributes are discussed, along with possible opportunities on which to capitalise. Finally, the threats—both previous and current—are explored. The current threat concerning the restructuring and/or functional review as a consequence of the delinking process of UNIMA Colleges into stand-alone universities, and the implications thereof, is explained.

Samson Kambalu

Samson Kambalu is an artist and writer working in a variety of media, including site-specific installation, video, performance, and literature. His work is auto-biographical, and approaches art as an arena for critical thought and sovereign activities. Born in Malawi, Kambalu's work fuses aspects of the *Nyau* masking culture of the Chewa, the anti-reification theories of the Situationist movement, and the Protestant tradition of inquiry, criticism, and dissent.

Kambalu's first book, an autobiographical novel of his childhood upbringing in Malawi, *The Jive Talker*, was published by Jonathan Cape in 2008 and toured around Europe for four years. He has been featured in major exhibitions and projects worldwide, including the Dakar Biennale (2014, 2016), Tokyo International Art Festival (2009) and the Liverpool Biennial (2004, 2016). He was included in *All the World's Futures*, Venice Biennale 2015, curated by Okwui Enwezor. His public sculpture *Antelope*, featuring the Malawian Baptist preacher and Pan-Africanist John Chilembwe (cf. above), was selected to go on the Fourth Plinth in Trafalgar Square, London, in 2022.

Kambalu attended Kamuzu Academy (1989-1995), then studied at the University of Malawi (BA Fine Art and Ethnomusicology). In England, he continued his studies at Nottingham Trent University (MA Fine Art) and then Chelsea College of Art and Design (PhD Fine Art). Having begun his academic career at the University of Malawi, he has won research fellowships with Yale University and the Smithsonian Institution and is now a Professor of Fine Art at the Ruskin School of Art and a Fellow of Magdalen College, Oxford.

His elephantine contribution to this book forms Chapter One. He makes a case for the view that Kamuzu Banda's political thinking was informed by Aristotle's analysis in *Politics* Book Five, regarding what factors make sole rulers/tyrants effective and their regimes durable. Aristotle's "aporetic method has driven Western appetite for knowledge since antiquity," Kambalu observes. The discussion of Banda, informed by Freud's thinking on the "primal father," is located within a historical exposition of what it means to be a Chewa—as Banda was, and as Kambalu is—and how the Great Dance (*Gule Wamkulu*) is where the "Nyanja identity is revealed as part of the larger scheme of things." After reflecting on the formation of modern Malawi through the trauma of resistance to colonial rule (in the days of John Chilembwe) and struggle over who would have the upper hand after independence (centered around Henry Masauko Chipembere), Kambalu places Banda as Malawi's Peisistratus. He follows the story of Banda's rule to the end and beyond, to the ambivalent monumentalizing of his rule—concluding by offering a new insight into "what [Banda] meant with the riddle, you are not educated until you know Latin and Greek?"

Emily Greenwood

Emily Greenwood is Professor of Classics and Comparative Literature, Harvard University. She spent a formative eleven-year period in Malawi as a child and teenager (1982–1993). In Chapter Three, she builds around Kamuzu Banda's founding of Kamuzu Academy, reflecting on his purposes and the "overdetermined legacy of Greek and Roman Classics in the modern world." She contrasts his hopes and values with how Latin was used by George Simeon Mwase in the service of a national consciousness, and comments on the circumstances behind Aleke Banda's clash with President Banda over the cost of the Academy— after Aleke Banda, co-founder of the Malawi Congress Party, endorsed Kamuzu Banda as leader of the Party in 1959. Greenwood finds that "the most salient mediating tradition" in the background of Kamuzu Banda's promotion of the Classics was the tradition of America's Historically Black Colleges and Universities—in this context discussing the contrasting kinds of thinking put forward by W. E. B. Du Bois and Booker T. Washington. Banda's unpublished autobiography, which exists in typescript in the H. K. Banda archive in Bloomington, Indiana, is drawn on in this chapter.

Michael Chappell

In Chapter Five, Michael Chappell (Lecturer in Classics, Chancellor College, University of Malawi) adopts a teaching-centred approach, basing his contribution around an account of his coming from the UK to Chancellor College in 1998 as an expatriate Lecturer in Classics. He is the longest-serving white member of staff in the Department, having left the College in 2001 but returning in 2013—since which time he has continued to teach there. He reflects on the role played by expatriate teachers at Chancellor College (and Kamuzu Academy). In connection with teaching epic, Chappell writes of teaching Genesis and *Gilgamesh*, the *Epic of Sunjata* (West Africa), and the *Mwindo Epic* (Congo): with epic, he asks, is one dealing with a "purely western construct based largely on Homer?" In answer, he points to the dual identity of Homer: as ancestor of written epics on the one hand, but, on the other, as a traditional oral poet—comparable to other oral poets worldwide. In the epic context, he comments on Aimé Césaire's *Cahier d'un retour au pays natal* and Derek Walcott's *Omeros*, outlining how his own praxis in teaching centres around equipping students with strategies of postcolonial reading. Chappell continues with an account of his priorities in teaching tragedy and in teaching

Greek and Roman religion: in general, he sees Classics teaching as "a fruitful way of looking at the relationship between colonial and postcolonial cultures."

Cybelle Greenlaw

Cybelle Greenlaw's sojourn at Chancellor College fell between Michael Chappell's departure in 2001 and his return in 2013. Her university education in Classics was followed by disillusionment after making a professional start in the museum world—and then, in 2006, an advertisement, recommended by a Dublin friend, led to a job offer from Chancellor College. Her first impression of Zomba was of natural beauty, marred by ugly reminders of colonialism.

In Chapter Six of the present volume, she offers a narrative commencing from her mother's primate sanctuary—first established in Tacoma, Washington and later relocated to Greenlaw's own house in Kansas City. She writes of relations with Malawi-based American diplomats: the strong and weak points of their understanding of what faced them in Malawi. She reflects with mixed feelings on a departmental retreat by Lake Malawi and on a visit to the home village of Loudon Umi Gama, her housekeeper. In a course she teaches on Greek philosophy, perplexing questions arise in a discussion of wealth and poverty, and an encounter with Apollodorus *Against Neaera* calls forth expressions of strongly contrasting views by women and men students. With a new acquaintance—a recipient of a Clinton Library grant to promote democracy in Malawi—Greenlaw attends an American Embassy reception, where she is introduced to the American ambassador. Baboons and vervet monkeys peek from behind every paragraph, and this rich chapter concludes with observations on the (in)visibility of people with disabilities in Zomba, on contrasting expectations at grading time, and on an encounter with the Malawi Police.

Esela Munthali

The path which led Esela Munthali to Classics began in Lusaka at the American Embassy School, then continued at Kamuzu Academy and Chancellor College as an Assistant Lecturer from 2008 to 2019, where her duties included teaching Greek democracy. She makes lecturers' side gigs the focus of Chapter Seven, commencing with her own avocation as a baker and her cake shop/café in Zomba. Her theme is how side gigs relate economically to an academic career—in Malawi and beyond. She summarizes what leads to success in the academic world: higher degrees and publications, but advancement via promotion and improvements in one's (inadequate) African academic salary can be no more than part of the matrix. One must strategize effectively, but there are other opportunities which may make an academic career worthwhile. The drawback is the danger of being distracted from delivering full value in teaching. Munthali writes of her own commitment as a trade union delegate, and the 2012 academic freedom campaign which cemented her certainty in the effectiveness of the academic union at Chancellor College in representing its members to the employer. But union activity is not exactly a side gig, and, in the case of the latter, Munthali finds optimistic conclusions implausible under present conditions in the African academy.

M. D. Usher

Chapter Eight, by M. D. Usher of the University of Vermont, builds on Usher's 2014 article in *Arion*, turning once more to Pier Paolo Pasolini's "Notes for an African *Oresteia*." Usher here figures Zomba as Malawi's Athens and recalls the factors which have drawn him towards it—back to his days as a graduate student at the University of Chicago. Communications with Dr. Henri de Marcellus, then Head of the Classics Department at the University of Malawi, were followed by conversations with Dr. Caroline Alexander and Prof. Moira Chimombo. Afterwards, while Usher was teaching at Willamette University in Salem, Oregon, he began to investigate Pasolini's interest in George Thomson and Thomson's *Aeschylus and Athens*. Academic visits to Chancellor College followed: the first in 2010, when he stayed six weeks and taught a seminar on the *Oresteia*; then further visits in 2011 and 2015. Usher interrogates the "intrusive gaze" of Pasolini's camera in Tanzania and Uganda, and reflects on his use of newsreel footage from the Biafran War. In the concluding part of this chapter, Usher reflects on R. M. Ogilvie's 1979 report, its recommendations, and two of the challenges which have arisen: recruiting well-qualified expatriate staff and—concomitantly—developing Malawian staff, in a country where no postgraduate education in Classics is available.

Ted Jenner

A prose poem responding to his own arrival in Zomba, by the late Ted Jenner (Chancellor College Lecturer in Classics, 1998 to 2001 and 2005 to 2007, and historian of the Department[96]), forms a coda to the book.

Careful Commentary

An Introduction should not reach a conclusion, and this one duly will not. Those who have taught Classics at Chancellor College represent a diversity of kinds of classicists: Father Hunter was a scion of the Universities Mission to Central

[96] Jenner 2001.

Africa[97]—a High Church Oxonian—and a man who could ride his bicycle in the opposite direction to the movement of a rioting crowd and remain untouched. It was no surprise when some came to think he had powers which went far beyond Latin accidence. There have been armchair classicists, some of them of the decadent type; romantic classicists, some of whom might be called *disillusioned* romantic classicists; American classicists of more-than-Alexandrian refinement; uppity classicists who saw in Malawi something very far from an ideal state; and subversive classicists who could not be reconciled, even provisionally, to prevailing conditions.

This book, therefore, constitutes a laying of cards on the table. Banda deputized Ogilvie, whose attitudes to empire and to race (as noted above) scarcely bear examination, to plan a Classics Department for him. Ogilvie was a disciple of Benjamin Jowett, who is credited with having said "Never retreat. Never explain. Get it done and let them howl." Howls have gone up—from Kerr and Mapanje,[98] for example. So, in the face of the issues raised by the continuing existence of an outpost of Classics teaching in the heart of Black Africa, some careful commentary, at least, is called for. This is what the Monumentalists offer.

[97] After 1968, United Society for the Propagation of the Gospel; since 2016, United Society Partners in the Gospel.
[98] Kerr and Mapanje 2002:80.

1

A Man Half Wicked

Banda, Aristotle, and the Malawian Political Imaginary

SAMSON KAMBALU

Prologue—*Bwalo:* What It Means to Be a Chewa

USING HIS UNDERSTANDING of the ancient animatic philosophy *Nyau*[1], the author would like to argue that the Chewa, or the Amang'anja of Malawi, are not really a tribe[2] but rather an elective community of sovereigns, a gathering of *virombo*,[3] as expressed in their *Nyau* masking: the *Gule Wamkulu*,[4] literally the "Great Dance" or the "Great Prayer."[5] Every Chichewa[6] speaker will know that the name Amang'anja is meant to enchant, summoning the primordial identity of this "non-tribe." More than the prosaic "people of the lake," Amang'anja speaks of a "people of an existential void." The *akumadzi*—literally "those from

---

[1] *Nyau* could simply be described as a Chewa philosophy of "excess." *Nyau* philosophy and its masking tradition *Gule Wamkulu* ("the Great Dance" or "the Great Prayer") are built around the work of negative energy (also known as "cool" energy among the Chewa): see Breugel 2001 or Morris 2000:137. *Nyau* religion is, thus, "animatic," from the Latin anima meaning "soul," rather than animist.

[2] The Chewa, or Amang'anja, are the remnant of the original Amaravi peoples of Southern Africa before the fragmentation of their society around 1400 into the various tribes seen in Malawi today, such as the Tumbuka, Yao, or Senga. See Phiri 1997:22–23. Elsewhere, the author has referred to the Amaravi of Nyasaland as Nyanja peoples—"lake peoples"—as *nyasa* is archaic for *nyanja*.

[3] To borrow from Hegel, the singular, or chirombo, could be translated as an "animal soul" to describe the human soul in its pre-ontological state.

[4] On Chewa *Nyau* masking and religion, see Breugel 2001.

[5] Not all *Gule Wamkulu* dance; ritual play is the basic premise of *Nyau* masks. See Boucher 2012.

[6] The language is also known as Nyanja (literally "lake") or Chinyanja ("of the lake").

the waters"[7]—is the pre-ontological vortex of being[8] from which the Chewa "Great Dance," *Gule Wamkulu*, emerges, *ex nihilo*. One deduces from the *Gule Wamkulu* that the Chewa are indeed the universal substance of the Amaravi tribes of Malawi and of humanity at large—at least conceptually speaking. One finds in *Gule Wamkulu* a retinue of all kinds of masked personages, *visudzo*, from Malawi history: primal ancestors (the so-called Akafula or the Amwandionerapati), Arabs (*Aluya*), Indians (*Amwenye*), slave traders, Angoni, Chinese merchants, European colonialists (*Atsamunda*), Muslims (*Achinasala*), Christians, uxorilocal men (*akamwini*), and so on.[9] It is as if *Gule Wamkulu* is a depository—a *dambwe*[10]—for all humanity and its ideas. *Gule Wamkulu* essentially reveals that to be a Chewa simply means to be a human being—*munthu*—in all one's basic "animality," existential excesses, and mystery. It is, thus, most fitting that, since 2008, *Gule Wamkulu* has been inscribed on the UNESCO Representative List of the Intangible Cultural Heritage of Humanity.[11]

The author would further argue that a real Chewa is an "individualist"—an egotist, even.[12] *Gule Wamkulu* symbolic casting and socialized theater[13] shows that a typical Chewa *Dasein* is a potentially disruptive player both in their community (*mudzi*) and the "cosmopolis" (*mzinda*),[14] a "*homo ludens*"[15] by default, even a "man-child" (*nthumbidwa*).[16] Chewa characteristic individualism is further evidenced within everyday life by endemic "petulance" in the form of pathological *nsanje* (envy) and covert egoism disguised as extreme altruism and asceticism among Malawians. Malawians themselves are aware of this *nsanje* phenomenon at the heart of their cultural and political identity. The Malawi national anthem includes an appeal to God to protect the nation

---

[7] See Morris 2000:134. The Chewa God of this primordial vortex is known as Chauta, "the pool" (Schoffeleers 1999:201).

[8] Or say the "night of the world." The author has again borrowed from Hegel here to describe humanity in its pre-ontological state as conceived by the Chewa.

[9] For a plethora of colorful *Gule Wamkulu* masks, see Boucher 2012.

[10] A *Gule Wamkulu* workshop, usually located at the graveyard.

[11] UNESCO n.d.

[12] Or say sovereign individual, not to be confused with the subject of consumerism and capital who one would argue is not truly an individualist. See Žižek's body of work for his general take on egoism and individualism in late capitalism.

[13] See Boucher 2012.

[14] The Chewa idea of an ethical city, *mzinda*, in many ways resembles the Greek polis in its regard of its members as elective individuals, as celebrated in *Gule Wamkulu*. See Boucher 2012.

[15] On the relationship between culture and play (that could apply to the Chewa Dasein), see Huizinga 1949.

[16] In *Nyau*, a *nthumbidwa* is an uninitiated subject, an unbridled egotist, naïve to the ways of the world, sometimes an outright neurotic.

from "envy."[17] Rampant individualism and egotism ultimately mark the Chewa commitment to a radical democracy.[18]

The Chewa as a matriarchal "non-tribe" have no "father," in the Oedipal sense: men and the core family are marginal, children are raised communally at *kuka,*[19] and, in *mphalas,*[20] their main guardian is their *nkhoswe.*[21] The Chewa also do not have any metaphysical big Other, such as the idea of God or the written law: Chewa chiefs are titular, and, where God[22] exists, he or she is at best otiose, indifferent, and resolutely materialist.[23] Taboo—*mdulo*[24]—marks the presence of God among the Chewa as a negative agency, or *Nyau.* The Chewa adherence to spiritual materialism is manifest as studied asceticism[25] and obsession with "purity" of character—the idea of *munthu wabwino,* universal man.[26] At initiation, the young adept is shown the vacuous underbelly of a tilted *Kasiya Maliro*—the principal *Nyau* demiurge, a theriomorphic womb structure disguised as an

---

[17] Malawi's national anthem as composed by Michael-Frederick Paul Sauka in 1964:
O God bless our land of Malawi.
Keep it a land of peace.
Put down each and every enemy,
Hunger, disease, envy.
Join together all our hearts as one,
That we be free from fear.
Bless our leader, each and every one,
And Mother Malaŵi.

[18] Russell 1930:90–91 posits envy as one of the prices to be paid for democracy—a horizontal system that replaces hierarchy with diversity.

[19] The *kuka* is where women communally prepare food and drink, raise toddlers, and socialize. It is the center of the everyday life in a Chewa village. See Power 2010:134. In *Our African Way of Life,* Banda and Cullen Young (1946) call the *kuka* "the talking place."

[20] *Mphala* is a youth clubhouse.

[21] A designated family advisor and guardian, male or female. See Phiri 1997:33–34.

[22] The fact that even the idea of God is parodied and traversed in *Gule Wamkulu* shows that the *Nyau* animatic religion is older than the idea of God. In *Gule Wamkulu, Chisumphi* appears as a fattened and protruded water python, *Thunga,* most probably alluding to an unresolved theological deadlock. See Linden 1979:187–188 and Boucher 2012:188.

[23] See Schoffeleers 1999:202.

[24] See Breugel 2001.

[25] Malawians will wear conspicuous poverty rehearsed in *Gule Wamkulu* as a badge of honor. See Breugel 2001. This has its reverse manifestation in contemporary times, as endemic dandyism.

[26] In olden and colonial times, the obsession with subjective purity among the Chewa was manifest by frequent outbreaks of *mwabvi* ordeal events orchestrated by a medicine man (*sing'anga*), where villagers drank a poisonous solution made from *erythroplaeum guineense* (the ordeal tree) to prove their purity. It was a risky challenge that frequently resulted in death. See Breugel 2001:220–222.

antelope[27]—and is told by the elders *"Kulibe!"*, "There is nothing!",[28] thereby making it clear to him that a Chewa God does not "exist."[29] The adept's ego is crossed out by *mphini* markings on his body, and he is run through a gauntlet of various purges[30] and trials to prepare him for a lifetime of inevitable suffering and recurring subjective destitution, which he will affirm and traverse in the jouissance of a ritual *Nyau* dance (*Gule Wamkulu*) and acts of prodigious generosity (*kufupa*) at *bwalo*[31] ("the clearing"). The initiate then joins "adulthood" and "community."[32]

The Chewa commitment to the "atheology" of the "clearing," and to radical democracy, can be witnessed in historical grassroots resistance to *Chisumphi*, priests, Islamic and Christian patriarchy, colonialism, and indeed any other attempts at social, religious, or political centralization throughout Amaravi history.[33] The Chewa, as a "non-tribe," only renounce their characteristic individualism for community temporarily, and often only superficially: for example, when the *Gule Wamkulu* is in session at *bwalo* and in various social interventions or ritual ceremonies, such as the coronation of a chief, commemoration of the dead (*mpalo*), or female initiations (*chinamwali*).[34] The Chewa will occupy themselves in communal rites and ritual acts of prodigious gift-giving and potlatches

---

[27] In Chewa ontology, all aspects of sexuation encapsulated in *Kasiya Maliro* indicate that only one sex exists, manifesting in varying degrees either as man or woman—hence the principal Nyau womb structure *Kasiya Maliro* disguising as a male antelope. The womb's Fallopian tubes are disguised as antlers. From another perspective, the womb appears as the pubis area but upside down—see Boucher 2012:106–107. In *Gule Wamkulu*, masked characters, visudzo, are animated by historical time while theriomorphic structures allude to cosmological time; see Morris 2000:140. *Kasiya Maliro* dances round and round, usually at night. During the day, she can often be seen accompanied by children. Children are an important part of the *Nyau* performance which often employs "interpassivity" (a surrogate form of belief—see Pfaller 2017) and the make-believe for effect.

[28] Author's personal experience. Also see Smith 2001.

[29] Here the author would like to disagree with Slavoj Žižek that Christianity is the only "materialist" religion in the world that arrives at a post-metaphysical "atheist" God through a philosophical or theological deadlock (Žižek 2008:liv–lviii). The Nyau religion has no hidden story: the main message relayed to the initiate is that the mask at *bwalo* hides "nothing." For this reason, it is no wonder that the Chewa have identified plenty of parallels between kenotic Christianity and the *Nyau* religion. See Boucher 2012 and as explored in this study.

[30] See Morris 2000:136.

[31] *Bwalo* is an "ancestral arena," usually a dusty clearing in the bushes, where *Gule Wamkulu* "spirits" gather to perform and where village disputes are settled with mediation from the chief. A previous chief's skull is buried there, at the consecration of the arena. The author has identified *bwalo* as an embodiment of Schelling's primordial "ground of being"/"vortex of drives" (see Žižek 1996)—the *Nyau* itself—where the Chewa come "to be" and to reaffirm their commitment to radical democracy.

[32] For a description of *Nyau* initiation, see Breugel 2001 and Morris 2000.

[33] See Schoffeleers 1999, Breugel 2001 and Boucher 2012.

[34] Schoffeleers 1999:151.

then.[35] When the *Gule Wamkulu* are back at *dambwe,* the primordial "waters," the Chewa are once more an elective community of sovereign individuals at "play," following and performing their own egotist desires and potentially disruptive actions: pursuing the "good life"; taking part in various social games animated by taboo and transgression, elaborate etiquette, rules, and manners (*miyambo*), and participating in politics and an economy of exchange driven by the problematic of gift and necessity. The Chewa essential free-spiritedness and ludic approach to life and community is reflected in a colorful array of oral literature[36] and the metapolitics of *Gule Wamkulu,* which star theriomorphic structures—*nyama*—whose lord of the "dance of life" is the "elephant" (*Njobvu)* or the "lion" (*Mkango).*

Dr. Hastings Kamuzu Banda (1896–1994)—a Chewa, political scientist, physician, and self-styled "Lion" and "Life President" of Malawi from 1964–1994—understood what being a real Chewa meant[37] and it spurred him to work in a post-independence Malawi, for his own political ends. As this "short circuit"[38] study will demonstrate, Aristotle's musings on tyranny were the perfect ready-made tool for this task.

---

[35] Duff 1969—*Nyasaland under the Foreign Office*—is a thoroughly wretched and dehumanized rendition of Malawi under colonial rule. But the book has moments of clear insight on precolonial Amaravi society as animated by an excess of the "gift," or gift economy: "Hospitality ... is exhibited in a marked degree by all Central African natives. Both men and women may constantly be seen sharing their maize or cassava with others who have no food. If a delicacy, such as a cigarette, be given to any one man, he will pass it on to each of his companions in succession, and in the same way practically everything that they have is enjoyed more or less in common. The reception which the natives accord travelling Europeans is singularly hearty and charming, and is extended without stint to all the members of the European retinue, who are at once received into the village circle, supplied with beer and corn, and given quarters for the night. To the European himself the Chief of the village will always present a goat or a sheep, a few fowls or basket of bananas; and if the illustrious friend has no tent, then the best hut available is forthwith placed at his disposal. No doubt in a case of this kind the native casts his bread upon the waters with the assurance of finding it again...".

[36] See Schoffeleers and Roscoe 1985.

[37] An early take on Chewa culture by Banda is *Our African Way of Life* (1946), a book he co-edited with the anthropologist and missionary Thomas Cullen Young.

[38] The author borrows this "short circuit" speculative technique from the Slovene philosopher Slavoj Žižek. Žižek has described the short-circuiting procedure as "to take a major classic (text, author, notion) and read it... through the lens of a 'minor' author, text, or conceptual apparatus ('minor' should be understood here in Deleuze's sense: not 'of lesser quality,' but marginalized, disavowed by the hegemonic ideology, or dealing with a 'lower,' less dignified topic) ... If the minor reference is well chosen, such a procedure can lead to insights which completely shatter and undermine our common perceptions." See Zupančič 2017:vii.

1. *Gule*

It appears that for Aristotle, philosophy is, first and foremost, a sovereign activity. There is a certain jouissance running through his musings transcending the good and the bad, the useful and the useless. As a philosopher, he will consider everything "from deductive inference to detailed descriptions of animal species."[39] Most important, however, is that he thinks, writes, and disseminates. His aporetic method has driven Western appetite for knowledge since antiquity. His relentless analysis and systemization betray an unsettled hysteric, contradicting his call for temperance in everything. He is a ready *Gule* of thinking.

In *Politics,* Aristotle offers advice not only on good governance by the rule of law but also on tyranny—the latter is relayed in an elated tone, as if it is nothing to him as a philosopher. In the same book, he exalts the merits of the "good life" over those of mere living, utility, and the empty pursuit of money and profit for its own sake,[40] yet he also offers insights into the most callous way to gamble and turn a good profit! Aristotle even justifies slavery! So long as it serves (noble) "action" rather mere "production," he says.[41] Clearly, for Aristotle, philosophical action is the most important of all human endeavors. It is as if, for him, philosophy is a political act.[42] It most probably is. As a foreigner and non-citizen in Athens, the Stagira-born Aristotle was not allowed to vote or take part in the city's political process, despite his praise of political action as a precondition for human flourishing in *Politics.*[43] Philosophy was probably the only way he could exercise any real "action" in Athens, and he held on to the discipline religiously, pegging his hopes on posterity by penning numerous tomes. In this regard, Aristotle resembles the marginalized men of the Chewa matrilineal and uxorilocal system (*akamwini*), whose only real influence in the Chewa village (*mudzi*) or cosmopolis (*mzinda*) was through the metapolitics and ritual sovereignty of the *Gule Wamkulu.*[44]

The pursuit of philosophy as a sovereign activity and form of political action is not an entirely impossible common denominator between a philosopher and a dictator.[45] Aristotle's mentor Plato regarded philosophy as an activity "far

---

[39] Everson 1996:xi.
[40] For instance, see Aristotle *Politics* 5:1331b–1332a.
[41] Aristotle *Politics* 1.1254a–1254b.
[42] Althusser 2008:91 has described philosophy as "class struggle in the field of theory." Aspects of German Idealism employed in this study via Hegel, Freud, Lacan, Žižek, and others have also approached philosophy as political praxis. See Žižek 2012:xx.
[43] See Everson 1996:xi.
[44] See Breugel 2001.
[45] See Popper 2005.

more important than democracy"[46] so that for him, as proposed in his *Republic* and *Laws,* an ideal leader of a community would be an enlightened despot—a "philosopher-king."[47] It is at the murky crossroads between philosophy and politics that we must encounter Aristotle with Dr. Hastings Kamuzu Banda,[48] the self-styled *Ngwazi*[49] of the Republic of Malawi from 1964 to 1994.[50]

2. Banda the Hellenophile, or Banda as a Reader of *Politics*

Banda was a Hellenophile.[51] He used to say that you are not educated until you know Latin and Greek and frequently peppered his conversations with Greek[52] and Latin phrases. In 1981, he opened a lavish grammar school, Kamuzu Academy (often dubbed the Eton of the Bush), in Mtunthama, Kasungu, in the middle of "nowhere," where Malawian students from diverse backgrounds and on full scholarship were taught Latin and Greek, exclusively by European teachers. This was intended to create an elite of "future leaders" of the country.

By Banda's standards, the author of this study is learned. As a teenager, from 1989–1995, he attended Banda's Kamuzu Academy and was subjected to Latin and Greek for those six years. On Founder's Day, he had to take part in Greek and Latin plays by Aeschylus, Aristophanes, Plautus, and the like, performed before Banda; the President watched them intently. The author once asked his Greek teacher, Monsieur La Rouche, who was close to the President, "Can Banda really understand Latin and Greek?" Monsieur La Rouche said, "No."[53] It was strange and puzzling. Did Dr. Hastings Kamuzu Banda, a US and UK trained physician with a background in political science, then consider himself not educated?

---

[46] As for example, Plato *Republic* 9.591c–592a.

[47] Plato was sold into slavery in Syracuse while trying to apply praxis to his ideal of the philosopher-king. He was luckily ransomed for twenty minas by a well-wisher, one Anniceris, and sent home (Diogenes Laertius *Lives of the Philosophers* 3.19–20). Some of his followers, though, such as Dion and Callippus, did manage to become tyrants at Syracuse under the pretext of philosophy. Aristotle's own mid-career patron was a former slave and tyrant Hermias of Atarneus (Diogenes Laertius *Lives of the Philosophers* 5.1.5), and the peripatetic philosopher tutored the (then a child) imperialist Alexander of Macedon (Plutarch *Alexander* 7.1-5).

[48] An early comprehensive biography of Banda, especially on Banda's dual heritage of Africa and the West, consulted in this paper is Short 1974.

[49] A Ngoni title meaning "conqueror" or "wise leader" that Banda adopted upon coming to power.

[50] See Alexander 1995.

[51] For an introduction to Banda's enthusiasm for the Classics, see Alexander 1995.

[52] Mgawi 2005:26. Contrary to Mgawi's claim, there is no evidence that Banda actually studied Greek.

[53] Banda studied Latin as part of his high school studies at Wilberforce Institute near Xenia, Ohio. See Short 1974:20.

It turned out Kamuzu Academy cost over one third of the national education budget.[54]

But why did the most famous Chewa in the world prostrate himself before the classical canon with such a costly project? One could only speculate. He perhaps wanted to make it as a complete man of letters by establishing this school. After reading Aristotle's *Politics,* the author has come up with another possible thesis: maybe Kamuzu Academy was an homage to the Greeks for helping him stay in power for so long! As a political scientist and self-styled statesman, Banda might have seen a parallel between the turbulent political life of Aristotle's Greece as it adjusted from "closed" tribal life to democracy[55] and that of his newly independent Malawi—and learnt from it. As this study will specifically show, Banda's "colorful" Life Presidency is a near perfect appendage to Aristotle's nonchalant musings on how tyranny can be preserved. Even where Banda appears to be transgressing Aristotle's rules, he is animated by them and appears deliberate. And just as Aristotle promised (if one followed his rules), Banda's tyranny lasted—for over thirty years.

The price of Banda's exercise in tyranny, though, is that it killed both his own spirit and that of the Amaravi nation, as leader and subjects locked themselves in what the philosopher Achille Mbembe would describe as "mutual zombification" for almost half a century.[56] Malawi is still recovering from the aftermath. Gone are the days when Malawi, as a place of radical democracy, produced leading progressive and revolutionary political and religious figures throughout Southern Africa, such as the Baptist Pan-Africanist John Chilembwe in Nyasaland, trade unionist Clements Kadalie in South Africa, and socialist visionary Oscar Kambona in Tanzania.[57] The Young Turks, as led by Masauko Chipembere in the fight against colonial rule, appear as the last glimmer of true political radicalism in Malawi. Malawians of Banda's political legacy have been described as lethargic, "lacking the spirit of assertiveness,"[58] and prone to bad faith—and the youth as politically indifferent. The introduction of multiparty politics has failed to exorcise a tendency towards anti-democratic practices, which have been evident in a succession of post-1994 governments. By studying Banda's specific political technique[59] through the lens of Aristotle, the author will attempt to map out a possible route to a real political revaluation and recovery for himself and his native country.

---

[54] On the cost of Kamuzu Academy, see Emily Greenwood's chapter in this book.

[55] See Popper 2005.

[56] On the complex relationship between the African dictator and his subjects, see Mbembe 2001.

[57] See Mwakasungura and Miller 2016:12 and Chakanza 1998.

[58] See Mwakasungura and Miller 2016:231.

[59] The author's speculative tools in this endeavor include aspects of Freudian and Lacanian psychoanalysis as expounded by Slavoj Žižek and others.

3. Two Ways to Preserve Tyranny[60]

Aristotle suggests two main opposed and contradicting ways to preserve tyranny: by force, which is the "conventional method" for tyrants, and by the simulation of kingship—"a tyrant should not appear like a tyrant in the eyes of his subjects, but like a king and a manager of a household; not a person who is out for his own gain but as a trustee of the affairs of others, aiming not at a life of excess, but one of moderation."[61] The objectives of ruling by force are to keep subjects in check by depriving them of power, stir up strife among the people to keep them poor and low in spirit, and work up an "extreme form of democracy" where subjects have no confidence in one another. The preservation of tyranny by kingship tactics has one objective: to guard the power of the ruler and thus enable him "to govern not only those who wish him to but also those who do not."[62] The peculiar and heterogeneous nature of Malawi's precolonial and post-colonial political terrain allowed Banda to deploy both methods on the Malawi peoples over his thirty-year rule. The former was modelled on the caprice and brute force of colonial rule; the latter, which we must look at first, on precolonial Amaravi/Malawi "Kalonga" kingship under the Chewa title *Ngwazi*—meaning conqueror, "dynamic and wise leader," or, in other words, "philosopher-king."[63]

4. Where Did You See Me?

Pre-colonial Malawian history[64] is oral. It is often a muddle when set in written text.[65] One needs to introduce some form of framework to make sense of it. This study employs a psychoanalytic framework borrowed from Sigmund Freud's writings on the place of the figure of the "primal father" in tribal kinship in *Totem and Taboo* (1903) and *Moses and Monotheism* (1939) and further expounded by Slavoj Žižek[66] and others. Freud's paternal exception appears to animate the early history of Malawi and throws light on Banda's basic political strategy.

---

[60] The translation of Aristotle's *Politics* quoted in this chapter is that of Sinclair and Saunders 1981, except where noted otherwise.
[61] Aristotle *Politics* 5.1314a–1314b.
[62] Aristotle *Politics* 5.1313a.
[63] Under Banda, Malawi was often portrayed as "one tribe," an Amaravi tribe ruled by one "king." See Short 1974:266 and 281.
[64] The main texts on Malawian pre-colonial history employed here are Schoffeleers 1999 and Phiri 2004.
[65] Schoffeleers and Roscoe 1987:11 put "survival" of the tribe as the rationale behind the versatility of the Malawian oral narrative approach. The author believes the Malawian oral tradition is about social accommodation—oral history is a form of gift giving.
[66] See Žižek 1999.

Nobody knows where the Amaravi peoples came from—there are only spec-ulations.[67] When the Amaravi appeared in southern Africa—around 900[68]—they found the Akafula peoples, also known as the Abatwa or the Amwandionerapati, there. The red-skinned Akafula were short, hot tempered, and prone to violence. One popular folktale narrates that when you came across an Akafula man, he would ask you, "Where did you see me?" When you answered "*Pompano*, just here," he would jump on your back and kill you.[69] The right answer was "*Uko*, from over there!" You pointed at the horizon where you first saw him, for such was Akafula's ego and *Dasein* that, despite his diminutive size, he covered the whole horizon (*dziko*). It is among the Akafula that we find the Amaravi primal father. One can deduce from Akafula behavior that, similar to Freud's paternal exception, he was territorial and that, like a vicious silverback, he terrorized his horde, marginalized his sons, and kept all the women to himself.

The disappearance of the Akafula after the appearance of the Amaravi peoples coincides with the ascendancy of the Amaravi matrilineal system installed by Akafula's sons, the Bandas ("those who live in the open plain"). Having killed their father (and most probably eaten him as a sacrament),[70] the Bandas set up a radical, democratic, matrilineal society ruled by spirit-wives housed at rain shrines scattered high-up in hills and mountains throughout Amaravi territory. [71] There, various sacrificial rites and potlatches were carried out in ritualized play affected by *Nyau* masks and the spirit-wives, who commu-nicated God's messages in dreams and ecstasies.[72]

5. *Gule Wamkulu*

The Bandas most likely established the *Nyau* secret society[73] that exists to this day as a form of social construct and to expiate the guilt of their father's murder. The Amaravi primal father's exceptional behavior animates *Nyau* masks—collectively

---

[67] Accounts vary from Schoffeleers 1999 to Phiri 2004. They have included attempts to deduce a detailed account of early Amaravi history from Herodotus' histories of Africa—see Phiri 2004:14–15.

[68] See Phiri 1997:22.

[69] See Lamba 1983:1 and Phiri 2004:14.

[70] *Bwalo* (the "clearing"), an arena where the *Gule Wamkulu* gather to perform, always has the skull of a chief buried there—see Breugel 2001. The *Gule Wamkulu* and its adherents dance over the chief's skull. Here Freud's theory that the primal father was killed and probably ritualistically eaten by his sons—as is re-enacted in Christian communion—is accommodated.

[71] See Schoffeleers 1999:151–153.

[72] See Schoffeleers 1999:153.

[73] While the genealogy of the *Nyau* secret society can be worked out from its function among the Chewa, the origins of *Nyau* masking are unknown—see Morris 2000:132. The Chewa say where there are people, there is *Nyau*. See Breugel 2001.

known as *Gule Wamkulu*—in dramatic choreography and performance routines, which are, at once, intimidating, petulant, and lascivious.[74] *Gule* sings in an otherworldly falsetto, like a castrato backed by a comforting chorus of women, to mark his sublime impotence, which he makes up for in ritual sovereignty and jural immunity: what one does while wearing a *Nyau* mask is beyond good and evil and beyond the reach of the law[75] and everyday customs.[76] His driven dance and song are usually cut in midair by the *tsabwalo* (master of ceremonies) who shouts *"Kwawo! Kwawo!"* ("Time to go home!") in an apparent re-enactment of his primal castration.[77]

Within the *Nyau* rite of passage explored earlier, the Amaravi primal father is revealed as a spoilt man-child who should be renounced by the boy upon entering adulthood.[78] From there, the primal father will haunt the boy's entire adulthood as an insatiable "ancestral spirit" in many guises, and as a mediator between the living and the undead, and who has to be constantly negotiated with and appeased in sacrifices, libations, and ritual *Nyau* dances.[79]

Gule Wamkulu, where the Nyanja identity is revealed as part of the larger scheme of things,[80] expresses the Chewa affirmative jouissance even in the face

---

[74] A comprehensive description and photographic documentation of the *Gule Wamkulu* is found in Boucher 2012. The catalogue, though very informative, is also an unwitting charting of how elements of the Western mimetic tradition and missionary moralism and didactics have come to dominate contemporary conceptions of *Gule*. *Nyau* appears in danger of losing its ancient penchant for real abstraction.

[75] See Morris 2000:137 and Schoffeleers 1999:151.

[76] A standard description of Chewa *Nyau* animatic religion is by Breugel 2000:125–168.

[77] This enactment of the primal father's "castration" or say "fall" is, in the author's opinion, the most significant part of the *Gule* performance. The cut marks the moment when a Chewa man gives up on his infantile indulgences and fantasies to join an elective community as a responsible sovereign individual.

[78] As observed by Short 1974:9. In *Our African Way of Life* (1946), Banda and Cullen Young edit a piece by a young Malawian writer named Kambalame on the *Nyau* initiation process. Banda's description of *Nyau* as a "primitive masonic brotherhood" and "carnival" reeks of missionary moralism and does not go far enough. *Nyau* might look carnivalesque in *Gule Wamkulu*, but its ritual application is much deeper and darker than mere entertainment, commemoration, or male bonding. As argued earlier, *Nyau* is the very pith of the Chewa Dasein.

[79] Thus, unlike other tribes where the "name of the father" is "real" and demonstrated through circumcision as is seen among the Yao—see Morris 2000—the Chewa never really disavow their childish ways upon entering adulthood. This is what is revealed in the *Gule Wamkulu* petulant libidinal dance that the Chewa society need to constantly traverse and "cut" on to remain a community. Many aspects of modern Chewa culture remain resolutely "anti-Oedipal" (see Deleuze and Guattari 2019). The author portrays his Chewa father's struggle with modern patriarchal fatherhood in his satirical coming of age memoir *The Jive Talker, or How to Get a British Passport* (2008).

[80] For the author's personal experience of the *Nyau* initiation process, see Kambalu 2008:229–246.

of extreme suffering.[81] Although exclusive to men—and elected women beyond childbearing age, usually one woman per *dambwe*[82]—the *Nyau* allegiance to the matrilineal system and prodigious gift giving is seen in its principal masquerade structure, ominously named *Kasiya Maliro* ("that which lays down the dead"), which is a womb disguised as an antelope. It is a symbol of the radical generosity which lies at the heart of the Amaravi society.

6. Of the One Who Packs the Heads of the Dead

For hundreds of years, the Bandas lived in clusters of stateless villages until another phratry of Amaravi, known as the Phiri, appeared on the scene— some speculate around the fourteenth century[83]—bringing ideas of the "law" and centralized governance. The Phiri were led by the all-conquering warlord Kalonga ("one who packs heads of the dead"), who bore all the mythical brute attributes of the Akafula pygmy and the ritual sovereignty of the *Nyau* masks[84]— it is as if the banished Amaravi primal father had returned to take revenge on his sons with interest; and it is said that when Kalonga asked you, "Where did you see me?" and you pointed at the horizon, he killed you and added your head

---

[81] See Short 1974:10. The philosopher George Bataille, in his last interview, published in Richard 1998, explains a link between existential laughter, masks (the grotesques, the *danse macabre*), suffering, and death: "In portraying death under comical features people sought to escape its terrible aspect..." (Richard 1998:225).

[82] See Schoffeleers 1999:150. This is as *Gule Wamkulu* appears to the lay person. In fact, all Chewa people can be said to belong to the *Nyau* secret society. There can be no *Gule Wamkulu* without the involvement of women, as chorus and as central members of the Chewa "non-tribe." See Bruegel 2001:132. We can here borrow from Lacanian sexuation, as is further expounded by Žižek 1993 and Zupančič 2017: Chewa woman, as the "primal sex," already wear a mask, and so, in *Gule Wamkulu*, only the men wear the mask, and the women provide the chorus. The counterpoint to the male space of the *bwalo* is the women's *kuka*, where the women dominate everyday life in a Chewa village. The *kuka* has a form of masking called *chinkhome*, performed by women, but this is more an amusement and narrative theater—see Breugel 2001:133. At *bwalo*, the *Gule* negotiate with women through the chorus for meaning, while at the *kuka*, the women have to contend with ongoing disruptive potlatches by roaming *Gule* who will seek to interrupt the women's sedated camaraderie, stealing their food, turning over their cooking utensils, and interrupting their storytelling. This is from the author's own experience of *Nyau* at Misi, his father's home village, in Dowa District.

[83] Schoffeleers 1999:150 describes the Phiri as "a group of royal invaders." His reading is probably led by colonial justification. This study would like to propose that the Phiri appeared on the scene out of the Amaravi class antagonism common to growing communities. The splitting of the Amaravi into Banda and Phiri phratries most likely happened in an attempt to resolve a political deadlock.

[84] Deduced from folklore description of Kalonga from the author's childhood and Mwase 1967:13–14.

to his collection.[85] The right answer, rather, was to point at the sun and the stars, for such was Kalonga's confidence of his place in the universe. Kalonga banished the Banda high priestess, Makewana ("mother of the children"), the spirit-wives, and *Nyau* masks to the fringes of Chewa society and introduced blood sacrifices at the rain shrines, which his priests came to run. God of the primordial vortex, *Chauta* was replaced by a new metaphysical "High God" *Chisumphi*. To consolidate and integrate his power among the Bandas, Kalonga married a Banda queen (*mfumu kazi*), Mwali, a former spirit-wife.[86]

Kalonga ruled through headmen, who replaced the offices of the spirit-wives. He demanded taxes in elephant tusks and opened the Amaravi region to trade, including trade in slaves.[87] His clan, the Phiri ("those who live on a hill"), became the ruling class. Any resemblance to a modern nuclear family to be found among the Chewa most probably took root around this time. New myths and histories of the origins of the Amaravi peoples[88] had to be propagated by Kalonga's officials, along with new codes of morality. Kalonga had numerous wives, who ensured offspring to sustain his kingship after his death.[89] Soon enough, the Amaravi Kalonga kingship met resistance from the grassroots, spearheaded by a spiritual leader ("rainmaker") named Mu'ona,[90] whose martyrdom haunts the Malawian political imaginary to this day—as this study will argue.

---

[85] Such folklore on Kalonga's appetite for carnivalesque violence and as communicated by Mwase 1967 was prevalent in the author's childhood in Malawi.

[86] This was a decisive moment in power relations between the Banda and the Phiri. By marrying Mwali, Kalonga identified himself as a nkamwini—in effect, a "foreigner"—to the Chewa matrilineal and uxorilocal system. In time, Kalonga was seen more as a prince consort than a king. See Schoffeleers 1999:194.

[87] Phiri 2004:16.

[88] See Phiri 2004.

[89] Through his pathological autocratic deeds, Kalonga appears to have mistaken or exploited the ritual sovereignty and jural immunity of *Gule Wamkulu* for real power. It is, thus, possible that Kalonga was a *nthumbidwa*—a man-child or even an outright neurotic who was never initiated into the *Gule Wamkulu*. Another possibility is that he was a naïve *nkamwini*, who believed in the possibility of a "real society." The story of Kalonga shows the precariousness of the Chewa elective community aimed at accommodating social antagonism through *Nyau*. It might also why explain why the Chewa are suspicious of "strangers" and villagers who have not "bought the path" into the *Nyau* secret society.

[90] See the "Rainmaker" episode below. The rainmaker is now popularly known as Mbona, which, in the author's opinion, is a derogatory and disparaging derivative of the Nyanja Mu'ona or Muwona meaning "seer," or "the one who sees"—Schoffeleers 1999:162. In order to invite a revaluation of this very critical figure in Amaravi history, this study has reverted to the seer's original name, Mu'ona.

7. *Nkamwini* King

In time, the Amaravi radical democracy and matrilineal system returned, albeit in a synthetic form:[91] Kalonga's authority lived on as a weakened institution represented by less powerful tributary kings, as the Amaravi peoples fragmented once more, but this time into various tribes ruled by titular chiefs.[92] Banda priests—from the Mbewe clan—were placed at the rain shrine,[93] and the high god *Chisumphi* was synthesized and radicalized as a restless water python spirit, *Thunga*.[94] *Nyau* was rehabilitated as the "people's prayer."[95] Among the Chewa and Mang'anja, each titular chief was ironically known as *mwini dziko* ("owner of the land") and *mwini dambwe* or *mwini mzinda* (the "owner of the *Nyau*")[96]—in a more descriptive way, "the manager of the polis or cosmopolis."[97] They had libidinal counterparts in *Gule Wamkulu,* such as *Chadzunda, Njobvu* (elephant), and *Mkango* (lion).[98] The chief ruled as a necessity, in consultation with the people and his *nduna* (an executive committee), and mediated on legal matters (*milandu*) at the *bwalo*. He was also, thus, along with the *Gule Wamkulu* masks, the principal agent of the Chewa (*eudaimonia*), and an executor and manager of prodigious gift giving, which guised in many forms, including complex bureaucratic institutions (*unduna*), politics (*ndale*), spiritual and creative revelations, elaborate rituals and etiquette, taboo and ritual transgression, *Nyau* acts, interpretation of dreams, and ongoing *Gule Wamkulu* interventions and raves at the *kuka* and the *bwalo*.[99]

The troubled *Chadzunda* (meaning "one who is deprived of authority" or "the miserable one")[100] bore the carnivalized despotic and petulant traits of the deceased Kalonga as the "lord of the dance." As is said in his song, *Gule Wamkulu n'Chadzunda* ("The Great Dance of *Chadzunda*"), his real name is *Chadzunda*, meaning "There

[91] On the recovered prominence of women in the Kalonga aftermath, see Linden 1979:189.
[92] See Lwanda 1993:2.
[93] See Schoffeleers 1999:153.
[94] The protruded Thunga, as portrayed in *Gule Wamkulu* (see Boucher 2012:188), can be likened to Kraken, the legendary gigantic (squid) sea monster of Scandinavian folklore—see Žižek 2016— and a symbol of radical ontological difference, the *Nyau* itself. As will be seen in the "Rainmaker" section below, Thunga, with his restless tentacles, came to disturb the centralizing metaphysical religion of Kalonga, further diminishing his hold over Chewa peoples.
[95] See Schoffeleers 1999:151.
[96] The Chief is more an honorary member of *Nyau*, which is a society independent of his bureaucratic authority. See Morris 2000:133.
[97] Whereas the localized Chewa polis (*mudzi*) can be identified with clusters of early Amaravi settlements in Southern Africa, the cosmopolis (*mzinda*) marks the Chewa opening to a bureaucratic democracy and "internationalism" in the aftermath of Kalonga.
[98] Boucher 2012:124.
[99] For detailed aspects of the Nyanja general economy, see Breugel 2001.
[100] See Boucher 2012:95.

is only one *Gule*, *Chadzunda*, and *Gule Wamkulu* is but his impossibility."[101] It was in the style of the post-Kalonga titular chiefs that Banda fashioned himself as *mwini dziko* and *mwini mzinda* upon his return from Europe to lead Malawi to independence from the British. It was a prelude to his real return as "the one who packs heads of the dead." This was a political tactic that enabled him to apply Aristotle's contradicting methods for preserving tyranny on the ready peoples of Malawi in the most effective way.

8. Tyranny by Kingship

Aristotle renders the ideal tyrant by kingship as follows: he looks the part of a king and plays it well; he presents himself as a religious and pious man; he is a man of the people but is also friends with notables; he appears more as a steward and manager of his people; he exercises moderation in his appetites; he treats women and children with respect; he posits himself as a protector of women and cultivates a loving relationship with the youth; he refrains from harming women and children; when he punishes his followers, it appears to be out of fatherly love; he refrains from anger in proceedings; he refrains from upsetting men of honor and those with nothing to lose; he punishes men of achievement gradually, not at once; public works in his honor appear as a gift from the public; he appears to work for the common good; he encourages open accountability, keeping public records of finance; he keeps his wealth hidden in the open as a public purse; when he taxes and extracts gifts from the public, it is as if for the public good; he conducts himself with dignity; he creates images of valor in battle; and he honors his men lavishly but does not single out favorites.[102]

As we shall see, Banda's political strategy as "Kalonga" is, from the beginning of his political career, animated by these rules. Where the rules appear to have been transgressed, Banda was laboring to adapt them to modern times and to a specific Amaravi context, some of which we have outlined so far.

---

[101] *Chadzunda*, thus, shows the Chewa primal subject as divided—between their symbolic identity and an unfathomable ego. His descendants—man or woman—are marked by the same identity expressed in the affected hysteria of *Nyau* dance. Following on from Chewa ideas of non-binary sexuation apropos Lacanian psychoanalysis, it could be deduced that the nankungwi or *wakunjira* ("of the path")—the single woman allowed at *dambwe*—represents the "castrated" *Chadzunda* himself as lord of his impossibility, the *Gule Wamkulu*.
[102] Aristotle *Politics* 5.1314a–1315b.

9. Messiah

Banda's return to Malawi in 1958 to take over the leadership of the struggling Nyasaland African Congress (NAC)[103] is sold as messianic.[104] He anticipates this narrative with widely circulated pastoral letters to his followers, urging them to take heart in their fight against colonial rule as deliverance is "at hand." Messengers are sent to the remotest parts of Malawi to proclaim his imminent return.[105]

There is a false start on 29 June 1958: there is a riot of 10,000 people when a British plane lands at Chileka airport in Blantyre but does not produce a messiah.[106] Then, on 6 July 1958, people gather once more at Chileka, but this time Banda appears out of the sky and lands on Malawi soil after forty years abroad—to ululation and jubilation. Chiefs are there to welcome him, bringing with them a civet cat, a garland of flowers, and other gifts.[107] Wearing a homburg hat, trench coat, and three-piece suit, the messiah looks like a film star. There is magic in the air.

Banda says he has come to act as a bridge in the "gap" between Africans on the one hand, and Asians and Europeans on the other, and between the "old and the new"[108]—in other words, as a "mediator," or an Amaravi chief's role among the living, and the *Gule Wamkulu* role among the living and the dead.[109] He has, in effect, announced himself as a *Nyau* leader. But little did the people know that he meant an exceptional leadership that would be animated by a pseudo-Amaravi radical democracy on the one hand and, on the other, outright Kalonga despotism modelled on colonial rule. He shouts "*Kwacha!*," signifying that the dawn has come, and is whisked away in a long convoy. The whole country catches fever from his "second coming," but he still needs to convince the many political factions that he is the ideal person to lead the Amaravi peoples against colonial rule.[110] This is where he has to prove himself as "adept at playing a king." Banda applies himself meticulously to this end.

---

[103] Infighting by self-serving leaders, and conflicting visions for the direction of the party, are some of the main reasons for the party's failure to master effective popular support. See Chipembere 2002:217–238.

[104] Chipembere 2002:293–316 is an extended account of Banda's messianic strategy.

[105] See Chipembere 2002:315.

[106] Chipembere 2002:328.

[107] Power 2010 lists more gifts, including a chair and broom from Clair Masache of Zomba, for Banda to "sweep away" the Federation of Rhodesia and Nyasaland.

[108] Chipembere 2002:333. Various clips of Banda's speeches from around this time also bear witness to this mission.

[109] See Breugel 2001.

[110] Chipembere 2002:333–356.

10. Setting up Court

To set up his simulated kingship, he cultivates "loving relationships" with the youth:[111] he surrounds himself with young Church-educated political agitators—the so-called "mission boys"[112]—who act as his entourage of advisors, secretaries, bodyguards, and panegyrists at his political rallies. Included among these "Young Turks" are the rebellious colonial legislators Masauko Chipembere and Kanyama Chiume, journalist Aleke Banda, and the militant Chisiza brothers, Dunduzu and Yatuta. Banda's avuncular relationships inspire loyalty in these young men as if they were his sons. They are prepared to die for him.

His return hailed across the country as the second coming, Banda already has plenty of political capital to do as he pleases with the moribund Nyasaland African Congress. With his intelligence and charisma alone, he marginalizes the former leaders of the party, including T. D. T. Banda, Manoa Chirwa, and Orton Chirwa. In 1959, having been appointed President General of the NAC, he demands absolute control of the party in the name of the "common good," or the nation's struggle against colonial rule.[113] He sets up *nduna*, a central executive committee, flanked by the Women's League (*mbumba*) and the Youth League as a sanctified chorus for his royal political designs. He controls the party with a considered arbitrariness, as if in parody of the arbitrariness of colonial authority, hiring and firing senior members at will. His orders are impulsive, delivered with a stiff upper lip and in the Queen's English. He barks at journalists questioning his political motives in interviews,[114] like an angry Akafula man. He has an intimidating nervous twitch when he gets angry, something of Dr. Mabuse of Weimar films. He pre-emptively rebukes his adversaries and calls colonial policy "stupid" at every opportunity.[115] His subversive persona rouses mass public enthusiasm in politics.[116] Party membership soars.[117]

---

[111] See an insider account by Chipembere 2002, one of Banda's Young Turks.

[112] In *Nyasaland Under the Foreign Office* (1903), the colonial administrator Hector Livingstone Duff writes regarding the "mission boy": "Personally I am bound to confess that I have no liking for the type of native who actually spends his life under missionary tutelage. He always strikes me as being an awkward, self-assertive, and somewhat sanctimonious person, lacking in proper respect for his superiors, and in that pleasant simplicity and gaiety so characteristic of the aboriginal Bantu. Some of these mission boys have turned out thorough rascals too; but on the other hand I dare say that many of them are sincere Christians according to their lights, and that their defects, however offensive, are no more than skin-deep" (Duff 1903:376).

[113] Chipembere 2002:352.

[114] Brown 1962.

[115] For instance, see Banda's take on punitive colonial farming methods in Chipembere 2002:358.

[116] Chipembere 2002:340.

[117] Chipembere 2002:349.

11. Drumming up Independence

Banda's speeches, which are Homeric in style[118] and delivered with the cadences of an African American preacher,[119] are repetitive[120]—as if moved by the spirit. In fact, the speeches borrow freely from Chewa lyrical oral tradition.[121] He blasphemes like a Ngoni general,[122] as a sign of his resolve to get independence from the British with or without God's approval.[123] He speaks through a translator like a colonial officer, and his speeches are double-edged, delivering a blistering criticism of colonial rule and the establishment of the Federation of Rhodesia and Nyasaland in English, while in Chichewa translation they are often reduced to carnivalesque stand-up comedy, parodying colonial officers, so as to entertain the crowds.[124] Banda, furthermore, frequently corrects his translator to show his total command of the *Nyau*—of both the Western and Chewa dialectal discourses.

Of piety, it is said that he is an ordained elder of the Church of Scotland and that he is actually a pious person despite his apparent excesses.[125] His is an African form of piety. He is a Malawian Moses. He dances well, "like a gentleman," and sings with his *mbumba* in a booming lyrical voice and fluent archaic Chichewa, dispelling rumors that he is not really a Malawian, and adding to his messianic mystery.[126] He encourages his followers to dance from *boma* to *boma*, undermining colonial values of decency, moderation, and industry.[127] Syncretic dances such as *Beni*, *Malipenga*, and *Mganda* further satirize colonial bureaucracy and protocol, and parody British military discipline and hierarchy.[128] Banda advocates a non-violent struggle while imploring "my people" to do away with his political opponents and colonial authority quietly—like *chiswe*

---

[118] See Lwanda 1993:80.

[119] Chipembere 2002:348.

[120] Chipembere 2002:345.

[121] Lwanda 1993:4.

[122] For description of a "blasphemous" war dance led by a Ngoni general see Schoffeleers 1999:135.

[123] In Short 1974:111, Banda is quoted: "If the God of the Christians does not look after us then the spirits of our ancestors will."

[124] See samples on the comedy of mistranslation employed by Banda's populist translators to entertain the crowds in Mgawi 2005:38–39. "For example, when Dr. Banda said, 'I want my people to be free,' the interpreter said, '*Ndifuna anthu anga azikhala atatu*' (I want my people to be in threes)... When Kamuzu said, 'I met the Queen,' the interpreter would say, '*Ine ndinameta Queen!*' (I shaved the Queen)."

[125] Schoffeleers 1999:96.

[126] Mgawi 2005:36.

[127] McCracken 2012:373.

[128] McCracken 2012:156–158.

(termites).[129] He keeps his hat on in front of Europeans,[130] some of whom function in his entourage as his "notable" distinguished friends.[131]

He is so well educated it has turned him into a sorcerer (*mfiti*):[132] it is said that the mark for his surgery exams at Meharry Medical College in the United States was an impossible 99.45%.[133] His name Kamuzu ("a little root") identifies a man with the magic to defeat the white man in Nyasaland[134]—just as it helped Kwame Nkrumah defeat the white man in Ghana. His personality and identity are, thus, at once heterogeneous and a mystifying disguise. His performative and spirited leadership style is more that of the *Nyau* demiurge *Chadzunda*, a libidinal counterpart of the Chewa paramount chief:[135] mystery, contradiction, political transgression, excess, and paternal jouissance are all part of his act. It is a political language and a democratized spirit of the "clearing" that Nyanja peoples understand well, and they welcome him as their titular post-Kalonga king (*mwini dziko, mwini mzinda*) and savior (*mpulumutsi*). With a vacuous film star image and the depth of an ancient *Nyau* mask, he inspires unity and a spirit of radical democracy and political ferment, which the colonials cannot contain.

On 26 October 1959, there is stoning of European traffic around the clock tower in Blantyre,[136] and a rebellion all over Nyasaland ensues. Banda and his protégés are soon jailed by the colonial government at various places around the Federation of Rhodesia and Nyasaland,[137] with Banda and Dunduzu Chisiza in Gwelo,[138] Southern Rhodesia. This only galvanizes the will of the Nyanja peoples for self-determination. In Banda's absence, after the banning by the government of his Nyasaland African Congress, his Secretary-General Orton Chirwa resurrects the Party as the Malawi Congress Party.[139] Banda is made the party's Life President upon his release in 1960. In 1964, a reenergized and insurgent Nyasaland becomes

---

[129] Schoffeleers 1999:23.
[130] During those days, for the African to keep his hat on in front of white people was an act of subversion. Many were punished for this act. See the Chipembere hat incident, below and in Chipembere 2002:104.
[131] See, for example, an episode with Fergus Macpherson, Principal of the Livingstonia Mission and a long-term friend of Banda, in McCracken 2012:347.
[132] See Breugel 2001:217.
[133] Short 1974:27.
[134] Chipembere 2002:327.
[135] For a political interpretation of Banda as *Chadzunda*, see Boucher 2012:95–96. Bakhtin (1984) has explored the power of the carnivalesque and the grotesque to undermine authority—Mbembe 2001 applies this phenomenon to explore how African political leadership have employed the grotesque, the comedic, and the carnivalesque to parody colonial authority even after independence to galvanize popular support.
[136] McCracken 2012:347 and Short 1974:96–98.
[137] McCracken 2012:353.
[138] Now known as Gweru.
[139] McCracken 2012:366.

independent from the British, with Dr. Hastings Kamuzu Banda as its first elected Prime Minister. The next step is for Banda to consolidate himself as the absolute ruler of the Amaravi peoples, and here Aristotle's tyranny by kingship strategy becomes most convenient.

12. Malawi

The country's new name, "Malawi," is taken from an area where Maravi kings (the Kalongas) erected their headquarters, south of Lake Malawi.[140] This was purposeful, as on a national level, Banda is seen as more than a titular Nyanja chief:[141] for uniting the Amaravi peoples once more and freeing them from colonial rule and narrow tribalism, he is the new Kalonga himself, and Banda welcomes the mantle.

Banda dresses in three-piece suits and a homburg hat in all weathers, a nod to his film star status and his days as a fashionable physician in London. However, he indicates his newly sanctioned role as *mwini dziko* with a flywhisk, and this is where Banda deploys rule by force, modelled on colonial caprice and brutality, to consolidate his power.

13. Tyranny by the Conventional Method

Regarding ruling by force, Aristotle prescribes the following for the self-sustaining tyrant: he is to "lop off the eminent" and get rid of independent spirits; eat with foreigners rather than with citizens of his own state; prohibit mass gatherings in messes (clubs), education, or similar that would inspire confidence and a desire for independence in his subjects; he is to make sure there are no places for scholars and intellectuals to gather; subjects should not get to know each other, so they do not develop the mutual confidence that leads to solidarity; he must keep dwellers in the city on view; he will keep an ear to everything that is said in the community and let the subjects know there are listeners (eavesdroppers) everywhere, so that there is an overarching sense of paranoia; he will look to stir up strife among his subjects by setting friends against friends and the rich against the poor; he must keep his subjects working and poor with heavy taxes so his bodyguard is affordable; he is to affect "extreme democracy" amongst his people, where there is "dominance of women in the home, and slack control of slaves";[142] he is sustain the mob with flattery and cultivate the

---

[140] See Boucher 2012:4.
[141] Short 1974:89.
[142] Aristotle *Politics* 5.1313b.

baser sort in his company; he is to encourage an obsequious spirit with mutual compliments; he is to assign base deeds to the base mob; he is to have no friends and must be ready to make war so he can use this as a pretext for taxes; he must position himself as defender of his people.[143]

14. Of the Tallest Ears of the Corn

After Banda is released from Gwelo prison in 1960 and wins a landslide election with the Malawi Congress Party in the Legislative Council, there are a few "men of spirit" and "eminent men" —especially the so-called "mission boys"—he must lop off like the "tallest ears of corn" in the field before consolidating his power as the modern day Kalonga of the Amaravi peoples. There is, for example, Gilbert Pondeponde,[144] a former member of the MCP who formed the Christian Democratic Party in protest against Banda's appointment as Life President of the MCP upon the latter's release from prison. He was killed by Banda's white-uniformed bodyguards, or "icemen," in 1963, about which Banda says on national radio that Pondeponde was killed by a lover's jealous husband.

Previously, in 1962, hot-headed young political scientist and MCP General Secretary Dunduzu Chisiza was killed in a car accident in Namadzi, and the Malawi Youth—Banda's dreaded red-shirted base multitudes, the "termites" (*chiswe*)—are suspected of killing him, as Chisiza had been arguing with Banda on the direction of the Party for some time.[145] In 1961, as if in support of Pondeponde's Christian Democratic Party, Chisiza had published a pamphlet titled *Africa: What Lies Ahead*, which warned against a future dictatorship and called for the Church to strengthen its political role to ensure that equality, human rights, and justice would prevail in the new nation. He then published *The Outlook for Contemporary Africa*, which he defiantly delivered before Banda at a symposium on African governance in 1962. A few months later, he was dead.

That same year, the trade union leaders Chakufwa Chihana of Commercial and General Workers Union (CGWU) and Suzgo Msiska of Transport and Allied Workers Union (TAWU) were suspended from the MCP party when they warn the government to refrain from interfering in labor matters. They were eventually exiled, precipitating the death of the labor movement under Banda's rule.[146]

Chisiza and Pondeponde, the trade unionists, and indeed many of the "mission boys" in the MCP, such as Chipembere, preferred a communalist and subsistent economic policy marked by a grassroots democracy and diplomatic

---

[143] Aristotle *Politics* 5.1313a-1314a.
[144] For a detailed account of Pondeponde's political philosophy, see Schoffeleers 1999:85–90.
[145] For an exploration of Chisiza's political philosophy vis-à-vis Banda's, see Schoffeleers 1999:61–90.
[146] See Power 2010:178–179.

relations with communist China and the USSR, opposing Banda's preferred spectacular industrial state capitalism, drummed-up by his political jouissance as
lord of the dance and presided over by himself and an elite coterie that included
former European colonialists.

15. The Church Is Silenced

By the time of Pondeponde's death, Banda has already moved to tame the Church
and any aspiring "mission boys." His Young Pioneers and reified *Nyau* adherents
harass and exile the Jehovah's Witnesses to Mozambique for not submitting to
the MCP government, and they burn the house of Chester Katsonga, leader of
the Christian Liberation Party, and bring him to publicly recant and submit to
Banda's paternal authority.[147]

Banda uses the *Malawi News* to counter criticism from the Catholic Church,
which accuses him of "communist tendencies," and the paper is the propaganda
arm of the MCP, under the direction of one of his "boys" and a fellow share-
holder in the paper, Aleke Banda.[148] Aleke presents Banda as a savior, and calls
for a national church in Kamuzu's name and the nationalization of all mission
schools. He ensures Banda's image and hymns of praise are more ubiquitous
than those of Jesus Christ around the country. He implores Malawians not to
trust foreign missionaries in their struggle against colonial rule.[149]

By 1963, all parties backed by the Church are dismantled. Soon after, Banda
bans multi-party politics as "unAfrican" and "wasteful."[150] Malawi's real political life is, thus, short-lived, as Malawi quickly turns into a police state where
everybody is kept at Banda's "gates." The Christian Church, the seedbed of
progressive Nyanja society since the mid-nineteenth century, goes silent in
exchange for "religious freedom"—that is, as long as the Church does not inter-
fere in politics and remains in its neutered cell, Banda lets it be. The purge is
thorough. It would take thirty years before a regrouped Church saw to Banda's
political demise.[151]

16. Cabinet Crisis

Next, Banda moves to lop off "eminent men" from the struggle against British
colonialism, especially those he owes the most—the architects of his return

---

[147] McCracken 2012:371.
[148] McCracken 2012:69.
[149] Schoffeleers 1999:34.
[150] Short 1974:261.
[151] Schoffeleers 1999:121.

to Malawi as messiah—by seemingly breaking Aristotle's rule for sustaining autocracy:

> ... abstain from all ill-treatment in all its forms and in two in particular: offences against the person and the youth. This precaution must be taken especially with regard to ambitious men: for while the money-loving chiefly resent slights which affect their money, the ambitious and the respectable resent attacks on their honor.[152]

It is a pretext that most of his young protégés fall for. Perhaps they are as naïve as he makes them out to be. Banda preys on their passions, sense of honor, and the age-old Malawian tendency for *nsanje* (envy) to sow discord among them and to drive them to rushed actions fueled by anger and malice. He resists Africanization and employs the British colonial infrastructure to consolidate his political power.[153] He keeps many colonial expatriates in high-ranking positions: one of his cabinet ministers is a Scot, Colin Cameron; the Secretary to the Prime Minister and to the Cabinet is Peter Youens; Colonel Peter Lewis heads the army; and Peter Long, the Malawi Police Force. He puts one John Savage in charge of training the new Malawi police, which includes many British officers, in brutal methods of torture and interrogation, to be used on his political opponents.[154]

His favors to the Young Turks are uneven, sustaining the colonial technique of "divide and rule." For example, he gives less than ministerial jobs, such as parliamentary secretaries, to big egos, including the begowned impresario barrister Orton Chirwa (Justice) and the hot-headed political philosopher Yatuta Chisiza (Finance).[155] On the other hand, he leaves out others, apparently because they lack "good" English (Lawrence Makata) or for being too young (Aleke Banda). Despite his championing of women's right to vote, there are no women appointed in any senior ministerial or administrative roles,[156] as Rose Chibambo is only a junior minister. Banda gives himself several ministerial portfolios and does not consult his fellow ministers on policy—while interfering in theirs. He personally handpicks MPs, regardless of merit.[157]

He suspends the Youth League leader and independent spirit Jomo Chikwakwa, and splits the organization into two more subservient organizations: the Malawi Young Pioneers (MYP) and Malawi Youth, the former being

[152] Aristotle *Politics* 5.1315a.
[153] Mwakasungura and Miller 2016:18.
[154] Mwakasungura and Miller 2016:18. In the same book, on page 215, the Malawian exile Mordecai Gondwe displays a head scar from a wound inflicted on him by Inspector John Savage.
[155] Chisiza's "stubborn" disposition is recounted by Chipembere 2002:355.
[156] McCracken 2012:372.
[157] McCracken 2012:430.

his personal militia and bodyguard.[158] He encourages people and the police Special Branch to report on cabinet ministers directly to him through anonymous letters and reports. He cites preventive detention laws from colonial times and proposes detention without trial of potential dissenters. He isolates those who oppose him in that endeavor.[159] He asks his base supporters to "deal" with his enemies wherever they may be found.[160] The Scottish cabinet minister Colin Cameron resigns.[161] It is an early sign that his strategy is on course, and he is encouraged.

At every opportunity, especially when showing off before his already patronizing European colleagues, acquaintances, and notables, he calls his Malawian ministers and ambassadors "my boys," no doubt to break their confidence and deny them any honor.[162] He, furthermore, admonishes them for excessive drinking[163] and speaking to Europeans, while he himself keeps European company at sumptuous banquets. He won't let the Young Turks use the toilet at his house.[164] He won't eat the traditional communal meal, *nsima*, with them. He excludes them from transitional talks with the colonial government, leaving them sitting outside the door,[165] until some, like Chipembere and Chiume, lose their temper and patience, much to Banda's advantage.

When, within a month of independence (on 26 August 1964) they call a meeting to complain of his autocratic rule and colonial paternalism, Banda takes a calculated gamble and offers to resign.[166] The rebelling minsters, some resigning in protest, some hanging on, fail to agree on an alternative leader to take things forward—so they reject Banda's resignation. Banda then becomes more decisive. He expels the whole cabinet and goes to war against eminent members of the community by claiming autocracy is the "African way." He deploys ethnicity to further wedge division among his opponents.

In these acts, he is supported by Ngoni and Chewa ministers such as John Z. U. Tembo and Richard Katengeza. Aleke Banda and Gwanda Chakuamba also side with Banda, in direct contrast with many of the rebelling politicians who, like them, are from the North.[167] Cabinet members Chiume, Chirwa, Chokani, Chipembere, Chibambo, Chisiza, and Bwanausi are sent into exile. In these

---

[158] McCracken 2012:371.
[159] McCracken 1981:431.
[160] Meaning they should kill them. See Mwakasungura and Miller 2016:15.
[161] McCracken 2012:431.
[162] Short 1974:197–198.
[163] McCracken 2012:430.
[164] Mwakasungura and Miller 2016:15.
[165] Mwakasungura and Miller 2016:13.
[166] Chirwa 2007:64.
[167] Mwakasungura and Miller 2016:13.

actions, Banda is backed by his powerful Western friends, colonial police, the army, the traditional authorities and chiefs, and the Malawi Young Pioneers, who side with him for advantage in newly independent Malawi.[168]

17. Republic

In the aftermath of the cabinet crisis, Banda chooses less educated and less eminent ministers ("party bosses") from the Nyasaland African Congress, both of whom are more accustomed to submitting to authority during colonial times than the Young Turks. He employs two hatchet men—over-enthusiastic Ngonis from Ntcheu—to draw up lists for ongoing political purges:[169] Focus Gwede, as new head of the Special Branch of the Malawi Police Force, and Albert Muwalo as Minister of State.

Soon after, Malawi becomes a republic, seemingly under a mixed constitution reminiscent of the chastened Plato of the *Laws,* with grassroots democracy on one hand and Banda as a benign philosopher-king on the other. In reality, there is only one constitution in the country, and it is Banda himself. His pretensions to a Platonic communitarianism are a mere charade.

Ensuring that everybody is in view and kept at his gate, Banda builds himself a £1.5 million palace on top of Sanjika Hill, in Malawi's commercial capital Blantyre.[170]

18. Discretional Alignment

Banda's foreign policy—often seemingly petulant[171]—carries the mark of his political jouissance as "lord of the dance," or of *Chadzunda* himself.[172] He calls his often contradictory and transgressive foreign policy "discretional alignment."[173] Its aim, apparently, is to make himself and Malawi a "mediator" in Africa and in Africa's relations with the rest of the world.[174] As a committed Hellenophile, it is not entirely impossible that he sees the Malawian as a modern day Greek, poised to unite the modern world in the name of "democracy" and "reason." He, in fact, makes Malawi a pariah in the Pan-Africanist workings of the Organization

---

[168] For a picture of *kuthana*, political strife among Banda's politicians in the aftermath of the cabinet crisis, see Power 2010:177–201.
[169] Lwanda 1993:186.
[170] See Short 1974:282.
[171] Short 1974:307.
[172] Short (1974:161) describes Banda's *Nyau* political approach as "a deliberate polarization" using the "reasonable" and "pig-headed" sides of his character.
[173] Short 1974:173–196.
[174] Short 1974:187.

of African Unity (OAU), and a slightly eccentric nation at the United Nations. With his "pig-headed" approach, Banda will go anywhere for capital and political expediency, including smooching with scheming former colonial masters, all for the sake of his exceptionally "poor" people.

His relationship with fellow African heads of state is pre-emptive. He treats them with disdain and in a patronizing manner, calling them "ignorant little boys," "hypocrites," and "cowards" when they question his methods. He even boasts that he is worth ten Kwame Nkrumahs.[175] His dreams of African unity,[176] and of recovering the ancient borders of the Amaravi Empire[177] in Mozambique, Tanzania, and Zambia through a political and economic union are thereby quickly scuppered.[178] He instead makes trade deals and pacts with colonial Mozambique,[179] a rogue Rhodesian government, and apartheid South Africa. His new capital of Lilongwe is built by the government of apartheid South Africa. He says he does not mind making a deal with the devil if it is in the interest of Malawi.[180]

He represents himself as the protector of his country from communism and refuses financial aid from China, and yet his rule has many traits of Maoism,[181] especially with regard to the dictatorship of the "proletariat" (his "people") over which he presides,[182] and which is enforced by the Malawi Youth and Malawi Young Pioneers (his own Red Guards), who terrorize relatives of his exiled opponents as deterrence. The ubiquitous personal presence of Banda's Special Branch hatchet man Gwede in every Malawi embassy in the world, as if by magic, unsettles political exiles. Many disappear after being questioned by Gwede at the embassies. Banda's unpredictable policy declarations and political purges recall aspects of Stalinism.[183] While he talks about African liberation and pride in African culture, he is an Anglophile and maintains close ties with

---

[175] See Power 2010:183.

[176] Short 1974:177–178.

[177] The inconvenience of arbitrary colonial borders to the Malawian should not be underestimated. The author's home village of Chingoni in Ntcheu District is divided in two by a huge border road between Mozambique and Malawi. Throughout his childhood half of the village, the Mozambican side, was ravaged by civil war.

[178] See Short 1974:192.

[179] See Lwanda 1993:11 on how Banda pursued a costly foreign policy with colonial Mozambique having been promised the northern part of Mozambique as a buffer against the black states in the north.

[180] Short 1974:290.

[181] See Lwanda 1993:173.

[182] On Banda's "base" political support over any specific tribal affiliation, see McCracken 2012:447. McCracken's view fits the author's theory that Banda in essence operated a non-tribe *Nyau* strategy adopted from the Chewa.

[183] See Žižek 2016.

Britain and America while marginalizing bona fide Malawian traditional titular authority.

Malawi's economy improves dramatically amidst Banda's ostracization from the Organization of African Unity—during the first ten years after Malawi independence annual economic growth is five to six per cent.[184] Because of this, some African leaders warm to his "pragmatic" statesmanship.

19. Rainmaker

As mentioned earlier, after the marginalization of the spirit-wives, the *Gule Wamkulu,* and the destruction of Chewa radical democracy under the Kalonga, there manifested a grassroots resistance led by a spiritual leader, former Phiri priest, and rainmaker named Mu'ona ("seer," or literally "the one who sees"), whose shrines can still be seen today in parts of Southern Malawi.[185] When Mu'ona appeared on the scene, there was continued rivalry for the control of the rain shrines between Phiri and Banda priests, as the latter (mostly coming from the Mbewe clan) checked Kalonga's control (now assumed by warlike Lundu chiefs) from within. *Thunga,* the Banda radical rendition of the all-powerful high God, *Chisumphi,* shook his tail, and the kingdom showed signs of extreme spiritual alienation and social fragmentation, manifested in endemic slave raids and trading, rampant individualism, blood sacrifices, and in independent spirit possession cults[186] propagated by itinerant prophets and dancers (*Avirombo-a-Chisumphi*),[187] who, for a price, would speak God's will in tongues.[188] Under Kalonga, the Chewa religion had thus been displaced from the impersonal and mechanical involvement of *Nyau* and *Chauta* to the more personal and charismatic spirituality of *Chisumphi* and *Thunga.*[189]

Alongside these independent spiritual movements were the "rainmakers," performance artists and interventionists of sorts who came to replace the *Nyau* masks banned by Kalonga at the rain shrines—Mu'ona was one of these rainmakers, or at least his legend evolved amongst them. Accused of witchcraft by Lundu priests at Kaphirintiwa, when he beat them to rainmaking by a happening

[184] Power 2010:199.
[185] For a basic account of Mu'ona's resistance against Kalonga centralization employed in this study, see Schoffeleers 1999:147-178. It is often not clear whether Mu'ona was a man or a woman. See Phiri 1997:24.
[186] For a study of proto-Chewa religious alienation under the Kalonga, see Linden 1979:186–207.
[187] See Linden 1979:198.
[188] It is here we must associate the rise of Kalonga with new trade (capitalism) brought by Arab and Portuguese slave traders from the East and early Dutch settlers in South Africa. It is most likely that the religion of Mu'ona had an early Christian influence. See Schoffeleers 1999.
[189] See Linden 1979.

alone,[190] Mu'ona was hunted down and killed—only to appear again in various other parts of the Kingdom as a divinized man performing miracles, including bumper harvests, for those who would call on him.[191]

Mu'ona's deeds demonstrate that he sought the sublation of Chewa radical religion after Kalonga, by showing how "the whole," peace and harmony (the domain of *Chisumphi* and Phiri priests), could co-exist with "the exception," or ontological difference (the domain of *Thunga* and Banda priests), through understanding and compassionate deeds. He taught that everyone could reach God without the mediation of the priests, through creative and ritualized play as a member of a universal community. Like the *Gule Wamkulu* of old, the "people's prayer," Mu'ona brought about "rain"[192] through dance and creative happenings without the blood sacrifices of the defenseless before the insatiable *Thunga* and *Chisumphi,* as was done by the Lundu priests. Where Mu'ona orchestrated a rain event and slept during his flight from the Kalonga priests, flowers and trees grew, and *Mulungu* (the Holy Spirit) prevailed: that is to say, community blossomed.[193]

---

[190] The rain sacrifice, *mfunde,* of Kalonga priests which required a sacrificial victim for the High God *Chisumphi* and his counterpart *Thunga* contradicts the more performative approach of the kenotic rainmakers.

[191] The Malawian protest against the introduction of bunding by the colonials cited the fear that Mu'ona might trip while moving among the crops as he blessed them. See Schoffeleers 1999.

[192] "Rain" here should not always be understood as literal rain but rather as a metaphor for faith in humanity and generosity in times of want. A telling description of rainmaking as a form of gift giving through play as means of excluding debt (see Wark 2011) can be found in Linden 1979:191. He shares this account, given by Chikaole and Paima: "When the rains were late Sosola told Mbuzimaere and Mbuzimaere informed Chikaole... Every family was obliged to give one cob of maize and one head of millet. When all the offerings had been collected and prepared, a day was set apart for the brewing of beer. Meanwhile a completely black goat was sought. When the day was drawing near young boys and girls were chosen and made ready for the sacrifice. On the day itself, the boys were sent to cut wood for the building of the spirit-house (*kachisi*). They chose only one kind of wood (*kapangale*). Everybody was asked to bring one piece of grass. The boys and girls were told to bring charcoal (*mikala*), which was ground up in a pot (*phali*) mixed with water and made into black paste. The girls smeared it on the children to make them very black. Mbuzimaere sat down cross-legged, and the circumference of his body formed the outside of the spirit-house. The roof was fixed by resting it on his head. Mbuzimaere poured the beer which was passed to him by Chauma who remained standing. The boys and girls went to the stream to collect sand (*mchenga*). They had to sit on their heels when they offered sand; even Chauma had to kneel when he offered it to Mbuzimaere. Mbuzimaere spread the sand (*mwalawaza*) on the floor of the spirit-house. Afterwards Chauma led the children back across the river, and wherever he went the children had to follow. They had to walk right through the water and were not allowed to lift up their clothes. As they were returning rain began to fall."

[193] Huizinga 1949 has explored indispensability of play in binding people together in every aspect of society including politics, religion, and law.

Martyrdom of Mu'ona weakened Kalonga's secular authority even further, and the cult of *Chisumphi* and his feverish counterpart *Thunga* waned.[194] Gradually the Amaravi secular empire disappeared, leaving clusters of independent communities in the region exposed to new invasions, including the Ngoni from South Africa, and lingering Yao, Arab, and Portuguese slave raids from the East. The Amaravi peoples resisted and most of these newcomers, such as the Kalonga rulers, were traversed in *Nyau* and assimilated into the Nyanja culture.

Mu'ona's apotheosis after death is the Malawi prototype religious event, akin to that of Christ uniting "the Jew and the Gentile" through the mysterious movement of his death and resurrection[195]—which the Nyanja peoples understand as a *Gule Wamkulu* event[196] on a cosmopolitan scale. It is said that Mu'ona was *Thunga* himself and died according to his own volition, out of love for humanity. When Lundu's priests tried to kill Mu'ona with arrows, knives, and muskets, the ballistics fell off his body harmlessly. They managed to behead Mu'ona only when he indicated to them a piece of grass which could cut him like a knife with a caress.[197] Mu'ona's skull was kept in shrine by his spirit-wife, a priestess named Salima, at Khulubvi in Nsanje, and he spoke to his followers through her to reveal the day and place of his next appearance as a happening.

By the end of the nineteenth century, *Nyau* and rainmakers were everywhere, and the Nyanja peoples were more than ready for the next challenge thrown up by an awakened *Thunga* in the pool: British colonialism, which had come under the pretext of ending slave trade, pacifying the tribes, and introducing the Nyanja region to civilization though Christianity and commerce.[198]

---

[194] Linden 1979:201.

[195] As extrapolated by Saint Paul. See Badiou 2003.

[196] The assimilation of Christianity into the Mu'ona movement has been explored by Schoffeleers (1999). Father Boucher appears to have seamlessly incorporated the Christian message into his *Gule Wamkulu* project at the Catholic Mua Mission in Dedza, where Christ is considered on par with *Kasiya Maliro*, the *Nyau* principal mask structure. See Boucher 2012. Saint Paul's 'resurrected' Christ is seen by the philosopher Slavoj Žižek as what could be deduced as a *Nyau* figure—*Gule*: "... and what, ultimately, is Christ but the name of this excess inherent in man, man's extimate kernel, the monstrous surplus which, following the unfortunate Pontius Pilate, one of the few ethical heroes of the Bible (the other being Judas, of course), can only be designated as '*Ecce homo*'?" (Žižek 2003:143). The union between Christianity and *Nyau* has been celebrated in the partnered appearances and dances of *Chadzunda* ("the ancestor and progenitor of all the other *Gule Wamkulu* masquerades") and *Mariya* ('Virgin Mary,' who is now seen as his wife). See Boucher 2012:22, 95-96, 261.

[197] Folklore from the author's childhood—see Steve Chimombo's play *Rainmaker* (Chimombo 1978).

[198] David Livingstone was the first British explorer to set foot in the *Nyasa* ("lake") region now known as Malawi, in 1859. In 1889, the area became a British Protectorate, and it was named Nyasaland in 1907.

20. Antelope

It is no coincidence that the first Pan-Africanist to die resisting colonial rule in Africa is a larger-than-life Baptist, Nyanja preacher named John Chilembwe[199]— *Chilembwe* is the other name of the Chewa principal demiurge *Kasiya Maliro*, a theriomorphic womb structure in the guise of an antelope and a symbol of radical generosity, the kernel of Amaravi identity. Chilembwe lived up to his name, first as a charismatic preacher and later as a millenarian political activist.

Chilembwe was born in 1871, in Tsangano, Chiradzulu District. His father was a former Yao slave trader, and his mother, Nyangu, was a rescued Chewa slave.[200] Chilembwe trained at Blantyre Mission School under the apprenticeship of the radical British missionary Joseph Booth, then in the United States under the sponsorship of the Negro National Baptist Convention, where he was ordained at Virginia Theological College and Seminary in Lynchburg. Chilembwe toured America with Booth, trying to find sponsors for their missionary work in Nyasaland, but, after witnessing a spate of lynchings of black men and being subjected to a violent objection against their interracial relationship at Richmond in Virginia, the two went their separate ways. Chilembwe returned from the United States through the United Kingdom with nothing but a church bell and an undetermined illness (probably subjective destitution), but ready for a mission inspired by a mix of the teachings of Booker T. Washington and other Negro advancement movements. Chilembwe founded the "Achewa Providence Industrial Mission," which later became Providence Industrial Mission (PIM), at Mbombwe in Chiradzulu.

To the alarm of the colonialists, Chilembwe's industrial mission at Mbombwe involved not so much the teaching of normative Christianity and the production of commodities and profit, but also the tailoring of fashionable modern clothes, directed by his wife Ida, and the building of schools and churches to create a new generation of self-sustaining Africans educated and self-respecting enough to stand up against colonial injustices. Chilembwe's commitment to liberation theology as a preacher can be deduced from his acts and writings, which bear a kenotic reading event of the death and resurrection of Christ. A democratizing atheology of an impossible God and an elective community of believers would have been a familiar one to him as a Chewa, through the *Nyau* rite of passage, the apotheosis of Mu'ona,[201] and access to radical theology as a mission apprentice

---

[199] The three main references on the life of John Chilembwe employed here are Makondesa 2006, Shepperson and Price 2000, and Mwase 1967.

[200] Mwase 1967:17 communicates an oral history that Nyangu was in fact a "Phiri" of "the descendant of Kalonga the great."

[201] See Shepperson and Price 2000.

with Booth—prior to leaving for the United States, Chilembwe paid a visit to Mu'ona's shrine at Khulubvi as Booth's translator.[202] He would have also been encouraged by the successes of the millenarian preaching of the Tonga Elliot Kamwana in mobilizing grassroots revolt against colonial injustices in the North.[203] Chilembwe would have understood that, for the Chewa, what had died on the cross was not just Jesus (as in the days of Mu'ona) but also *Chisumphi*, the metaphysical God of the hereafter. The raising of a dead God on the cross was but the revelation of the obscene underbelly of a tilted *Kasiya Maliro* at *dambwe*: the very same absent God of the "pool" that manifested as the "Holy Ghost" (*Mulungu*) amongst an elective community of believers.

Unlike the colonial missionaries, who excluded many for economic gain and power, Chilembwe baptized everyone and promised them the "end of time" and a "future community"—the Kingdom come—where truth, compassion, and justice would prevail forever, in the here and now.[204] When, in 1915, Chilembwe came to rebel against the colonial government to usher in the "end of days," it was against a "tyranny by conventional method" akin to that described by Aristotle: Chilembwe was protesting, among other things, the burning of his churches and schools—a colonial effort to keep his followers from thinking and in menial and manual work; unpaid labor at European farms (*thangata*); the hut tax; the dismantling of African communal life; the "pacifying" of all dissenters; the ban on the communal rite of hunting; the sale of common land; the forbidding of Africans from wearing hats (the *Chotsa Chipewa* system),[205] shoes,[206] and speaking English before white people; and, above all, the continuing shedding of the blood of African soldiers (*askaris*) trafficked throughout the British empire to fight in wars whose causes they seldom understood.[207]

The reified Amaravi titular chiefs, now despots working for the colonials, refused to support Chilembwe's uprising, and it was the petty bourgeois, such as John Gray Kufa and Haya Peters, who had once supported his cause but who betrayed him in the end.

To ignite the uprising, Chilembwe needed to get weapons from colonials but things did not go as planned—perhaps they were not meant to, and his

---

[202] Langworthy 1996:46–49.

[203] See Shepperson and Price 2000.

[204] "End of time" and "future community" are terms the author has borrowed from Agamben 1999 to contextualize Chilembwe's messianic message as political subversion.

[205] Mwase 1967:32.

[206] Power 2010:18.

[207] More detailed grievances of Chilembwe's against the colonials are listed in Makondesa 2006:124–127, Mwase 1967:29–33, and in Phiri 2004:262–265.

uprising was more a "rainmaking" event, a portent happening.[208] A 2:00 a.m. assault on the African Lakes Company headquarters at Mandala in Blantyre, on 24 January 1915, led by his keen lieutenant David Kaduya, was botched when an attempt to negotiate a stealthy entry into the ammunition depot ended abruptly with the watchman screaming "*Nkhondo!*", "War!", to alert his colonial masters, and he was shot. The gunshot alerted other guards and the contingent was forced to scatter as someone was shooting at them from inside the house. Four of Chilembwe's men were caught. News of the uprising quickly spread, and Chilembwe's plans went largely unexecuted by his various collaborators around the country. His letter appealing for military assistance from the Germans in East Africa was delivered by his messenger Yotam but the messenger never made it back.[209] Chilembwe was killed fleeing into Mozambique by colonial police (*askaris*). He was identified by his characteristic reading glasses and striped pajamas over which he wore a blue coat.

Chilembwe was buried in an unmarked grave in Mulanje District, but his followers denied it was Chilembwe killed and buried there. Rather, they argued that Chilembwe made it to Mozambique and from there had gone back to the United States—like Jesus, he would come again to save his people. Fearing it was true that the real Chilembwe was still out there, the colonial authorities rounded up "trousered Africans," up and down the country, mostly teachers, and conscripted many of them for carrier duties in British World War I campaigns in various remote parts of Africa.

Chilembwe's martyrdom spread far and wide despite colonial attempts to tarnish his image by painting him as naïve, and essentially a savage. The colonial police said Chilembwe had preached his last sermon with the head of William Jervis Livingston (his abusive farmer neighbor at Mbombwe and a relation of the famed Scottish explorer David Livingstone), one of the three white people killed during the uprising, displayed in the church.[210] What was sure was that at that sermon, Chilembwe promised a "messiah" who would come after him to deliver Africans from the yoke of colonialism. Ironically, it was Chilembwe's uprising which gave traditional authorities ("men in blankets") more autonomous power from the colonial government through a new formalized policy of Indirect Rule, which aimed to marginalize "trousered" Africans like Chilembwe.[211]

---

[208] On John Chilembwe's not entirely logical approach to the uprising, see Mwase 1967. Mwase reaches a conclusion that perhaps Chilembwe merely sought a symbolic "blow" against colonial authority, akin to that of the American abolitionist John Brown.

[209] Mwase 1967:50.

[210] William Jervis Livingstone had deployed many tactics to sabotage Chilembwe's mission including breaking Chilembwe's church bell in a furnace having advised Chilembwe that the process would make the bell ring louder.

[211] Power 2010:20.

Chilembwe, a sharp dresser and a resolutely modern African, left us haunting and animating photographs to inspire fidelity to his message of self-respect, equality, and prosperity through education, creativity, and a life of prodigious generosity.[212] For Chilembwe, the way to resist the ravages of colonialism, capitalism, and modernity was not a retreat into cultural atavism but a full-on radical engagement and traversing of the new reality. In one of these photographs, the last one taken before his death, Chilembwe defiantly wears a gleaming white, felt hat twisted sideways for effect before a white person—his friend the British missionary John Chorley, who also wears a twisted hat in support. Chilembwe in turn inspired Negro advancement leaders, such as Marcus Garvey and W. E. B. DuBois, early Pan-African liberation movements in Africa, and the critical trade unionism of the Tonga Nyanja Clements Kadalie in South Africa.[213] Chilembwe's martyrdom and prophecy, for good and bad, is the guiding light for Banda, the Young Turks, and many of the "mission boys"[214] fighting for an independent Malawi.

21. Chipembere's Turn

Henry Masauko Blasius Chipembere was a typical "mission boy,"[215] who attempted to fashion himself after John Chilembwe. He succeeded, at least, in turning his own legend into a *Nyau* demiurge, which now appears alongside *Kasiya Maliro*.[216] Chipembere's grandfather, an enterprising fishmonger and trader in ivory, apparently took the name, which translates as "rhinoceros," "to strike terror in the hearts of his enemies and rivals"; and Chipembere's political eminence and enthusiasm for the struggle against colonial rule did worry Banda.[217]

Born a Chewa-Yao in Kayoyo near Kota-Kota, Chipembere's father was an Anglican deacon. Chipembere went to school in Mangochi, where, during a time of a political awakening, he was beaten by a white assistant native commissioner

---

[212] For a colorful description of Chilembwe's character and his American and Pan-African influences, see Mwase 1967:25–28.

[213] Shepperson and Price 2000:434–435. At the time of writing this study, the author is on the short list for a Fourth Plinth sculpture on Trafalgar Square with a proposal for a John Chilembwe statue.

[214] See Chipembere's fervent speech on Banda as the messiah promised by Chilembwe, made at the Nyasaland Legislative Assembly on 7 March 1963 in Chipembere 2002:386–387.

[215] Chipembere 2002:183–196 narrates his own experience with Anglican missionaries. At best, the experience left him with mixed feelings: he is proud of his father's dedication as a clergyman but otherwise finds the Anglican missionaries thoroughly "paternalistic" towards Africans, often petty, and ultimately self-serving.

[216] See Boucher 2012:57.

[217] Short 1974:142.

for not removing his hat as he bicycled past the officer.[218] From Mangochi, Chipembere went to university at Fort Hare in South Africa, where he immersed himself in the teachings of Booker T. Washington and Marcus Garvey.[219] Back in Nyasaland in 1954, and driven by the memory of the hat incident, he joined the Nyasaland African Congress to resist colonial rule.

After working for the colonial government in various posts, he became one of the first two Africans to be elected to the colonial Legislative Council—the other was the young Kanyama Chiume, a Tonga and a schoolteacher from Nkata Bay who went to school in Tanzania and had a degree from Makerere University in Uganda. Looking for a way to unite the various political factions and traditional authorities against colonial rule, Chipembere looked the world over for the messiah promised by John Chilembwe, a man who would be Malawi's own Kwame Nkrumah. He had seen photographs of Nkrumah.[220] The candidate had to have "grey hair" or be bald like Nkrumah or Kenyatta, for the Nyanja have an "almost superstitious adoration for old age."[221] Apparently, Chipembere himself, although charismatic, could not stand as leader—he looked too young.[222] But there was more to it. He was met with resistance from some observant elders of the NAC who regarded him and Chiume as *nthumbidwa*, as we have seen in *Nyau*, uninitiated and immature youths,[223] for their frantic approach to politics. As this study will show, perhaps the elders were on to something—but Chipembere ploughed ahead.

His first bet is a false start: the boastful theatrical antics and buffoonery of the recently elected NAC President-General T. D. T. Banda, who earned the nickname *Wakufuntha* ("the mad one"), are enough to galvanize popular support across the country but fall short of impressing the colonialists.[224] Eventually, Chipembere finds his messiah in the "handsome" London-based Nyasaland

[218] Chipembere 2002:104.
[219] Chipembere 2002:242.
[220] Chipembere 2001:141. Photographs in the press of Kwame Nkrumah, president of the first Black government in colonial Africa, appear to have made an impression on the young Chipembere.
[221] Chipembere 2002:297. From the author's experience of growing up in Malawi, the "remainder" or the "useless" is what commands reverence as this marks the presence of *Nyau*, the universal substance which is worshipped as God in *Gule Wamkulu* and in everyday life. Reverence of elders among the Amaravi comes with reverence for other "excesses" such as spirit mediums, mad people, witchdoctors, flowery language, and leftover food.
[222] Chipembere 2002:297.
[223] At the party conference in 1957, James Chinyama, a member of the NAC Central Executive Committee, ominously describes the young Chipembere and Chiume as *nthumbidwa*: "As was his wont in time of deep emotion, one of his eyes wept a flood of tears, but this did not deter him" (Chipembere 2002:229).
[224] Chipembere 2002:309.

physician Dr. Hastings Banda, an already known Pan-Africanist and an effective communicator among diaspora Africans and Europeans.[225]

22. Banda

Dr. Hastings Kamuzu Banda was born Akim Kamkhwala[226] Mtunthama Banda in Kasungu in the late nineteenth century. He claimed he did not know the exact year he was born, but that it was around 1896, when the local Chewa Chief Mwase was pacified by British troops.[227] Banda's official birthday—much later— was fixed in 1906.

As a Chewa, Banda's childhood education would have included an initiation into the *Nyau* secret society[228] where, as we have seen, the initiate is shown the vacuous underbelly of a tilting *Kasiya Maliro* and put through a gauntlet of ritualized cruelty administered by various *Gule Wamkulu*, in order to prepare him for the trials and tribulations of life. These included recurring subjective destitution as a sovereign individual condemned to freedom in an elective community. The initiate is taught to seek solace in *Gule Wamkulu* and is introduced to the metapolitics of *Nyau* and the Chewa idea of radical democracy.[229] Despite his allusion to *Nyau* knowledge in *Our African Way of Life*, inexhaustible personal initiative, and the fact that he was welcomed back to Malawi by some members of the *Nyau* secret society,[230] a study of Banda's detracting political career and life, when faced with moments of personal revaluation, casts doubt on his initiation into the *Nyau* secret society as a youth,[231] and we shall explore this later. We can, however, be certain that, as a youth, Banda attended the newly opened primary school run by the Church of Scotland missionaries, where he was introduced to the Western canon. At the age of sixteen, after his disqualification from sitting an examination at his school due to cheating—diminutive in stature, he said he was only trying to see the blackboard—Banda walked from his village to South Africa via Southern Rhodesia in search of further education without notice.[232]

---

[225] For a detailed account of Chipembere's search for the "Messiah," see Chipembere 2002:14.

[226] Kamkhwala, later changed to Kamuzu by Banda, means a "little root" or a "little medicine." Banda was so named because he was conceived after his mother sought fertility treatment from a witchdoctor.

[227] See Short 1974.

[228] See Short 1974:9.

[229] Short 1974:8–10.

[230] See Ross 2009:221 and McCracken 2012:372.

[231] The author has already questioned Banda's moralized interpretation of *Nyau* as a kind of carnival or primitive masonic brotherhood in *Our African Way of Life* (Banda and Cullen Young:1946).

[232] The missionary who dismissed Banda was Thomas Cullen Young, Banda's co-editor in *Our African Way of Life*. It is not clear in the book that Cullen Young remembers the incident.

In 1925, Banda found his way to the United States, first under a scholarship from the African Methodist Episcopal Church (AME) to the Wilberforce Academy in Ohio, as a noticeably twenty-seven-year-old high school student, where he was introduced to Classics. He then attended the universities of Indiana and Chicago, where he trained in political science and history. He went on to study medicine at Meharry Medical College in Tennessee. From there he moved to the United Kingdom, where he obtained another medical degree in order to practice in the British Empire. In all this, Banda remained indebted to the various patrons and well-wishers he had encountered on his quest for a Western education.[233] Denied jobs in Nyasaland, including at Livingstonia where white nurses refused to serve under an African doctor, Banda worked in Liverpool and Tyneside during the war as a conscientious objector, before settling as a highly successful physician in London. [234] It was around this time that he began to give back and became known for his generosity in treating many poor patients—Black or white—for free while also financially supporting his family, friends, and fellow political activists back home in Nyasaland.[235]

His medical practice was then derailed by a scandal that bore all the marks of sudden subjective destitution and self-sabotage: he began an affair with his secretary, Mrs. Merene French,[236] who was married to a British army officer. In 1953, fleeing the disgrace of having been publicly named in divorce proceedings,[237] he moved to Ghana with his lover and their new child, David.[238] This relationship with Mrs. French ultimately did not work out, likely because time and circumstance revealed that the man she fell for—this highly polished Black physician—did not exist, and even more so once the support of her husband was out of the equation. With the characteristic "petulance" that would come to the fore in his later years, Banda refused to be a "father," probably in an attempt to reassert his Chewa identity,[239] refusing to become a British *nkamwini*. Banda became withdrawn and temporarily severed contact with Nyasaland. Mrs. French and child returned to the United Kingdom.

---

[233] These included financial support from Pepsodent toothpaste philanthropists Mr. (Douglas) and Mrs. (Emaroy) Smith.

[234] Short 1974:39.

[235] Short 1974:41–51

[236] Short 1974:76 names her Margaret, but McCracken 2012:326 and others call her Merene.

[237] Short 1974:76.

[238] Lwanda 1993:13. It was a common rumor during Banda's time in office that he had left a lover and a child in the United Kingdom, although this was never officially verified. Mrs. French kept silent about her relationship with Banda until her death in 1976. Since Banda's death, several people have come forward to claim him as their father, but none has been accepted by Banda's estate.

[239] See Deleuze and Guattari 2019.

Banda's medical license was revoked for a time by the Ghanaian Medical Council for "schizophrenic" conduct and running an abortion clinic. When he was called to return to Malawi, to lead the Nyasaland African Congress, he had been abroad for over forty years, and his reputation as a physician and a man abroad was in tatters[240]—gone *Nyau*, as some Nyanja would put it. His hysterical conversion registered in a nervous twitch on his face. It was to his advantage that Malawians back home in Nyasaland did not know much about him,[241] as his next project (politics) had to work—and he was well prepared.

23. The Doctor Knows Best

Banda's classical education at Wilberforce and political science degree from Chicago would have given him a vision of a modern Malawi state radically transformed by its encounter with colonialism. In the history of ancient Greece and the Amaravi, he finds ready models for a cultural and political transition for Malawi—from the tribal to the modern. In the Greek regard for the individual, self-worth, and the good life, he recognizes his own Chewa identity as essentially a *chirombo*, or an autonomous member of an elective community. As for the marginalized Aristotle at Athens, philosophy and politics would become Banda's new source of empowerment and a way to reassert his own identity as a Chewa in a modern world.

Linguistic and anthropological work with Professor Mark Hanna Watkins at the University of Chicago,[242] consultation work on Nyasaland with various missionaries at Edinburgh, and the book he edits with the missionary and anthropologist Thomas Cullen Young, *Our African Way of Life*, in 1946, spell for Banda a modern Malawi where "the old and the new" would manifest in a new synthesis.[243] This new Malawi in *Our African Way of Life* is necessarily bleak: represented by a crocodile, aspects of the Nyanja matrilineal culture are presented with the awareness of a growing, new, and unforgiving system of "government police, taxes and other things."[244] In this dynamic new world of calculation, ignorance, sentimentality, and carelessness are fatal. Other people cannot be trusted, and the moral road is mortally risky.

---

[240] Lwanda 1993:9.
[241] Power 2010:129.
[242] See Phiri 1998:155.
[243] The book charts aspects of the Chewa matrilineal system with an awareness of a growing new patriarchal system (capitalism). Banda would later sample aspects of Chewa culture in this book for his autocratic regime.
[244] Banda and Cullen Young 1946:127

His familiarization with Pan-Africanist ideas,[245] and membership of the Fabian Colonial Bureau and the Labour Party in London, give him insight into the work of modern politics with regard to colonial Africa. His far-reaching education, combined with real world experience in the capitalist West,[246] sets him ahead of his young supporters whose thinking of Pan-African politics is based on abstract ideas of African communalism. Furthermore, Banda would have learnt a lot about the practicality of Pan-African philosophy from the mistakes or successes of Kwame Nkrumah, his host in Ghana.[247]

Dazzled by Banda's intellectual range, experienced grey head, and polished self-presentation,[248] it is Chipembere's lead that gives Banda autocratic power in the Nyasaland African Congress, telling those who doubt that "the doctor knows best."[249] It is Chipembere, as self-appointed *tsabwalo,* who encourages the Nyanja peoples to see in Banda the fulfilment of Chilembwe's prophesy of a Malawian messiah. It is Chipembere who encourages Banda's incendiary speeches against colonialism and the "stupid" Federation of Rhodesia and Nyasaland. It is Chipembere who threatens violence against anybody opposing Banda, and he is prepared to go to prison for it.

Between 1961 and 1963, Chipembere is in jail for inciting violence.[250] Chipembere and the Young Turks use Banda as a ready whip against the colonials and to appease and unite traditional authorities, but only because Banda is willing—Banda has his own plan. As Banda is given a mandate to negotiate Malawi independence from Britain following the general election in 1961, he willfully allows Chipembere to languish in prison.

24. Bush Conference

Chipembere appears to have been what Hegel would call a "beautiful soul,"[251] unaware of the cunning of reason in the work of history, as is revealed in his

---

[245] Banda attended the Manchester Pan-African Congress, where he made acquaintance with leading proponents such as Jomo Kenyatta and Kwame Nkrumah. He also frequented Pan-Africanist meetings in Soho and would often host these meetings at his own house in fashionable Brondesbury Park, London. See Short 1974:28–54.

[246] While living in London, he joined the brotherhood of Freemasons, invested in real estate, and gambled on the stock market. See Short 1974:51.

[247] Short 1974:199. See also White 2001.

[248] Chilembwe, who visited London in 1899 on his return from his studies in the United States, had already demonstrated that fashion was more than mere mimicry of Western mannerism—an African kind of dandyism could be a place where a new African identity could be communicated. See McCracken 2012:346.

[249] Chipembere 2002:352–354.

[250] Short 1974:142.

[251] See Hegel 1977:383f.

fervent advocacy of the abstract idea of "Africanization." Had Chipembere and the Young Turks been politically thorough, they would perhaps have been prepared for dealing with the shadow of colonial rule already looming over Malawi via Banda's autocratic approach in decentralizing and radicalizing the colonial power infrastructure and edifice. Either that or, perhaps, out of envy, the Young Turks themselves wanted to be dictators—the new Kalongas!

At the now infamous Bush Conference of 1959,[252] Chipembere and the Young Turks plotted violence against the colonials should they assassinate Banda, as was feared when Banda's campaign sparked nationwide political insurrection. There, however, no political direction was mapped out with the exception of a Jacobin committee led by Chipembere and Chiume that would assume power collectively to carry out revolutionary revenge for Banda. No quarter would be given for the colonials and their stooges—the so-called *kapilikonis*. The Young Turks revealed themselves then as "infantile"—*nthumbidwa*, as some elder members of the NAC had suspected—and more interested in power and rebellion than the more mundane, aftermath task of creating a new working country.

Lacking a unifying vision beyond the excess of militant struggle, personal ambition, and political enthusiasm, they left the future of an independent Malawi to chance. It was Banda, excluded from the Bush conference, who learnt from history to map out a version of a pseudo-localized democracy to serve his autocratic political ambitions.[253]

25. Sorcerer

Banda, thus, returned from abroad a changed man, perhaps even "de-tribalized" and permanently "Westernized." He had witnessed a lynching of a Black man in Tennessee[254] and had experienced the all-consuming virulent dance of capitalism (the modern manifestation of *Thunga*)[255] that saw everything "solid melt into the air,"[256] from the United States to Europe via South Africa and from Europe back to Nyasaland via Ghana. *Thunga* had re-awakened in the guise of British imperialism to shake the Malawi pool, once more demanding bloody sacrifices. Banda's traumatic encounter with Mrs. French revealed a man conflicted with himself, and cynical politics would be the fetish to cover his alienation and impotence as

---

[252] See Chipembere 2002:372–383.
[253] In Short 1974:202, Banda narrates how, for instance, the Young Turks left it to him to draft the new constitution of post–independence Malawi with the colonials in London.
[254] Short 1974:25.
[255] Žižek 2016:3 likens the virulent dance of capitalism to the sea monster Kraken, which, in this study, identifies as *Thunga*, the Chewa water python spirit.
[256] As described by Karl Marx and Friedrich Engels in *The Communist Manifesto* (2012; org. pub. 1848).

a colonial subject. He would be the new Kalonga, the messenger of *Thunga*[257]—
the "one who packs heads of the dead!" A *nthumbidwa* king!

Like a sorcerer diverging from the traditional social and economic circles
and localized politics, Banda now seeks to forge his destiny as an individual[258] by
way of modern magic. He now sees the reality of capitalism (money) as the new
Nyau,[259] beyond good and evil, to which morality, the law, and democracy were
subject—an endless parade of commodities is the new *Gule Wamkulu* without
kwawo! In this new witches' dance, totally spectacular and independent of the
actuality of community, generosity, "democracy," and social alienation are now
opportunities to be exploited for personal gain and self-enrichment, and he
moves to capitalize on his messianic political image.

As a keen political scientist, Banda would have been aware of the dialectical
nature of the movement of history, as put forward by Hegel: that after the revolution, the revolution itself must be negated if a revolution is to bring real change.
The insightful Gwelo prison writings of his young political scientist, Dunduzu
Chisiza, warned of the dangers of strongman leadership overstaying its purpose
after colonialism was vanquished,[260] and these alert Banda to his own impeding

[257] Banda, as a messenger of *Thunga* (which is to say of capitalism and social strife), is relayed from
a legend popular on the school playground of the author's childhood. It was said if you went into
Banda's room at Sanjika Palace while he was in another part of the country making a speech
at a rally, you would see him there sat next to his bed polishing a huge python, *Thunga*, like a
spirit-wife.

[258] One sociological definition of a witch is somebody who has broken out of communal obligation
to carve out destiny on their own and independent of their community—see Mauss 1972. This
definition of a witch is accommodated by the Chewa—see Breugel 2001:223. *Nyau* can be considered a form of witchcraft if employed for individualistic ends—Morris 2000:137. Ultimately, the
figure of the witch is ambivalent among the Chewa—see Breugel 2001:211-231.

[259] In contemporary times, when *Nyau* is under siege from "witchcraft," one can simply buy the
path into the *Nyau* secret society. See Morris 2000:135.

[260] See Mwakasungura and Miller 2016: 14, Schoffeleers 1999:69-70, Short 1974:201-202, and
McCracken 2012:410. Chisiza (1962:14f.) writes, in a tone reminiscent of Aristotle, "The seventh
danger is that of dictatorship. Three things will bring about a dictatorship in Africa: (1) too
much trust, (2) too little trust, and (3) neurotic ambition. Of the three causes, the third presents
the least problem. A man who makes up his mind to be another Napoleon, Hitler, or Mussolini
in these changed times, can be certain that resurgent Africa will deal with him the way Europe
dealt with the European misanthropes. People cannot heave off the yoke of colonialism and then
fail to pulverize under their feet a demented individual who wants to sit on their necks.

"The real problem is posed by those leaders who will lapse into dictatorial tendencies
either because their countrymen trust them too much or because they trust them too little.
When too much trust is reposed in a leader (sometimes) the thing goes to his head and makes
him believe that he is infallible. Such a man is not likely to brook criticism or to welcome alternative suggestions. It is his idea or nothing. On the other hand, when a brilliant, self-assured,
well-meaning leader is begrudged trust or is dealing with an illiterate populace, he too will tend
to force his measures through in a dictatorial manner believing that the masses will appreciate
what he is doing later."

negation. Chipembere's short-sighted, even naïve, Jacobin arrangement for the transfer of power should Banda be assassinated by the colonials only galvanizes Banda's own ruthless approach to dealing with anybody standing in the way of his "political" ambitions. It is, after all, a means of self-preservation.

In 1964, barely two months after independence, Banda pre-empts the inevitable negation of his Chewa kingship style by the new, free nation of Malawi by expelling his young ambitious cabinet before they could overthrow him, now that their messiah had served their political ends. In any case, in his specific game plan, these "notables,"[261] the so-called Young Turks, have to go.

26. A Martyrdom Denied

When rumor spreads across Malawi that Chipembere is armed with the most potent magic for invincibility[262] in the theater of war, he launches an audacious guerrilla war against Banda—with a plan to strike at the center.[263] However, when his plans fail to capture the imagination and enthusiasm of Malawians for a nationwide armed conflict, he settles for what appears like a symbolic attack modelled on John Chilembwe: Chipembere dresses fashionably in a trench coat and marches with 200 men on the Malawi army headquarters in Zomba. His march is ill-timed, as when he reaches the river at Liwonde, the ferry is on the opposite side, and the Malawi security forces are able to catch up with him as he waits for it. Chipembere and his army scatter in panic.

A list of Chipembere's followers is found at his abandoned "Zambia" camp in Mangochi.[264] These followers are hunted by the Malawi Young Pioneers, and Chipembere gives himself up. Even here, Banda pre-empts Chipembere by denying him martyrdom. Rather, as if advised by Aristotle, Banda sends him with a "fatherly pardon" into exile in the United States, disguising him in humiliating Blackface make-up, apparently to conceal his identity on the plane.[265] A contrite Chipembere resurfaces in Tanzania two weeks later, begging Banda to take him back, but Banda tells him he has reached a point of no return and withdraws his contact. Chipembere later dies of diabetes, although some allege by

---

[261] Aristotle (*Politics* 5.1311a) warns "the notables are the source of conspiracies (against tyrants)—some because they want to be rulers themselves; others because they do not want to be slaves." See Aristotle (1996:211) as translated by Ernest Barker.

[262] McCracken 2012:448.

[263] McCracken 2012:442.

[264] McCracken 2012:443.

[265] As McCracken 2012:453 points out, Chipembere's flight was actually organized by the British Special Branch, most likely employed by Banda to provide his cynical political operations with an "aura of British respectability." Black paint from the Zomba Dramatic Society was employed.

poisoning, in 1974 in the United States, as a doctoral politics student at UCLA, no doubt having grasped where Banda's political cynicism might have come from.

Following the cabinet crisis, the fate of the rest of the Young Turks is equally tragic: first, there is disunity in exile in Tanzania because of the familiar Malawian *nsanje* (jealousies and envy) out of Malawian covert egotism. In Tanzania, Chipembere heads a new party—the Pan-African Democratic Party (PDP)—but not all the ex-ministers join him, choosing instead to form their own parties. Leading his Congress for the Second Republic (CSR), Kanyama Chiume partners with friends from his student days in Tanzania to undermine Chipembere's political influence in exile. It is under Chiume's malicious instigation that Chipembere is thought to be a CIA agent and forced back into further exile in the United States. The Tanzanian police give Chipembere a disrespectful and thorough frisking before boarding the plane at Dar es Salaam airport.[266]

The gung-ho Yatuta Chisiza forms his own *Ufulu Umodzi M'malawi* (UUMA) and goes to China to train in martial arts and guerrilla warfare. He returns to Malawi via Zambia, with an army of ten men and an assortment of fancy combat weapons,[267] and attempts to start a coup d'état from Mwanza in 1967.[268] Chisiza is killed by the Malawi army (with support from the Rhodesian air force)[269] in a fierce two-hour firefight while trying to enter Malawi.[270] He is the first of the rebels to die, which demoralizes his small army,[271] and his body goes on public display in the North. No one, not even his mother and relatives, is allowed to publicly mourn him.[272]

A penitent Chirwa goes to Blantyre to try to get an audience with Banda behind his friends' back. In a clear manifestation of subjective destitution, as the law could no longer protect him, Chirwa arms himself with traditional medicines for self-protection (sourced from a witchdoctor in Mulanje) but is beaten by Banda's icemen and sent into exile in Tanzania, where he ekes out a living teaching law. Breaking from Chipembere and Chiume, he founds a political party, the Malawi Freedom Movement (MAFREMO). Years later, in 1981, he

---

[266] Mwakasungura and Miller 2016:78.

[267] See Malawi Historic Pictures 2017.

[268] Apparently having read a booklet by Che Guevara and Fidel Castro that said it was possible to spark a revolution with a small determined guerrilla army.

[269] Mwakasungura and Miller 2016:188.

[270] It is said a bazooka grenade that Chisiza exploded accidentally caused pandemonium in his camp, and that, in that cloud of confusion, an enemy crept behind Chisiza and shot him in the stomach when he turned around—"He was hit in the tummy. He went up. The air inside takes you up. I saw him going up and I knew he was hit," says Frank Jiya, a surviving member of the botched guerrilla campaign. See Mwakasungura and Miller 2016:192.

[271] Frank Jiya says that their stealthy movement was betrayed by noisy baboons. See Mwakasungura and Miller 2016:192.

[272] McCracken 2012:445.

is kidnapped by Malawi security forces while visiting Eastern Zambia, who say he was trying to enter Malawi illegally. Chirwa and his wife Vera are tried in a traditional court in Malawi, which, in a cruel irony, he had established as a justice minister in 1962 to counteract cumbersome colonial laws and judicial procedure. They are tried by chiefs and village headmen as *chigawengas*, using "common sense," and without lawyers or witnesses.[273] They are found guilty of high treason and are sentenced to death, but this is commuted to life imprisonment after an international outcry. Chirwa and his wife are taken on a tour of the country in chains to bear witness to the successes of Banda's development initiatives before they are taken back to prison, where Chirwa dies in 1992.[274] His wife, Vera, is granted clemency months later when Banda comes under further pressure from the donor community.[275]

Kanyama Chiume eventually settles in Tanzania as a journalist and writes and publishes numerous books. He returns to Malawi after Banda's fall in 1994. In old age, he has no appetite for politics and serves briefly as the director of the Malawi National Library and Malawi Book Service before retiring to the United States where he dies, depressed, in 2007.[276]

27. Elephant I

In 1970, Banda is mounted on the back of the elephant *Nyau* structure (*Njobvu*) at the crossroads to Mchinji and, thus, formally made a post-Kalonga titular chief.[277]

It is, in essence, a desperate attempt to limit his power, coming all too late. As a self-declared modern day Kalonga (*Ngwazi*), he had, by then, already exiled the de facto heir to the Kalonga throne, Chief Mwase of Kasungu, to Mulanje

---

[273] *Chigawenga*—literally "rebel"—translates more as *homo sacer* (see Agamben 1998) within the Malawian cultural and political context. The author was about eight years old and in primary school when, against his parents' advice, he attended Orton and Vera Chirwa's trial at the Southern Region Traditional Court in Njamba, Blantyre. He remembers the police bringing in Orton Chirwa in heavy chains on his hands and feet, out of the back of a Black Maria. The chains rattled to his labored walk against the dead silence that greeted him outside the court. The gathered crowd only stared at him. Orton Chirwa's grey head hobbled on a flimsy body, but he put on a cheerful face, waving at the crowd seated under the jacaranda trees around the court. His chains gleamed against the sun. Still, there was no reaction from the crowd. Nobody waved back at him. Everyone was frozen with fear of repercussion for responding to the rebel, as political dissenters under Banda were called.

[274] Wikipedia n. d., "Orton Chirwa."

[275] See Lwanda 1993:107.

[276] Wikipedia n. d., "Kanyama Chiume."

[277] Former cabinet minister and Banda's right hand man John Tembo says it was the MCP regional chairman Chidzanja who arranged the ceremony. See Cruise 5 2018. Chidzanja was Banda's contact for enlisting *Nyau* members into the Malawi Congress Party. See McCracken 2012:448.

Figure 8. Njobvu structure. Lilongwe, 1960s.
Photograph by Noel Salaun.

District;[278] he also depoliticized and marginalized the Malawian matrilineal system and its prestation economy, replacing them with a pseudo-puritan Christian patriarchy and a spectacular Hobbesian society driven by an exploitative market economy[279] under the ironic slogan "Unity, Loyalty, Obedience and Discipline."[280] Banda's seeming political madness, virulent violence, and— following his assumption of the Kalonga kingship—his adoption of capitalism as the economy of *Thunga* over the local prestation economies, has a working rationale: a feverish capitalist economy is a perfect accompaniment to a tyranny that preys on the Nyanja concept of an elective community and prodigious praxis and thrives on cultural and political deterritorialization.[281] In 1971, Banda is made Life President of the Republic of Malawi.

---

[278] Lwanda 1993:45.
[279] The economy was driven by cheaper underclass labor. See Mwakasungura and Miller 2016:20.
[280] Short 1974:264.
[281] Deleuze and Guattari 2019.

His Kalonga regime takes the shape of a ready course: the caprice and arbitrariness of British capital-driven imperial rule. As a Hellenophile, Banda's models are most probably based upon the opportunistic early tyrants of the pre-constitutional politics of Solon's Athens—the colonial legislator, Chipembere, was his Solon, and he is the Malawian Peisistratus.[282] Those who protest his "people's dictatorship" are threatened to be "meat for crocodiles,"[283] an allusion to one of the Kalonga's traditional methods of human sacrifice practiced in precolonial times. Many are detained without trial—a method inherited from colonial times. As under Kalonga and colonial rule, all traditional authority is subject to Banda and acts as an instrument of his political and economic objectives in a blatant act of primitive accumulation.[284] Banda's word is the law[285] and its very transgression. As an elder of the Church of Scotland since his Edinburgh days, he has a reputation for piety, which allows him to lord it over the Church of Central Africa Presbyterian (CCAP)--and, impicitly, over the churches more broadly.[286]

He runs Malawi like a personal plantation[287] and boasts about this to his Western guests at state banquets. He says he is "an embodiment of the will and the spirit of the people"[288] and an expression of their constitution and sovereignty.[289] He turns former colonial lands into national farms under parastatal organizations, Press Holdings, and Admarc, which are in fact his own—his wealth is hidden in plain sight. He invests in South African property, and banks in Switzerland and Britain.

While enveloping Malawi in a new Western Presbyterian patriarchy, Banda pays lip service to the Amaravi matrilineal system by calling himself *Nkhoswe* (Uncle) Number One, promising women empowerment and protection. That really means, however, that all women and youth belong to him personally. and is a bold declaration of the paternalism last seen during the days of "the one who packs heads of the dead." Thus, the Amaravi primal father finds a living

---

[282] On Solon: Aristotle *Constitution of the Athenians* 5; On Peisistratus: Aristotle *Constitution of the Athenians* 13–17.

[283] Schoffeleers 1999:155. One of Banda's crocodile ponds was at Box 2 in Limbe. See Mwakasungura and Miller 2016:103.

[284] McCracken 2012:455 writes (following the Cabinet Crisis) "Banda embarked on a policy of selecting and deselecting chiefs according to his own interpretation of Malawian history. Chiefs, it was clear, were now to be recognized as authentic exponents of Malawian culture rather than as colonial stooges, yet they were expected to operate within the constraining context of the Banda autocracy."

[285] Short 1974:254.

[286] Lwanda 1993:11.

[287] McCracken 2012:433.

[288] Short 1974:253. "I am a dictator of the people. I dictate by permission, by consent."

[289] Short 1974:93.

reincarnation once more—this time in the equally diminutive, angry, petulant, and impulsive Banda.

His insatiable appetite for power thus betrays incessant Oedipal pathologies. Banda does not keep any friends.[290] Rather, he places trust only in himself, his Ngoni "official hostess" Mama Kadzamira, and her seemingly dopey uncle John Tembo.[291] He resists any prodding from the Church to marry his official hostess, a former nurse under his employment at a short-lived medical practice he opened in Blantyre upon his return from Europe. This "Mama," who towers over him in colorful Java Prints bearing his surly face, most likely replaces his long-deceased, real mother, Akupingamnyama, as an object of his unfathomable egotist desires. Banda is most comfortable among women—it is as if he never left the *kuka*.[292] His use of women to mobilize mass support for the MCP depoliticizes and marginalizes masses of Malawi men. His rallies—the only political gatherings allowed—are accompanied by his *mbumba*, or dancing women who wear his sneering, frozen photographed face all over their bodies, like "Mama," and sing praises of him as conqueror, Messiah, and "wise leader."[293] These *mbumba* are a live "cinema of attractions,"[294] a form of modern

---

[290] Short 1974:198. Since the cabinet crisis Banda had recused himself from any informal relationships with his supporters or cabinet.

[291] Manning a student art exhibition, the author once met Banda, Mama Kadzamira, and John Tembo in person at one of Banda's sumptuous Founder's Day visits to Kamuzu Academy. Banda gave him a firm handshake and passed him on to also shake the official hostess's hand. Their hands were extraordinary soft. Banda's survey of the exhibition in the VIP lounge was enthusiastic but brief. What the author remembers most vividly from the encounter, though, was the balletic and machine like nature of how Banda's bodyguards scaled and moved about the room, in response to the president's every movement—it was an impressive dramatization of the *Dasein* and authority of an otherwise frail little old man. Then there was the sudden disappearance of Banda and his entourage from the lounge and the completely unheralded appearance of John Tembo to see the exhibition on his own. Tembo wore a smart grey suit and horn-rim glasses, but one of his shoes was completely worn out, a part of its sole coming off and trailing behind him. John Tembo looked and moved like a ghost. It was probably this most elusive trait he had about him that enabled him to be the sole member of cabinet to survive Banda's autocratic regime from the beginning to the end. Recent interviews with John Tembo reveal a man who was very aware of Kamuzu's *Nyau* method. Tembo describes Banda as the "man" who climbed the back of an "elephant" (structure). See Cruise 5, 2018.

[292] Banda's use of *kuka* politics to mobilize mass support has been explored by Power 2010:133–134.

[293] The author remembers these rallies vividly. In fact, one of his earliest memory is the sight of a *Gule Wamkulu* mask, Chimbano, languishing in the sun in stifling costume, waiting to dance for Banda, in Kasungu. The mask panted like a thirsty animal, and the author saw anguished human eyes in its mouth. His mother and sisters were often out rehearsing or dancing at these rallies and travelling, inconveniencing the family, but there was nothing that the family could do about it. In Chewa matriarchal society, the nuclear family is not so important: children are raised communally in *mphalas*. Banda made full use of that to mobilize even modern Malawian families to his political ends.

[294] An African form of the so-called "cinema of attractions," as described by Gunning 1990, was also popular in Malawian makeshift cinema houses. Western films were heavily edited in Malawi

day *chinkhome*, or a *kuka* derivative of *Gule Wamkulu*. Banda flickers and bounces off their gyrating bodies like *Chadzunda*,[295] declaring himself *"mwini mzinda,"* not for the sovereignty of the people but for political expediency, zombifying entertainment, and capital.

During the independence celebrations, school children in Kamuzu Stadium roll out a giant hypnopompic xerox of Banda's surly face from the stands in carefully choreographed cinematic swipes. On Soche Hill in Blantyre, three words in the Pan-Africanist colors of black, red, and green flicker in succession: Long Live Kamuzu. Banda's spectacular cinematic dispositif comes complete with membership cards, t-shirts, and badges that bear his name and are a form of tax, as they are compulsory. The same dancing, vacuous photograph hangs on the walls of every building and office, public or private, keeping everyone in "view" of Kamuzu. The gyrating and ululating women sing *Zonse zimenezi ndiza Kamuzu Banda*, "Everything belongs to Kamuzu Banda."[296] The Messiah has come to represent the *Nyau* itself—just like Jesus Christ.

28. Elephant II, or Lion

To keep his civil service further under control and in crippling poverty, he cuts their allowances and expenditure on social services, in the name of frugality. He publicly lectures them on how to dress: no mini dresses or trousers for women. Men are to keep their hair short and their facial hair trimmed. He also imparts advice on personal morality and continence.[297] The policing of dress and manners across the country, including for foreigners,[298] becomes a way of keeping the nation "at his gates."

Furthermore, many of his subjects remain landless. Swathes of land confiscated in the late nineteenth century, during Sir Harry Johnston's drive to settle

---

either through Banda's strict censorship or because of the projectionist's desire for a more "action packed" non-linear presentation, which was most popular. In other words, a James Bond film would suddenly change into a Bruce Lee one in the next frame. "*Nyau* cinema," as it was called in the author's childhood circles, was a lively and interactive form of cinema that generated the same levity and an atmosphere of generosity in the audience as *Gule Wamkulu* masks in the villages. The Catholic hall at St. Pius in Blantyre was one popular venue for *Nyau* cinema. Banda, like many modern Africans, understood the power of film and photography for generating *Nyau*.

[295] An early observation of Banda as the mask of the nation is by Short 1974:282: "As Malawi's President and later Life President, Banda no longer has to hide behind a mask; rather he became the mask. Everywhere he went the party and government machines surrounded him with pomp and ceremony and matters of statues and protocol became increasingly important."

[296] McCracken 2012:370.

[297] Short 1974:280.

[298] Mgawi 2005:30.

European farmers in places like Thyolo and Mulanje, remain in the hands of a minority of expatriates.[299] He gives contracts to big business and multinationals, such as Lonrho. He makes friends with Tiny Rowland. He expends wealth on spurious monuments, projects, and social activities, as well as on office buildings, palaces (thirteen of them), prisons, rallies, houses for his *mbumba*,[300] and on his pet school Kamuzu Academy. He grants favors to his grassroot supporters and senior politicians who support him without question.[301] Some—like Tembo, Aleke Banda, and Gwanda Chakuamba—become conspicuously rich. The Malawian idea that persists today, that politics is one way of enriching oneself and one's relatives,[302] dates to these times.[303]

To keep people busy and servile, the dreaded colonial *malimidwe* farming methods, such as the time-consuming bunding, are reintroduced[304]—this is the Malawian equivalent of erecting the pyramids. During the presidential crop inspection tours—most probably modelled on the acts of ancient Greek tyrants aimed at keeping subjects in check[305]—a portion of the harvest and money is gifted to the President. The districts compete on who gives the most to the Life President. Anticipation of these tours keeps everybody working throughout the year and too "low in spirit" to rebel or engage in social bonding pastimes, as they did during colonial times. It is a crime if your garden is left unattended and Banda sees it.[306] *Bao*, a popular board game with the Yao and dandy Tonga men, is banned, in order to force the men back into the fields.[307] There could only be one gentleman in Malawi now, and his name is Kamuzu.

Banda traffics his *mbumba* amongst the political elite and civil servants, from district to district, as a "gift giver" in ongoing political potlatches, that see family ties relaxed,[308] men emasculated and suspicious of their wives,[309] women objectified and kept at his feet, and traditional dances instrumentalized as political propaganda.[310] Military-inspired Malawi syncretic dances, such as *Beni*, *Malipenga*, and *Mganda*, previously at the forefront of resistance against reification during colonial rule, are now vilified as the superfluous pastime of

[299] McCracken 2012:455.
[300] Mwakasungura and Miller 2016:173.
[301] Banda's politics of patrimonialism has been explored by Power 2010:198–199.
[302] For the so-called "politics of the belly," see Bayart 1993.
[303] Mwakasungura and Miller 2016:21.
[304] For an account of "punitive" colonial farming methods, *malimidwe*, see McCracken 2012:318–324.
[305] Aristotle *Politics* 4.1295a.
[306] The author's personal recollection of Banda's yearly crop-inspection tours.
[307] Lwanda 1993:53.
[308] Banda's rallies had a dark orgiastic underside which might have contributed to the virulent spreading of Aids in Malawi in the 1980s.
[309] See Lwanda 1993:51.
[310] See Mkamanga 2000.

"lazy men."[311] The now marginalized Amaravi matrilineal system is symbolized by Mama Kadzamira, who accompanies him everywhere like his mother—an Amaravi spirit-wife in exile. The metapolitics of *Nyau* as under Kalonga are marginalized, even banned from Banda's reified *kuka* politics. *Gule Wamkulu* is reduced to a license for police violence[312] and amusement during Banda's exhausting ongoing political rallies and tours.

29. Strife—*Kuthana*

Like Kalonga and the colonial rulers before, Banda employs class and latent social antagonism as a political weapon. He employs elements of the *Lumpenproletariat*—penniless youths from the villages, the Malawi Youth, and Malawi Young Pioneers—to reinforce his autocratic rule. It is these people with "nothing to lose" that Banda claims to be working for. During Banda's political rallies, these young enforcers take over Malawi society like *pinimbira,*[313] and antagonize the civil service[314] and traditional authorities with arbitrary interventions, with Banda himself as the lord of their misrule. In this way, Banda keeps his civil service in check, as well as by constantly shuffling his educated personnel, who now work under his watchful hypnopompic portrait, everywhere, up and down the country.

Citizens are encouraged to turn on each other and family members against each other, as the whole family, even tribe, is punished by Gwede if one of its members is found to be involved in subversion. Muslims are marginalized and banned from visiting Mecca, citing the fear of their returning with polio.[315] He denies Europeans and Asians automatic citizenship, to stir up racial tensions and xenophobia.[316] He presents himself as the bridge between the classes—Africans on one side and Asians and Europeans on the other—but, in fact, he

[311] Lwanda 1993:53.
[312] McCracken 2012:418.
[313] A "swarm" of *Nyau* masks that occasionally invade Chewa villages from the graveyard to carry out a destructive potlatch of excess property at the *kuka* and elsewhere. See Boucher 2012:126.
[314] The author, son of a senior civil servant (his father Aaron Elisa Kambalu was a medical officer), once witnessed an encounter between his parents and the Malawi Youth. Coming back from one of Banda's political rallies in Blantyre in the family car, his father entered a junction too early, seemingly oblivious to an oncoming truck full of Kamuzu's *mbumba*. The truck swerved to avoid a crash and stopped ahead. A red-shirted Malawi Youth approached the family car to rebuke him, and the author's father prostrated himself before him like the lowest peasant. The language he used to plead forgiveness from the Malawi youth, his hands held tightly together, was most base. The author, sitting in the back of the car, could not recognize his father: it was a very uncanny moment. His mask had completely slipped.
[315] Lwanda 1993:12.
[316] McCracken 2012:457.

follows Aristotle's advice for the tyrant "to thoroughly embrace" the "strong side," which, in the modern Malawian economy, are Asian traders and European expatriates.[317]

Official Hostess Mama Kadzamira starts *Chitukuko Cha Amai M'malawi* (CCAM), an organization of middle-class women that extorts free labor from the subaltern classes. Although, upon his arrival in 1958, Banda pledged "to build a state in which color, race or creed will mean nothing,"[318] he instead entertains racial hierarchies left behind by the colonials. Only white people can teach at his beloved Kamuzu Academy[319] or head his Press Holdings. He has many white expatriates, with some of whom he shares fellowship in Freemasonry, working as farm managers and heading hospitals, the army, and the police. Asians are made the trading class in cities and town trading centers, and social interactions with Malawians are discouraged. His own "tribe," the Chewa, as under Kalonga, are elevated to be the ruling tribe—"those who live on the hill"—while the other tribes below, the new Bandas, serve. Special Branch eavesdroppers are everywhere, and one does not know who is listening.

Education is basic, covering farming, utility, and manual work. Banda demands that university education be tailored to "the conditions in the country."[320] He enlists Chewa students and staff as spies on University campuses.[321] He has low regard for the "half educated" and praises the wisdom of the villager. Academics, "grey haired lecturers and bald-headed men at universities," who attempt to raise a questioning or a speculative spirit among the students and populations, are jailed or sent into exile. In the seventies, Banda's Young Pioneers detain eighteen statisticians from the Bureau of Statistics when they earn praise from the World Bank for painting an accurate picture of Malawi's economic performance.[322] The floodlights of the dreaded Mikuyu prison can be seen from the Chancellor College, and many academics are sent there without trial.[323] The Malawian poet and academic Jack Mapanje becomes world-famous in exile, writing thinly-veiled verses criticizing Banda's rule.[324] Banda's elite school, Kamuzu Academy, has an alien syllabus rendering education at the school superfluous. Banda calls the youth "born frees" for political expediency, but in fact this too is mere representation:

---

[317] Aristotle *Politics* 5.1314b.
[318] Short 1974:157.
[319] Lwanda 1993:187.
[320] Short 1974:279.
[321] Mwakasungura and Miller 2016:76–77.
[322] Mwakasungura and Miller 2016:64
[323] Mwakasungura and Miller 2016:77.
[324] See Mapanje 2011.

he taxes them through party membership cards and[325] free manual work at school, and during Youth Week, they are involved in infrastructure work, repairing and cleaning dusty roads.[326] He reintroduces the notorious colonial hut tax. Government messengers and the Malawi Youth enforce the hut tax: one often sees men running away from their mud huts when the tax collectors swoop on a village.[327]

There is heavy censorship of the dissemination of information, and there is no television. There is only one radio station, the Malawi Broadcasting Corporation, whose transmitter is a donation from the government of apartheid South Africa. There are two newspapers, both belonging to the Malawi Congress Party. Banda subjects the Malawian political imaginary of Chilembwe to his Kalonga designs: Chilembwe was but a prelude to his own second coming as the Amaravi messiah.[328] His mother tongue, Chichewa, is imposed as the second official language after English.[329] He deploys Byzantine state bureaucracy to bamboozle the populace. He shows his admiration for valor in the theatre of war, through lengthy speeches on the Zulu warrior Shaka, whose pathological and gory kingship[330] he would like to be identified with as *Ngwazi*. He subjects Malawians to the work of history[331] and their sovereignty to an abstract idea of the Malawi state. Every major development project is named Kamuzu: Kamuzu Highway, Kamuzu Stadium, Kamuzu College of Nursing, and so forth[332]—these are all gifts from the *Ngwazi* to keep the nation under obligation and in crippling debt.

---

[325] For the author's own childhood experience with the MCP membership card, see Kambalu 2008:35. Here, the author comes under the spell not only of Banda's vacuous photographic portrait but also his gestural signature. Chipembere (2002:349) narrates how many Malawians saw the MCP membership card as a "passport to personal salvation."

[326] From the author's own childhood experience.

[327] When the author was around ten years old in Thyolo District, one of his father's "servant quarters" tenants, a "messenger," was stabbed in the chest trying to collect tax in the villages. He came back from work that evening covered in blood. When he recovered, he was promoted by the District Commissioner and given a new well-ironed khaki uniform in which he proudly paraded about the neighborhood.

[328] Short 1974:89.

[329] Phiri 1998:163.

[330] See Phiri 1982:21–56.

[331] Short 1974:256.

[332] Power 2010:201.

30. Preservation of Monarchy:
Zombie State (*Ndondocha* Republic)

According to Aristotle, when kingships are destroyed, it is often from within and in two ways: the first, "when those who participate in the royal rule form factions among themselves; the other, when kings try to run affairs too tyrannically, claiming powers more than they are legally entitled to."[333]

By the end of the seventies, Banda's Kalonga Life Presidency is well established, having thoroughly subjugated his court to his will and put away the key witnesses and potential adversaries. His notorious hatchet men Muwalo and Gwede, now rivals of Tembo and Kadzamira, are quietly dealt with, tried by the "traditional courts" for treason.[334] Muwalo is hanged, and Gwede is detained for life. In 1981, Banda opens the doors to Kamuzu Academy in what appears as an homage to his real secret weapon: the Classics—according to this study, more specifically, the disturbing middle passages of Aristotle's *Politics*. Banda is graced with visits from the UK's Queen Elizabeth II in 1979, and by Prince Charles and Margaret Thatcher. The visits are reciprocal: Banda is processed and hosted by Elizabeth II's court and her Prime Minister. In footage of one of these sumptuous banquets, a tuxedoed Banda, a known teetotaler, flanked by the Queen and the Queen Mother, appears to be making a drunken speech to entertain the bemused guests.[335]

By the mid-eighties, his rule and political approach tend towards greater moderation, but even here, he is not far from Aristotle: "The fewer those spheres of activity where the king's power is sovereign, the longer the regime will inevitably survive undiminished. They themselves become less like masters and more like their subjects in character, and therefore arouse less envy among them."[336] Banda appears to have reached his political *telos* then. His speeches during his crop inspection tours have become mundane, more like stand-up comedy as rehearsed before the Queen in England. He allows his officials to be criticized by the plainspoken Mai Manjankhosi of the League of Malawi Women. He enjoys watching himself and his defeated adversaries parodied by *Gule Wamkulu* performances.[337] He passes on the running of the country to his right-hand man John Tembo of the warlike Ngoni tribe, a "noble" rival of his own "formidable" Chewa non-tribe in precolonial times; this is a break with Aristotle's rule that, should the tyrant choose a favorite, they "should not be

[333] Aristotle *Politics* 5.1313a.
[334] Power 2010:158.
[335] Mandini 2017.
[336] Aristotle *Politics* 5.1313a.
[337] The author's personal recollection of Banda's late regime.

of bold character."[338] Tembo is shrewder than Banda realizes, or Banda could simply be getting old. Tembo and his niece Mama Kadzamira gradually isolate Banda from the general population, until he loses touch with the everyday life of most of his grassroots supporters.[339] Places he visits are set up to make him think everything is working perfectly[340] when in fact, since 1979, the Malawi economy has been through several "shocks," and living standards are steadily deteriorating.[341]

Meanwhile, political violence appears to lose agency, becoming a form of sadomasochistic pastime for the political elite and their grassroots henchmen. Every Malawian is a potential victim of the Malawi Young Pioneers' violent network—it all depends on the whim of any politician in a position of power, as they all have now fashioned themselves after the *Gule* image of their autocratic master. There is a large jail in each of Malawi's twenty-four districts[342] full of the sounds of sadistic beatings and prisoners wailing like *ndondocha* (zombies), capturing the deadening political deadlock of Banda's late dictatorship. The most abominable of these prisons is Dzaleka ("come and quit") in Dowa, where political prisoners are stripped naked, beaten, and chained up to be "eaten" alive by mosquitoes. All over the country, prisoners on hard labor are put in ironically angelic, white uniforms, and their shining chain gangs can be seen at work under the scorching sun throughout the country, against protest from Amnesty International. Shadows of respectable men are seen at work in the fields, barefoot and in humiliating colonial bermudas.

Malawian secret agents take to sending out parcel-bombs to political exiles abroad. The leader of the Socialist League of Malawi (LESOMA), Attati Mpaka, loses eight fingers in Mozambique, before he is shot dead in Zimbabwe. The house of the exiled journalist Mkwapatira Mhango[343] is fire-bombed in Lusaka. The Malawi Young Pioneers purge the senior service of northerners, mostly Tumbuka, scapegoating them for the gathering economic woes and political satiation; they are deported by the busloads. The crocodile pools at Box 2 foam forth with Banda's disappeared political victims.

---

[338] Aristotle *Politics* 5.1315a.

[339] It was observed by one government official that "He [Banda] withdrew, like Tiberius did to Capri, and left the running of his empire to his minions." See Alexander 1995.

[340] See Alexander 1995 and Kambalu 2008. At one point the author's dusty family house in Nkolokosa, Blantyre, was painted white on the front only, to make the passing Banda think the infamous "location" was habitable.

[341] These included drought in 1980, 9% loss in GDP, high interest rates for borrowers, and a disastrous foreign policy with Mozambique which led to Malawian imports and exports being redirected. See Lwanda 1993:168–169.

[342] Lwanda 1993:165.

[343] See Lwanda 1993:107.

Poets for and against Banda write verses spiting each other. "Bad verses from yonder" reads one headline in the Malawi *Daily Times*.[344] Banda's *mbumba* take to conspicuous shopping trips to New York, Paris, London, and Johannesburg, and make news headlines around the world.

31. The Fall

The nation is "pacified" and feeling secure in the early 1980s but under pressure from the World Bank and the IMF, who were calling for structural adjustments on what was perceived as economic excess, mismanagement, and lack of accountability. In response, Banda entertains thoughts of democratic reform, probably imagining a situation that mimics the British constitutional monarchy. In 1983, he calls a debate regarding this possibility with his cabinet ministers, and panics when there is enthusiasm for a more decentralized form of government and no reverence for the status quo amongst his ministers.[345] Banda is awakened from his political slumber, and his nasty "petulant" side takes hold once more. He dissolves parliament, dismisses all ministers, and sets out to marginalize those who had shown enthusiasm for reform. Three of these ministers and an MP—Dick Matenje, Twaibu Sangala, Aaron Gadama, and David Chiwanga—are killed in a mysterious "accident" in Mwanza.[346] It is the beginning of the end of his rule.

Five years later, the Berlin Wall comes down, and, along with it, Western support for the so-called Cold War dictators. From 1991, sanctions ensue from donor countries, including the United States and the United Kingdom. Banda resists, but a papal visit to the country reenergizes the Catholic Church, and the bishops write a pastoral letter mobilizing popular sentiment against him. His exiled political opponents begin to return one by one, beginning with a spectacular landing at Kamuzu International Airport of the long-exiled trade unionist Chakufwa Chihana. Faxes of anonymous letters criticizing the Banda regime stream into government offices and companies throughout the country. Riots ensue, targeting Banda's Press Industry stores and MCP offices.[347] The army disarms the MYP. Twenty-two people die in the clashes dubbed "Operation Bwezani." On 14 June 1993, Banda loses a referendum after a senile campaign for a one-party state. He would soon undergo brain surgery in South Africa—but return to office after two months, much to the dismay of the opposition.

---

[344] See Lwanda 1993:174.
[345] See Wikipedia n. d., "Hastings Banda."
[346] See Van Donge 1998:21–51.
[347] See Power 2010:1–7.

He is over ninety. Sixty-three per cent vote for multi-party politics. In 1994, Banda is deposed. All government funding to Kamuzu Academy is cut.[348]

Banda's political purges had been thorough—most of the politicians in the opposition party, the winning United Democratic Front (UDF)—including the president Bakili Muluzi (rumored son of Banda's witchdoctor)—are his former ministers.[349] They deploy his own political techniques on him, such as the projection of traditional chieftaincy, posturing speech, and the mobilization of grassroots women and the youth to consolidate political advantage.[350] Banda gracefully acquiesces to the transfer of power and retires.

By 1997, he is dead, having spent the rest of his days mostly under house arrest to answer for his political crimes, including the murder of the three ministers and the MP in Mwanza, although he was eventually acquitted for lack of evidence[351]—Banda never wrote anything down, instead depending on the Malawi tradition to pass on his orders,[352] and by the time he was taken to court, critical witnesses had been eliminated.[353] Furthermore, the Inspector General of Police, McWilliam Lunguzi, who is said to have passed on Banda's orders, was dead. Banda was coached by his English QC, Clive Stanbrook, to simply say, "I'm afraid, because it is such a long time ago, I have no information." 161 witnesses could not implicate him.[354]

Banda was given a state funeral in Lilongwe attended by thousands. The author saw his body laid in the casket, slight but determined even in death. It is said they found a photograph of Masauko Chipembere, the architect of his messianic return to Malawi, in Banda's room.[355] In the grainy black and white photograph, the fugitive Chipembere at his "Zambia" bush camp in Mangochi wears a trench coat and carries an umbrella.[356] He looks like a film star.

32. A Man Half-Wicked

For Aristotle, a tyranny that simulates kingship delivers at least a "partially evil man," and perhaps this is why Banda remains an ambivalent figure in Malawian

---

[348] The author experienced Banda's fall through the gradual deterioration of conditions at the school. Banda's expensive European staff often went unpaid for months, and the quality of the food in the dining hall steadily declined. Soon after the author finished his A Levels in 1995, the school was privatized.

[349] See Lwanda 1993:187.

[350] See Kayambazinthu and Moyo 2002:87–102.

[351] See Van Donge 1998:21–51.

[352] See Mapanje 2002.

[353] Power 2010:194.

[354] Alexander 1995.

[355] Boucher 2012:58.

[356] See illustration, Chipembere 2002:15.

history: "If he acts thus, his rule is bound to be not only better and more envi-able (he will not be hated and feared, and his rule will be exercised over better men, not men reduced to impotent submission), but also more lasting; and he himself will have either right of disposition or at least a half-good dispo-sition with respect to virtue, a man not wicked but half-wicked."[357] Banda is revered[358] and loathed[359] in equal measure—one only has to look him up in the news. Those who knew Banda as a person say that his cynical approach was just a political tactic[360] and that, in private, he exuded "dignity" and the "refined manners" of good missionary training and exercised "moderation" in everything. A teetotaler and a vegetarian, he chose his food for good health and not luxury. Those who visited him at his retirement home in Mudi say he was more interested in discussing the Classics than politics, making up for his short-term memory loss by reciting from his favorites, Cicero and Caesar.[361]

As an elder of the Church of Scotland, Banda showed himself "more obvi-ously earnest than anybody else" for political ends—but his real religion was driven by a grounded pragmatism, and he generally showed disregard for material wealth: for example, although a cherry-red Rolls-Royce was always at his disposal as head of state, he preferred to travel in his old Land Rover. His seeming dandyism was but a flipside of an underlying "tramp," and the Chewa idea of a "pure man"—*munthu wabwino*. He identified with farmers, peasants, and villagers and, as self-appointed "*Nkhoswe* Number One," he was a protector of women and children. In truth, he disdained corruption and refrained from grandiose projects associated with Africa's "big men." He looked after his rela-tives, patients, and friends.[362] Away from politics, he encouraged Malawians to enjoy their freedom, and popular culture from home and abroad flourished. Bars, taverns, and *gumbagumba* were everywhere.[363] The various tribes of the nation were allowed to practice many of their ancient traditions and religions. Banda was, in fact, a man of extreme generosity and good intentions, who placed the future of Malawi in the youth of the nation, the "born frees." Some called him "probably the most remarkable man in Africa today."[364]

---

[357] Aristotle *Politics* 5.1315b.

[358] For a sample, see a panegyric on Banda by Mgawi 2005. Mgawi once served as the Chairman of the Malawi Censorship Board under Banda.

[359] For a sample, see Makasungura and Miller's oral history, a compendium of Banda's atrocities, 2016.

[360] See Short 1974.

[361] See Alexander 1995.

[362] See Mgawi 2005:20–32.

[363] See the author's satirical take on Malawian popular culture under Banda in his memoir (Kambalu 2008).

[364] See Short 1974.

33. Nyasaland Analysand

The inference to be drawn from this study is that what people saw in Banda as Christian piety, good manners, and a ready generosity merely came from an inherited asceticism and altruism that hid a typical Chewa egotism left untraversed by a disrupting and fundamentally transforming encounter with colonialism and the modern world.

The fact that Banda was prepared to pervert the metapolitics of *Nyau* for his autocratic political ends means that, like Kalonga, the *nkamwini* king of the Amaravi, he believed he really had it! Either that or, upon discovering that he did not have it, he did not know what to do, as his traumatic episode with Mrs. French indicates. Instead of traversing his subjective destitution by radicalizing his reified colonial identity with a real grassroot cause like Chilembwe, Banda chose to hide his seeming impotence as a colonial subject by becoming a dictator—the new Kalonga!

The author would conclude here that it is most likely Banda did not see the vacuous underbelly of a tilted *Kasiya Maliro* as a youth, left Malawi uninitiated and uninformed of the "path," and came back a ready sociopath—a "witch" even! He was, in the end, not so different from the fervent Young Turks he patronized and exploited as "children in politics": a man of unbridled "individualism," too lacking in self-confidence and real political experience to join an elective community of sovereign equals—a *nthumbidwa,* as the elders of the Nyasaland African Congress would put it.

Malawi is still paying for his sin.

34. Father of the Nation

Efforts to exorcise Banda's ghost from Malawian politics have often ended in failure, and, lately, the country seems resigned to live with the legacy of his detracting politics, manifest in current times as what some have called "Chameleon politics."[365] When Banda was deposed from power in the multiparty general election in 1994, many public works named Kamuzu were renamed by President Bakili Muluzi, including after Banda's adversaries: for instance, Kamuzu Highway became Masauko Chipembere Highway, and Kamuzu International Airport was changed to Lilongwe International Airport. By the early twenty-first century, Muluzi's successor, Dr. Bingu wa Mutharika, had reversed these changes: Lilongwe International Airport was reverted to Kamuzu's name, as were Masauko Chipembere Highway and other such

[365] See Englund 2002:18.

projects. The Malawi Pan-Africanist flag, which bore a partial red sun as homage to Nyanja synthesized politics, was changed to one bearing a full white sun by Dr. Bingu wa Mutharika and then quickly reverted to the red half-sun after his sudden death and after popular, nationwide protests against the new design.[366]

Recently, attempts have been made to rehabilitate Banda's role in Malawian history as the "father of the nation."[367] Such initiatives have often turned out to be a pretext for a return to anti-democratic governance. Banda's successors have embraced the so-called "politics of the belly,"[368] turning the presidency into a family and tribal enterprise. Bakili Muluzi's party, UDF, is now run by his son Atupele, while President Dr. Bingu wa Mutharika at his death was succeeded as Party President by his brother Peter Mutharika. Malawi's first female president, Joyce Banda (after the death of Dr. Bingu wa Mutharika in 2012), resisted public accountability for her policies and financial dealings, claiming presidential immunity that stretched back to Banda.

Various monuments have been erected around Malawi honoring Hastings Kamuzu Banda, including a large mausoleum bearing his embalmed remains in Lilongwe. The monuments have become the loci of religious pilgrimage and nostalgic political protest for former Malawi Youth and Young Pioneers.[369] Meanwhile, prominent historical figures, such as Chipembere, Muluzi, and Dr. Bingu wa Mutharika, have entered the pantheon of *Nyau* demiurges where they play second fiddle to Banda's *Njobvu*.[370] But what real modern political imaginary does Malawi have when not honoring or entertaining tyranny? What is the "end" of Amaravi history? Is a new social contract for a radical democracy and unrestricted economics possible for Malawi?

Like Banda, we would have to look within and beyond Malawi history for possible answers and a new synthesis. As the Chewa saying goes: *Ipha njoka, mfiti ifulura mowa*, or "Kill the snake but spare the witch, for it is the witch who brews the beer."[371] Perhaps we would have to become Hellenophiles, too, and build our own academy as a seedbed for the age-old Nyanja penchant for critical and speculative thinking, radical democracy, and prodigious praxis. It appears that even Banda himself, as a shrewd anti-politician, foresaw this new academy metaphorically built over his "skull" as "father of the nation" and pre-empted history. Could this be what he meant with the riddle "you are not educated until you know Latin and Greek?" The true academy for future leaders of Malawi

---

[366] See "Malawi Parliament Approves to Revert to Original Flag" 2012.
[367] See Kainja 2019.
[368] See Bayart 1993.
[369] As witnessed on the author's last visit to Malawi in 2017.
[370] Boucher 2012 is a comprehensive catalogue of *Nyau* masks, including Chipembere (57), Dr. Bingu wa Mutharika (51), and Banda (117–118).
[371] Lacey 1934:17.

is evidently not Banda's Kamuzu Academy, but rather what the lavish school hinted at with its "alien" staff and syllabus built around "dead" languages and discourses—right in the middle of the "bush" at Mtunthama.

Postscript

At the posting of this study, in 2020, Malawi has elected a new president: Dr. Lazarus Chakwera, a Chewa and leader of the MCP. It was the first time the party had been elected to power since the fall of Banda twenty-six years before. Chakwera appears to be a glimmer of hope in Malawian politics. What has made him especially popular and a unifying force is his background as a "man of God"—Chakwera was president of the Assemblies of God of Malawi for twenty-four years before a sudden turn to politics.

Born to subsistence farmers in 1955 in a village in Lilongwe, Chakwera speaks with an inflection of an American accent,[372] mastered from his years of ministry in an American brand of charismatic religion. His exotic accent is more than curious entertainment for Malawians: it marks their hope for a better future after years of political deadlock and deterioration in standards of living—Chakwera might after all bring them unity, pride, and prosperity last seen in the early days of Malawian independence from the British. *Thunga* appears pacified for now.

---

[372] Chakwera has earned himself a hashtag for a moniker, #Itsanana, from his Americanized enunciation of "It's an honor."

2

Classical Studies in Malawi:
Its Health, Purpose, and Reputation

STEVE NYAMILANDU

Introductory Remarks

IN THIS CHAPTER, I will discuss the history of Classics teaching in Malawi, and then the origins of the Chancellor College Department of Classics. Next, I will write of student numbers and recruitment, commenting on the Department's substantially increased numbers in recent years, and I will present information from surveys I have made of the attitudes of Classics students towards Classics. Following that, I will describe the Department's course offerings and present information from surveys I have made relating to Classics students' views of the relevance of classical studies to their (Malawian) culture. Towards the end of this chapter, I will record the names and times of service of staff in the Department, External Examiners, and visiting scholars, seasoning these lists with reminiscences of memorable events and circumstances, from the beginning until now.

Overview

There is not yet much literature about Latin, Greek, or Classics teaching in Malawi in general. The present book will supply a partial correction for this omission. The history of Classics in Malawi starts with Latin as an ancient classical language, which was the first to be used in Malawi before the inception of pure classical studies.

Roman Catholic Church orders, specifically the Montfort Fathers, were the first to use Latin, in celebrating Mass, in Nyasaland. But the actual teaching of Latin began in Malawi in 1924, when the oldest Catholic seminary, Nankhunda—also called Child Jesus Seminary—opened for the purposes of training Malawian

Catholic priests. At that time, training for the priesthood and Latin learning were inseparable.

The challenges facing Latin teaching in Malawi cited by the seminaries, specifically regarding the lack of teaching and learning materials and the inadequate number of qualified Latin teachers, are among the problems experienced by learning institutions in Malawi generally, touching almost all subject areas.

As a secondary school subject, Greek has been taught only at Kamuzu Academy, which has been a private high school since 1995. Currently, at the very least, ancient Greek in the form of New Testament Greek shows signs of long-term survival in Malawi through the theological colleges and seminaries, which will certainly continue to teach students as long as teachers trained in ancient Greek are available.

Classical studies in Malawi (both at Kamuzu Academy and the University of Malawi) were largely promoted by President Hastings Kamuzu Banda. It would, therefore, be appropriate to briefly review Dr. Banda's education to establish his Classics motivation.

Dr. Banda cultivated his love for Classics during his first years in America, when he was a high school student. Philip Short reports that, at the African Methodist Episcopal Church's Wilberforce Institute in Ohio, Banda studied Latin in addition to standard high-school subjects.[1] He later attended the Universities of Indiana and Chicago before he was admitted to Meharry Medical School in Tennessee. He then continued his medical studies in Edinburgh in 1941.[2] There is no indication that he, at any point, pursued a degree *in Classics*, as distinct from a general degree with some classical content. As Caroline Alexander wrote, however, he had the "belief that it was impossible to understand the mind of the West without knowledge of the West's psychological and historical heritage."[3] He may have been influenced in the direction of this belief by the strong culture of Classics in the universities in America and the United Kingdom in the 1930s and 1940s; Alexander reports that Dr. Banda used to read Cicero's speeches over breakfast.[4]

It is also interesting to note that, prior to Banda's return home to lead the liberation struggle, he stayed in Ghana, where Barbara Goff (writing on the "Classics in the British Colonies of West Africa") indicates there was a strong culture of Classics by the middle of the nineteenth century: "from the missionary activity resulted the introduction of formal classical education among

---

[1]   Short 1974:20.
[2]   Short 1974; Ó Máille 1999.
[3]   Alexander 1991:58.
[4]   Alexander 1991:58.

indigenous West Africans."[5] It might, thus, be safely concluded that Dr. Banda was inspired by his experience in Ghana (then Gold Coast), where he stayed with his friend Kwame Nkrumah, of the feasibility of having classical education in an African culture—and that could have propelled him to promote classical studies in Malawi. Prof. Wilfried Stroh of the Ludwig-Maximilians-Universität in Munich, during a visit to Malawi made at the invitation of President Banda, who was a zealous supporter of the "living Latin" tradition, presented an oration in Latin at Chancellor College and at Kamuzu Academy in 1988. The title of the oration was *De latinis litteris hoc tempore docendis* ("The Importance of Latin Studies for the Present Age")—and, at the end, Stroh complimented his host with a superlative adjective: *Floreat latinitas! Floreat cum duce latinissimo res publica Malavi!* (May Latin flourish! May the Republic of Malawi flourish with its Latinist leader!).[6]

The first opportunity for people in Nyasaland (now Malawi) to learn Classics was during the Federation of Rhodesia and Nyasaland that lasted from 1953 to 1963, when Classics was taught at the University College of Rhodesia and Nyasaland. Referring to that decade, Whittaker and Toubkin report[7] that, in August 1962, a conference was held at the University College of Rhodesia and Nyasaland to discuss the position of Latin in schools—at which, Prof. François Smuts of Stellenbosch University lamented, instructors of Classics had not offered enough to students, and that Latin suffered because learners were conditioned to see it as something to be translated, rather than as something to be read and understood in a natural way.[8] I myself have attempted a search at our National Archives here in Zomba to see if I could trace information related to Classics at the tertiary level during the Federation period, but to no avail. It would be interesting to know what Malawians (if any) studied in Salisbury at the Federal University of Rhodesia and Nyasaland, where some classical studies existed prior to the University of Malawi.

---

[5] Goff 2013:21.

[6] Stroh 1988:24. I was not present on this occasion. My co-editor Paul McKechnie heard the oration when it was given at Kamuzu Academy. I have the text of the oration in an unpublished pamphlet which a kind colleague from the Department of French at Chancellor College gave me. Stroh's placement of *duce* may invite reflection on the nature of the Life President's position in the late eighties—but few in the two audiences were likely to pick up the echo of Mussolini's Italy; and then the oration ends with *res publica Malavi*, concluding in a resonant and Ciceronian clausula (resolved cretic, spondee). For more information, cf. Nyamilandu 2016.

[7] Whittaker and Toubkin 1963:vii.

[8] Smuts 1962:56.

Origins

The late Dr. Hastings Kamuzu Banda, first President of the Republic of Malawi, promoted classical studies in Malawi. He was Chancellor of the University of Malawi when the Vice-Chancellor contracted Prof. Robert Ogilvie of the Department of Humanities (now the School of Classics), University of St. Andrews, to carry out a feasibility study on the viability of classical studies in Malawi. Ogilvie opened his report as follows:[9]

> In May 1979, I was invited by the Vice-Chancellor of the University of Malawi to serve as consultant to advise on Classical Studies at Chancellor College. The original inspiration for the promotion of Classical Studies was given by His Excellency the Life President, Ngwazi Dr. H. Kamuzu Banda, and a resolution to implement this was passed by the Annual Convention of the Malawi Congress Party in September 1978 which called for the establishment of "a Department of Classical Studies at the University of Malawi."

But the fact that the resolution to establish classical studies at Chancellor College was made at a Party Convention meant that the establishment of classical studies was innately political. After the feasibility study was undertaken, recommendations followed to establish classical studies in the College.

Classics at Chancellor College was first taught by Caroline Alexander, who arrived in Malawi in 1982 and started teaching in 1983 in the Department of Philosophy. It was not until 1 September 1985 that Classics was established as an independent department, following a resolution at an extraordinary meeting of the Faculty of Humanities on 5 June 1985. The Dean of Humanities, Mr. (later Dr.) M. Shumba, wrote to the Vice-Chancellor recommending to the Senate the establishment of a Department of Classics at Chancellor College from 1 September 1985.[10]

From the beginning of the department, Classics courses at Chancellor College have been of two types: (a) Classical Civilization courses, for which no knowledge of the ancient languages is necessary; and (b) Classical Language courses, which impart—and, beyond the introductory level, require—knowledge of Latin and Greek, as applicable.[11]

---

[9]   Ogilvie 1979:2.
[10] Shumba 1985.
[11] Alexander 1985:2.

Student Numbers and Recruitment

In his feasibility study, Ogilvie estimated that the total number of enrollees would range from ten to twenty at most per year,[12] which was indeed the case, as Alexander reported:[13] when the Department started to teach Classics courses, the total number of students registered for various Classics courses was twelve: five in Year One, three in Year Two, and four in Year Three.

Those pursuing a Bachelor of Education (Humanities or Social Studies) registered greater numbers than those from pure Arts, since more students are registered in Education; the Humanities Faculty shared a limited quota amongst the seven departments that existed at that time.

As of the 2019-2020 academic year, a total of 316 students have registered for courses in Classics, a much higher figure than that of 1985, when the Department opened.

The increase in the number of Classics students over the years can be explained as follows: the University of Malawi has expanded its student admissions to various programs; in addition to the routine admissions increases, the University has encouraged potential candidates to register via mature entry; and some new programs have been introduced—for example BA (Media Studies), BA (Communication Studies), BA (Media for Development), BA (Theology) among others. But even though the numbers appear to have risen tremendously compared to when the Department started, it is still worrisome that we do not have a decent record for Classics majors at Year Four. The current trend is that enrollees are very high in Years One and Two, but dwindle drastically in Years Three and Four. This is a serious development, and one that has not been fully addressed for a long time.

The current situation regarding Latin and/or classical studies at the secondary level in Malawi is that, with the exception of Kamuzu Academy (which is, following the decree of its founder—the late Dr. Banda—unique in that classical studies are guaranteed), Latin exists only in a few Catholic institutions—and even there, it faces challenges. These challenges range from the lack of qualified staff to teach Latin to the lack of teaching resources. However, they are not insurmountable.

This precarious position for Classics and Latin instruction at secondary school level is not unique to Malawi. The challenges are almost the same everywhere, though to different extents, as the subject is not offered in all secondary

---

[12] Ogilvie 1979:9.
[13] Alexander 1985:7.

schools. Our current Malawian situation compares favorably with that in post-colonial South Africa, where Latin is now taught in very few schools. Chancellor College Classics Department will need to bring together those interested in learning Latin, Greek, and Classics in general at secondary and tertiary levels to discuss emerging practices in Classics pedagogies. But to make progress on this front, it is necessary to persuade policy makers and educationists.

It is no longer the case that the majority of those coming from Kamuzu Academy, or the the few seminaries and secondary schools offering Latin, Greek, or Classics pursue these subjects at a tertiary level; rather, the situation on the ground is that almost all who enroll in the Classics Department at Chancellor College have their first acquaintance with Classics, Latin, or Greek at Year One level. Those who take Classics come from different backgrounds. This implies that, even if all secondary schools were to stop offering Latin, Greek, or Classics, enrolments for Classics at university level would not be adversely affected to worrisome levels. To that end, it is necessary that those teaching Classics at the university level do so in a manner that accommodates real beginners, especially for the Language courses.

Attitudes of Classics Students Towards Classics

The results of attitude assessments that I have conducted on Classics undergraduates at Chancellor College have revealed that, in general, learners have fairly positive attitudes towards Classics. Highly negative attitudes are more prevalent in the first two years than in the two final years. This can be attributed to the fact that most students at the start of their degree program have just begun their acquaintance with Classics, and are yet to fully appreciate what Classics is all about—unlike those in the final year, who have studied the subject for some years. This calls for a more serious orientation during Year One on what Classics is all about and the skills students can gain from learning Classics. Moreover, there is a need for thorough outreach programs to communities and schools (as is the case with some universities abroad), so that students will not only learn about Classics at the university level, but also understand what they will be getting themselves into. To some extent, students' attitudes towards Classics can be linked to what they believe the subject will teach them or has taught them, in terms of skills. Above all, there is a need to foster positive attitudes by offering more innovative courses.

Current Course Offerings

The Department of Classics offers Year One courses that introduce the history and politics of ancient Greece and Rome, and word origins from Greek and Latin elements. In Year Two courses, students study ancient mythology (Greek and Roman Mythology), epics (Sumerian epic of Gilgamesh, Homer's *Iliad* and *Odyssey*, and the West African *Epic of Sunjata*), and the writings and methods of ancient historians.

In Years Three and Four, students take courses on Greek and Latin literature in translation, ancient philosophy, Women (and Gender) in Ancient World, Ancient Greek and Roman religion, and Archaeology and Greek and Roman Art and Architecture. The Department also offers courses in Greek and Latin from beginner to advanced levels.

Classics Courses Liked by Malawian Classics Students

There is considerable appreciation for the Classics courses listed below.

Greek and Roman History: Politics and Society

At Year One level, most students choose to take this course. The course was initially known as "Ancient History," but following revisions to the semester system, the first semester was renamed "Greek History Politics and Society" (CLA111), and the second "Roman History Politics and Society" (CLA121).

It is interesting to note that when students first come to the College, they know little about Greek and Roman authors, but are familiar with some names, such as Alexander the Great and Julius Caesar. They might discover these figures in history lessons in both the primary and secondary levels of schooling. As a result, there is an ease of transition. Students always find it interesting to relate certain topics of Greek and Roman politics to the Malawi context, particularly since Malawi has changed from autocracy to democracy—a change which is still in progress. For the Department, Mr. Jozef De Kuyper and Dr. Maryse Waegeman sourced video cassettes and films (both now defunct technology) which helped "spice up" the lessons. These video titles are still fresh in my mind: *Spartacus* (whose main actor, Kirk Douglas, has died); *Troy*; the Jacques Cousteau *Odyssey*, Volumes One and Two; and *Greece: Playground of the Gods*.

Apparently, Malawian students like the Greek and Roman history, politics, and society course for the same reasons visible elsewhere. While studying at the University of St. Andrews, I stumbled upon a 1921 report from the Committee that was mandated to inquire into the position to be assigned to the Classics in the United Kingdom's educational system—the so-called Crewe Report. The Committee justified the promotion of History and Politics of Ancient Greece and Rome in the following way:[14]

> [...] for us the lines of communication pass through Greece and Rome, and we are beginning to realise more fully than ever that most of the questions that press upon us at the present day, in politics, sociology and economics, in law and government, in literature and art, and even in science, first presented themselves to Greek and Roman thinkers and statesmen. Many of the problems of democracy, of internationalism, of industrialism, to name no others, were known to the ancient world. Because the forms in which they then emerged were much less complex, because they can now be studied without reference to the passions excited at the time, and because Greece and Rome offer the spectacle of civilisations running their course from start to finish, the study of their history may form the best preparation for that of our own difficulties. For the children of the present day, who are to be the voters of the next generation, we cannot afford to ignore the experience of Greek political thinkers and Roman administrators in any form in which it can be made intelligible to them.

Most of the justifications cited above for learning ancient history, politics, and society also apply to Malawian learners.

English Word-Origins From Greek and Latin Elements

Following the arrival of some new staff members and minor curriculum changes, this course was introduced by Dr. Thomas Knight in the 1994–1995 academic year. Dr. Knight mentored Steve Nyamilandu, who later took over the course following the departure of Dr. Knight to the University of Zimbabwe, which offered him a better salary. The main text used was Ayers (1965). Prof .William Dominik generously sent Steve a copy of his *Words and Ideas* (2002), which Steve later used. When the course was introduced for the first time, the numbers were modest, but after publicity from the Department during subsequent First Year orientations, the course became very popular—so much so that many students

---

[14]   United Kingdom Government 1921:156–157.

enrolled at First Year level. The course was taken by both Humanities and Education students. The Department was forced to limit the numbers to double digits, in order to accommodate the departmental resources and classroom capacities that were allocated by the College teaching timetable. Those in the Mathematical Sciences, who were mandated to draw up the timetables, never anticipated that Classics class sizes would reach triple digits.

Greek and Roman Mythology and African Folklore

This course, which attracted large numbers of students at Year Two level, was introduced during the time of Dr. Thomas Knight; after his departure in 1996, Steve Nyamilandu and Dr. Michael Chappell took over. Malawi learners have consistently found Greek and Roman myths to be of interest, especially when classical myths are compared with African myths, broadly. This confirms that "mythical thinking is not the preserve of one culture and that regardless of his geographical location on earth, early man sought to explain the environment around him through mythical representations."[15] In that regard, J. S. Mbiti remarks that:[16]

> Stories, proverbs, riddles, myths, and legends handed down orally, which are found in large numbers among all African people, do serve a purpose. Some are there to give a mere record of historical events, but most of them are created by people's imaginations.

Mbiti outlines the specific purposes of African myths or stories as follows: "Some entertain, others warn, others stimulate the imagination of the listeners; some are told as a commentary of people's lives in a given period."[17] These observations by Mbiti, a Kenyan philosopher who taught at Makerere University from 1964 to 1974, corroborate the insights of Malawian students who study courses on mythology and epics.

As for the epics, Malawian students have enjoyed the *Odyssey* more than the *Iliad*. *Gilgamesh* has also been liked, and so too the West African *Sunjata Epic*, which was introduced by Prof. M. D. Usher of the University of Vermont when he came to teach for a semester in 2012; this course is currently taught by Dr. Chappell.

---

[15] Nyamilandu 2015:10.
[16] Mbiti 1975:7.
[17] Mbiti 1975:5.

Classical Literature in Translation

In this Year Three course, students have shown keen interest in studying the following areas: selections of Greek lyric poets; Greek tragedy, especially *King Oedipus* and *Antigone*; as for Greek comedy, *Lysistrata* tops the list; from the selections of Greek historians, students have shown a strong liking for Thucydides, and particularly the Periclean Funeral Oration; speeches by Lysias and Demosthenes (the *Philippics*) are also liked; Hesiod's *Works and Days*, particularly precepts addressed to his brother Perses, receive a good response (they are, in fact, timeless precepts addressed to all ages); the five ages of the world; and the myth of Pandora. On the Roman side, students have loved the poems of Catullus and the *Odes* of Horace; Cicero's speeches against Catiline, the *Philippics*; and Vergil's *Aeneid*, particularly Book Four, or the tragedy of Dido.

Women in Antiquity

This course was introduced in 2007 by Dr. Cybelle Greenlaw during the few months of her teaching at Chancellor College. She mentored Esela Munthali (née Gondwe), who took over the course after her departure. Starting with close to twenty students when it was introduced, the course numbers kept growing to around fifty, on average, per semester. Students perceive this course favourably: they regard it as one that helps them reflect on inequalities, some of which still persist in society. Specifically, students state that the course helps them look at the history of women from different cultures, their journey to this day, and how they relate to women of today in Malawian culture.

Ancient Greek and Roman Religion

The few who register for this Year Four course speak highly of it, noting that some of its topics offer many areas of comparison with traditional African religions—particularly on some rituals and practices which are still regarded as deeply rooted in contemporary culture.

Archaeology, Art, and Architecture

Year Four's most popular course, "Archaeology, Art, and Architecture" surveys works from the Near East, Mesopotamia, Egypt, and, particularly, Greece and Rome. This course was promoted by Mr. Jozef De Kuyper, who was, armed with real field experience himself, keen to develop studies in archaeology. He taught it with passion. The first semester deals with an introduction to archaeology, its methods, and techniques. Students love this course for the experience they gain from a mini archaeological dig they undertake, but, most of all, they are able to compare some ancient influences, and even similarities, with certain modern art and architecture, as well as architecture in the deep rural areas (villages) of Malawi. Students in this course appreciate that the knowledge gained is relevant to their lives. For example:

- They can easily pinpoint local examples: the corridors at Chancellor College, for example, were designed like stoas, or walking galleries where ancient philosophers used to hold discussions.

- Students are able to compare the decorative designs on ancient pottery and relate them to local examples, such as pottery works from Dedza and Malindi, which are not unlike the decorative vases of the ancient world.

- Students appreciate learning that the Romans were the "inventors of the two chief materials of modern building, brick and concrete," as Rushforth reports.[18]

- In Malawi, many people, particularly in the villages, cannot afford to build using fired bricks or concrete blocks—rather, they resort to building with unbaked bricks (*zidina*), or just construct mud-daubed houses which can take different shapes; round or rectangular shapes are the most common. The roofing of most such houses is grass thatch. Though these roofs moderate temperatures during hot weather, they are prone to leakages during heavy rains if not properly maintained, and sometimes they harbor scorpions and centipedes within the cracks (their stings are very painful: my relatives and I have been stung on several occasions— scorpion stings are a commonplace hazard of village life, and not unexpected). It is always painful to relate experiences of living in such houses.

Languages

Regarding the teaching of Greek and Latin languages in general, a brief recap is called for at this point. The Ogilvie report promoted Latin more than Greek to begin with, for the sole reason that Latin was already in the secondary school curriculum and so merited immediate promotion. It was Caroline Alexander who moved beyond the recommendations of the Ogilvie Report to introduce Greek at the second year for the following reasons:[19]

- Greek is an integral part of Classics; indeed, arguably the best of classical literature and philosophy is written in this language.

---

[18] Rushforth 1923:392.
[19] Alexander 1985: footnote C [unpaginated].

- Chancellor College graduates in Classics will find it difficult to be placed in overseas graduate programs if they do not read Greek.

- The fact that Greek is not generally offered at secondary school level should not deter its introduction at university level: nowadays, it is not at all uncommon for Classics majors to begin learning Greek as university undergraduates, as was also the case in the 1980s with the majority of North American undergraduate programs.

- Kamuzu Academy offers Greek (up to A level) as part of its Classics program: Greek at Chancellor College is necessary if Academy graduates wish to continue classical studies at the university level.[20]

The Place of Latin and Greek Languages

Malawian students of Latin and Greek languages are getting to realise the usefulness of studying these two ancient languages, not only in understanding the languages but also in making it possible for one to apply linguistic knowledge broadly. For example:

- In addition to Latin being the mother of the Romance languages (French, Italian, Spanish, Portuguese, and Romanian), Latin is also a good basis for the study of any language: for example, Latin can assist a student of German, because "… a striking similarity exists in certain instances between Latin and German syntax, thus making it easier for the student of Latin to understand the German construction,"[21] as with the dative case, an equivalent to that which is present in Chichewa in the form of the applicative (benefactive): cf. Table 1.

- Furthermore, as an inflected Indo-European language, Latin contributed parts of speech to several languages, including many African languages which have embraced the concept.

- The Roman alphabet is widely used not only in Europe but elsewhere: "… even many thousands of natives of Asia and Africa who never heard the sound of Latin language, use it."[22] So, too, we use the Roman (Latin) alphabet for all languages in Malawi.

It is, furthermore, easier for Greek and Latin students to decode etymological entries in dictionaries and even to understand the Greek and Latin prefixes that

---

[20] Alexander 1985:2.
[21] Sabin 1931:44.
[22] Bradley 1923:384.

German

Er	gibt	mir	das	Buch
He	gives	me [dat.]	the	book

Latin

Mihi	librum	dat	
Me [dat.]	the-book	he-gives	

Chichewa

Andipatsa [a-ndi-patsa]			bukhu
He	me [dat.]	gives	the-book

Table 1: Datives and Applicatives (Benefactives)

are used in many subject areas. For example, Malawi adopted the metric system, which is easy if one remembers that Greek and Latin prefixes are added to the standard units—meter (cf. μέτρον), liter (cf. λίτρα), and gram (cf. γράμμα)—to produce the multiples and submultiples: "deka-" ten; "hecto-," hundred; "kilo-" thousand; "deci-," tenth; "centi-," hundredth; "milli-," thousandth. Therefore, students taking the course "English Word Origins from Latin and Greek Elements" will be able to benefit in their everyday lives.

In addition to learning the classical languages *per se*, learners are expected to "build, reinforce, and expand their knowledge of other disciplines while using the language to develop critical thinking and to solve problems creatively."[23]

The overall need to maintain Greek and Latin languages has been thoroughly discussed in the resolution of the International Federation of Associations of Classical Studies (FIEC), created at a General Assembly of Delegates in London on 4 July 2019, in support of the registration of ancient Greek and Latin in the UNESCO List of Intangible Cultural Heritage. Below is their justification for keeping ancient Greek and Latin alive:

---

[23] Ramsby 2018:124.

The International Federation of Associations of Classical Studies (FIEC) supports the registration of Ancient Greek and Latin in the UNESCO List of Intangible Cultural Heritage. Those two languages have had a deep impact on the Mediterranean area (in a wide sense) over several millennia; this impact is still to be felt very strongly today, not only in that area, but also in the world at large.

Ancient Greek was the main language spoken and written in Archaic and Classical Greece, as well as in the whole Eastern Mediterranean from the Hellenistic period till the end of the Byzantine period. In contact with other languages (notably Semitic languages and Latin), it has gradually evolved without changing its basic structure, to become Modern Greek.

Latin started in the Italic peninsula and, as Roman power extended over the centuries, has spread to most areas of present-day Europe, where it evolved to produce the Romance languages. Through the process of colonization, Latin has also spread to other parts of the world, notably the Americas.

Ancient Greek and Latin were used by authors who wrote many texts that are considered as fundamental by people of numerous countries around the world. They constitute the origin of many forms of literature through more than two millennia, and they still have a considerable impact on today's literature.

Although Ancient Greek and Latin are no longer in use in modern daily life, the understanding of those languages is maintained in schools and universities everywhere. This knowledge must be preserved and deserves the active support of governments and of their teaching institutions.

Classics Students' Views on the Relevance of Classical Studies to their Culture

In student surveys, I have sought their views regarding the contemporary relevance of Classics. Many respondents related Classics to present day lessons, Malawian culture to classical culture, or Classics to skills. On the other hand, some did not see any relevance, were not sure, or gave statements which I take to be evidence of misconceptions (see Table 2 below). Some managed to pinpoint specific areas for comparison: for example, on myths, rituals, and forms of government. Respondents also cited various ways in which Classics could be made more relevant. The majority cited the need to incorporate some comparable areas of Malawian culture so that the teaching process could, as a whole, be improved. Almost all respondents decried the lack of teachers, learning resources in general, and other opportunities that would allow for student growth. However, a few respondents, particularly in Years One and Two, harbored misconceptions. The levels of misconceptions reduced dramatically in Years Three and Four, implying that, as students advance with their studies, they appreciate more about the subject.

Aspect of relevance   **A. Contrasting ancient and modern**

Year One	Year Two	Year Three	Year Four
Helps us to understand our past regarding the past of other people: how they went through their tragedies and misfortunes, and how they managed their fortunes. It is relevant through the lesson from Athenaze: some Greeks were struggling to earn a living; and, in our culture too, others also struggle to earn their living.	It is relevant in the sense that there are so many topics which we cover in the classroom and are found in our culture: for instance, the issue of religion, rituals, values, and norms. It helps me to be able to understand other peoples' culture and appreciate diversity.	Studying Classics has helped me to understand life in general; culture and religion as well as in the ancient world and comparing and contrasting with the modern world; and eventually one discovers that modern life is quite similar with the ancient world and yet also very different. It helps to look at the history of women from different cultures, their journey to this day, and how they relate to those of today in Malawian culture.	From classical ideas, we are able to recognise and acknowledge that cultural identity needs to be preserved: for instance, some of the elements like the folktales, music, and even the dressing patterns. On myths, it really sharpened my view of African myths and how they relate all over the world.

Aspect of relevance   **B. Improvements to teaching and learning**

Year One	Year Two	Year Three	Year Four
I feel it is important to incorporate our own history as Classics: for example, the stories of Mbona, Bimphi cult, and Chewa history (Maravi Kingdom). The way Latin is taught has to change. Most of us are learning it for the first time. Please try to make your students able to major in the subject not only just to minor.	The lecturers are supposed to present the lectures in a manner interesting so that students may be compelled to think of majoring in the course, not as they do. The lecturers should ensure that their topic is well understood by letting the students apply the knowledge to everyday situations. Make teaching and learning materials readily available. Lecturers should individually assist those with difficulties.	It should look at the link between whatever we learn which is classical to the modern society. This would help understand what purpose Classics has on modern thinking and ideas. Emphasis on the political systems of the ancient world in comparison with today's atmosphere. The classes should be made livelier and more interesting. For instance, showing videos that have been filmed to portray or are related to that particular lesson.	Lecturers should also concentrate a lot more on its application to life in the present time to show that the course is applicable and not just another history lesson. There is nothing that is done from the department that is inspiring. Perhaps that is the reason why you will find hardly a single student majoring in Classics. Blend in areas of Malawian/African civilization, instead of having a whole package of Western civilisation. Make it more applicable to the Malawian context.

C. Misconceptions

| It helps me to know where my culture came from and where it is now.

Classics teaches me to accept my culture and appreciate it more. Helps me to understand what goes on around me in my culture as a kid who rarely goes to rural places. | I don't think it is, because in my culture there's nothing like a belief in myths, which is mostly the center of Classics.

Classics is not necessary. I don't think what we learn is applicable to our day-to-day lives. If it is about the writing or oral skills, there are other courses that offer such things at length. | | |

Table 2: Ideas from student surveys

Classics Staff, External Examiners, and Visiting Scholars: Their Contributions to the Chancellor College Classics Department

Each person listed below—whether as teaching staff, visiting scholar, or External Examiner—has made a unique contribution to the University of Malawi Chancellor College Classics program: the purpose of this section is to give a flavor of what has been accomplished from the 1980s until now.

1982–1985: Caroline Alexander (later Dr.) was the pioneer classicist at Chancellor College and had the mammoth tasks of constructing the Department from scratch and hunting for far-fetched teaching resources on a very tight budget. In fact, much as the Department was touted as promoted by Dr. Banda, there was no special treatment in terms of financial support. Caroline Alexander was the lone lecturer while attempting to recruit additional staff. Unfortunately, her immediate replacements did not stay long enough to sustain the Department at the level she had modelled.

1986: Prof. Gloria Shaw Duclos (Fulbright Fellow) had to leave early because of illness.

1986–1987: R. L. S. Evans (later Dr.) from South Carolina in the United States, and Dr. Albert Devine from Australia both departed at the end of the academic year, before completing their contracts. While teaching at UNISA, Dr. Richard J. Evans, along with his colleagues (Profs. Martine De Marre and Philip Bosman), twice facilitated my attendance at conferences in South Africa. My BA in Latin (Honors) and MA in Ancient Languages and Cultures were substantially funded by UNISA. One of Dr. Evans' ex colleagues, Dr. Sira Dambe, played an important supervisory role and, more significantly, made it possible for me to benefit from the Ian Maclean Trust Fund.

1987–1993: The Rev. Rodney Hunter, formerly Fellow of Wadham College, Oxford, taught at Zomba Theological College, and he assisted the Department on a part-time basis. He acted as anchor for the Department whenever there was a staff crisis and sustained the Department as Head when Richard Evans and Albert Devine left. Assigned to teach Latin in Years One and Two, he taught using a rigorous grammar/translation approach. Students used to joke that those who took classical languages (Latin and Greek) did not want to enjoy any other life on campus apart from academic work.

Indeed, the rigorous teaching and learning of conjugations and de-clensions, as well as daily class and homework exercises in grammar, vocabulary, and exceptions to the rules, were not popular. Before the end of every lesson, we were given a few minutes to complete exer-cises on pieces of paper, about which, he would, in his baritone voice, joke "How many are suffering?" Then he would move around col-lecting the scripts from students. Depending on preparation, some would finish early, but others would languish, finishing late. In retro-spect, I strongly feel other language-teaching methodologies would have better facilitated the teaching and learning process. *Richie's First [and Second] Steps in Latin* were his favorite, of course supplemented with other Latin grammar and prose composition texts. At Year Two he introduced us to Caesar's *De bello Gallico*, Cicero's *In Catilinam*, and Vergil's *Aeneid*, all of which were in the original Latin language. I re-call that we were sixteen students in the beginning; after a few days, the numbers dropped to eight.

Rodney Hunter stopped teaching at Chancellor College after the three Staff Associates (including myself) were recruited. Caroline Alexander, in the *New Yorker*, referred to Reverend Hunter as the "immortal Reverend Hunter."[24] Sadly, this was over-optimistic: he passed on in 2006 in Nkhota Kota, in the Central Region, where he was in charge of an Anglican parish. The circumstances were mys-terious, and his nephew Mark Hunter (based in the UK) attempted to pursue litigation regarding the death of his uncle. One of his stu-dents, Andrew Banda, while studying at Mzuzu University, wrote a dissertation for his BA (in Theology and Religious Studies) entitled: *The Life of Rodney Squire Hunter and His Contribution to the Development of Indigenous Leadership of the Church in Malawi*. In the work, Banda examined Rodney's life, and how his involvement in the theological colleges and seminaries contributed to theological scholarship in Malawi and to the development of indigenous church leadership. In 2018, the Department of Classics created the Hunter Memorial Fund in memory of the Rev. Canon Rodney Squire Hunter. The pur-pose of the fund is to provide financial aid to help Chancellor Col-lege Classics students pay tuition.

1988–1993: During their tenure, Dr. Maryse Waegeman and Mr. Jozef De Kuyper, a couple funded by the Belgian government organization

---

[24] Alexander 1991:88.

VVOB, made major attempts at local staff development. They had to leave after the expiry of their funding period, since they could not sustain themselves on University of Malawi salaries alone. They used to receive double salaries—both from VVOB and from Chancellor College.

In fact, they were so generous that they used to organize frequent parties and outings for Classics students, during which they treated us to exotic foods. I should confess those were the first times some of us tasted olives, pizza, and several other foods. Of course, we also enjoyed wine—which most of us were not used to except for church communion wine. Reverend Hunter was the only one allowed to take care of the remaining bottles of wine. I was taught by both: by Dr. Maryse Waegeman (an astute professor—we never found her idle, and she was always reading something: for her, the rule was *nulla dies sine linea*) from Year One to Year Four. It was during my Third Year that I was joined by Eltrudis Nthete and Thokozani Kunkeyani, who were brought into Year Three, not only on the strengths of the Classics knowledge they had acquired at Kamuzu Academy but also because the expatriates, whose VVOB contracts were coming to an end, had to groom local staff to take future positions, as earlier efforts to develop local staff had failed to materialize. It was during the period of De Kuyper and Waegeman that the three of us were appointed as Staff Associates: I was the first to report, followed by the two others a few months later. I recall that our appointment letters indicated two vital points: that we were recruited on a month-by-month basis pending further training, and that we were to be mentored to teach by handling classes under observation of senior colleagues until we earned higher degrees. That observation by senior colleagues never eventuated; we were entrusted with classes, so as to mature quickly. Luckily for us, the University used to organize a workshop for new recruits on how to teach and meet the other requirements of the job. As for further training, that turned into a troublesome issue because, by the time we joined in the mid-1990s, opportunities for scholarships were diminishing. Nevertheless, after my studies at UNISA, I moved forward to a cotutelle PhD from the University of Malawi and the School of Classics at the University of St. Andrews, Scotland. Sadly, I am the only one of their students still with Chancellor College Classics.

1991: Krist Poffyn (from Belgium) joined as a Lecturer, but left early in 1992.

1991: Eric Ning'ang'a was the first Malawian Assistant Lecturer in Classics. He returned from studies in Germany in 1991, but then joined the civil service. He did not return from Germany with the requisite qualification and had to leave for other jobs.

1993–1996: Dr. Thomas E. Knight from Colorado State University took over the Headship, but left for the University of Zimbabin, in search of better pay.

1995: Dr. Franz J. Gruber from Germany, and Dr. Harold Donohue from the USA, author of *The Song of the Swan: Lucretius and the Influence of Callimachus* (1993), joined Dr. Knight, Thoko Kunkeyani, Steve Nyamilandu, and Eltrudis Nthete. Both Dr. Gruber and Dr. Donohue broke their contracts and left at the end of the year.

1995–1996: Dr. Henri V. de Marcellus from USA came and left after one year.

1997: Prof. R. Joseph Hoffmann replaced Dr. de Marcellus and teamed up with Dr. Michael Chappell (UK) and the late Mr. Edward Jenner (New Zealand). He then left for Kamuzu Academy. Prof. Hoffmann was someone who had a lot of experience in restructuring and even creating academic structures. He was consultant when Classics was rationalized at the University of Zimbabwe in the early nineties. He was also a consultant at the University of the Witwatersrand where Classics was effectively abolished.

1998: Mr. Edward Jenner arrived on the same flight with Dr. Michael Chappell. Ted, as we used to call him, taught Greek and Latin language and literature.

1998: Dr. Michael Chappell arrived for a Classics post from 1998 to 2001, returning to Chanco in 2013, where he is still stationed. Departmental records show that Mike is the longest-serving expatriate staff member teaching Classics at Chancellor College. We are encouraging him to apply for Malawian citizenship and to settle in Malawi.

2007: Dr. Cybelle Greenlaw (USA, Kansas) joined as a replacement for Mr. Jenner, but she left before completing her contract. She was frank in telling us that our advert was misleading. Her late mother used to have a sanctuary for monkeys, and she expected to see a lot more in Zomba. Unfortunately, due to heavy deforestation and the burning of the bush on Zomba Mountain, the population of baboons and monkeys dwindled. Cybelle will be happy to hear that we are now into serious afforestation, and small monkeys are even descending close to some homes. Mr. Loudon Gama, her ex-housekeeper (now employed by Dr. Chappell), keeps reminding me of one incident at Dr. Greenlaw's house when the door leading to the corridor of her bedroom jammed. Efforts to open it yielded no results. I was called in, but had no solution except to hunt for a carpenter. Cybelle didn't have time to waste waiting for a carpenter to come, so she commanded both Gama and me to move from the door. We obliged and were amazed to see her jump with a flying kung fu kick— the door opened with a bang. We were astonished. Surely, that was a lady nobody would want to mess with!

External Examiners in Classics

I thank God that I had the opportunity to meet and interact with almost all of the External Examiners who assisted with our assessment processes over the years, except Dr. Vella and Dr. Mader. All the External Examiners listed below have enriched the academic side of the Department of Classics, from various perspectives.

My meeting with Prof. Sjarlene Thom and Prof. Carl Thom of Stellenbosch University (a couple who took turns as External Examiners) occurred when we both attended the FIEC Conference at the Humboldt University in Berlin, Germany. We boarded the same plane back to O.R. Tambo International Airport, Johannesburg. I remain grateful to the FIEC Board, then under the leadership of Professor Heinrich Von Staden, who facilitated the first flights in my life. It was a nightmare, however, landing at Tegel Airport, Berlin, and finding my own way to the lodge. I reminded myself of the free basic German classes which I took under the tutelage of Dr. Franz Gruber at Chancellor College.

1986: Dr. H. C. R. Vella (University of Malta).

1988–89: Dr. G. J. Mader (University of South Africa).

1990–91: Dr. Paul McKechnie (Kamuzu Academy) visited from 23–25 June 1991.

1993–94: Prof. S. Dennis Saddington (University of South Africa) visited once when I was in my final undergraduate year. We talked at length, and he encouraged me to pursue my BA Latin Honors with UNISA, which I eventually did.

1995–98: Prof. William Dominik (University of Natal, Durban) visited Malawi on a self-funded trip for the love of Classics. He even took our two Classics staff (Mike and Ted) for a trip to Lake Malawi, generously paying all incurred costs. I think he knew something about the, at the time, low salaries, especially as compared to South African universities.

2008–10: Prof. Sjarlene Thom (University of Stellenbosch, South Africa).

2010–2011: Prof. Carl Thom (University of Stellenbosch, South Africa).

2013–2018: Prof. M. D. (Mark David) Usher (University of Vermont, USA).

Visiting Scholars and Their Contributions to Chancellor College Classics

A number of scholars visited the department and made some contribution to Chancellor College Classics, each in their own way:

Dr. G. Papademetriou, Head of Classics of the University of Athens, visited Chancellor College Classics in December 1985, in order to discuss possible links between the Universities of Athens and Malawi. These hopes, however, went unfulfilled.

Dr. Wilfred Stroh from the Ludwig-Maximilians-Universität in Munich visited Chancellor College in February 1988, as noted above.

Dr. Paul McKechnie taught for one semester in 2004 and sent some Classics books directly to the Chancellor College Library. He visited again in 2018 and taught for another full semester.

The Department hosted Prof. M. D. Usher, who has visited the Department three times. In 2010, he came for six weeks to screen Pasolini's *Notes Towards an African Oresteia* (1970) and teach a seminar on the film. He taught a full semester course and also brought the Department some new books, which we still use to this day. Prof. Usher afforded me the opportunity to participate in the academic life of the Department of Classics at the University of Vermont from 28 September to 14 October 2016. I stayed at his home in Shoreham, Vermont, as his guest. For the first time in my life, I was treated daily to a triple breakfast.

It was amazing to learn that he and his wife Caroline built their beautiful house on their own: I mean, using their own hands, resources, and intellect. They run a farm called Works and Days. That was where I learnt to drive a tractor within the farm to transport fodder for the sheep in preparation for winter. During my time at their home, I savored the collection of music belonging to their sons, Estlin and Gawain; I developed a liking for Johnny Cash, for Dire Straits, for Lead Belly, and for U2, and I enjoyed their collection of classical music. When listening to classical music, I am always reminded of being asked by some people in Malawi what I teach at the University. Before I can answer fully, they will follow up with, "Is it classical music?"

Concluding Remarks

The chapter has spelt out the efforts, the resolve, and the viability of Classics teaching in Malawi generally, and the University of Malawi Chancellor College Classics program, specifically.

Gratitude should go to all those, living and dead, who have invested their energies and commitment to Classics to enable the Chancellor College Classics program to weather the storms. Gratitude also goes to our most important stakeholders: Malawi Classics students, most of whom have taken or heard about Classics for the first time when they arrived at the University—but continue to study it and speak well of our discipline. All this has ensured continuity of classical studies in Malawi.

I will end by quoting my co-editor Prof. Paul McKechnie (who has taught Classics both at Kamuzu Academy and at Chancellor College)—a quotation which best summarizes the appeal for keeping Classics programs in Malawi:[25]

> The choice of Classics, which donors will not support, is a commitment to a larger and longer-term vision that involves Malawi's taking a place in the international community that it chooses for itself rather than one prescribed by donors' views of what a Black African country should have. The aim is to give Malawians access to the roots of Western culture and not just the branches where the short-term needs are. [...] its emphasis on the Classics aims at unlocking the heart of western civilization to Malawians.

---

[25] McKechnie 1992:143.

3

Classics in Malawi and the Translatability of "Black Classicisms"[1]

EMILY GREENWOOD

"Why the term Academy? Wilberforce Academy, Plato's Academy; not
Edinburgh Academy. I did not know there was Edinburgh Academy."

Hastings Kamuzu Banda, Founder's Day Speech,
Kamuzu Academy 14 November 1984[2]

IN 1981, KAMUZU BANDA (ca.1898–1997), then Life President of Malawi,
founded the eponymous Kamuzu Academy as an elite secondary school for
about 360 Malawian scholars. While Greek and Latin were enshrined in the
school's curriculum at its founding, the rationale for the classical curriculum
was complex and reflected the overdetermined legacy of Greek and Roman
Classics in the modern world, and in Black transnational traditions, in particular. This chapter offers a reappraisal of Banda's model of a classical education by contrasting it with anti-colonial engagements with Greek and Roman
Classics on the part of his Malawian contemporaries and by highlighting Banda's
indebtedness to debates regarding the value of a classical education in African
American thought.

[1]   *Acknowledgments:* I would like to express my gratitude to Mireille Djenno for assistance and
       advice in consulting the H. K. Banda Archive at Indiana University, and to Paul McKechnie for
       sage editorial feedback. An expanded version of this chapter will appear in a forthcoming book
       entitled *Conjugating Black Classicisms.*
[2]   H. K. Banda Archive, African Studies Collection, Indiana University, Bloomington, Indiana. Box 2,
       Folder 6, quoting from p. 11 of the typescript of Banda's speech. Subsequent references to this
       archive will be in the shorter form "H. K. Banda Archive."

Who Speaks for the Classics in Malawi?
Alternatives to H. K. Banda's Classical Vision

In interviews and speeches, and especially his Founder's Day addresses at Kamuzu Academy, Kamuzu Banda implied that he and his eponymous Academy were the sole conduit for a classical education in Malawi. This stance ignored the classical knowledge of his Malawian predecessors and contemporaries, as well as the fact that Classics was taught in colonial Nyasaland. George Simeon Mwase's account of the Chilembwe uprising of January 1915, one of the earliest literary expressions of Malawian national consciousness written in English, offers an indigenous use of a classical education that bears suggestive contrast with Kamuzu Banda's western-oriented classicism. Mwase's account, which survived as a typescript in the colonial archives of Nyasaland and, now in the National Archives of Malawi, was subsequently edited by Robert Rotberg and published by Harvard University Press in 1967 with the title *George Simeon Mwase: Strike a Blow and Die*.[3] This work defies easy characterization: part biography of John Chilembwe, a Baptist minister who led an uprising against the British in 1915, part self-reflexive memoir, part statement of Nyasa nationhood, and part commentary on the history of race relations between white and Black people in the Nyasaland Protectorate. Written in English, Mwase's second or third language, the "Dialogue" (Mwase's term for the work) also contains several prominent Latin phrases.[4]

Based on the available evidence, it is impossible to reconstruct George Mwase's education in full. His birth is dated to ca. 1880, and he is known to have attended a mission school run by the Free Church of Scotland at Bandawe.[5] His subsequent education is not attested, but he did not enter government employment until 1905, when he took up the position of postal clerk.[6] This interval, together with the fact that he was qualified for work as a government clerk, makes it likely that he studied at the Free Church of Scotland's Livingstonia Mission's Overtoun Institution, founded in November 1894 at the instigation of the Scottish missionary Robert Laws, with the express purpose of training native students for the clergy and for skilled employment in the colonial service.[7] In

---

[3] Mwase titled his account "A Dialogue of Nyasaland Record of Past Events, Environments & The Present Outlook Within the Protectorate." See Rotberg's Introduction in Mwase 1967:ix, xxxix.

[4] In an editorial note, Rotberg suggests that English would have been Mwase's third language after Tonga and Chinyanja (Rotberg in Mwase 1967:48n2).

[5] The Free Church of Scotland mission in Bandawe was established in 1881.

[6] See the biographical note provided by Rotberg in Mwase 1967:xxxiv–xxxviii.

[7] Banda (1982:1–15) gives an overview of the history of missionary education in Nyasaland in the period 1875–1926.

1901, the first headmaster of the Institution, James Henderson, introduced a three-year Arts course, so that students could gain a general education in the Arts preparatory to theological training. This course included basic training in Greek and Latin.[8] George Mwase's older brother, Yesaya Zerenje Mwasi (a variant spelling of Mwase), did attend the Overtoun Institution and subsequently entered the ministry: he was one of its better-known graduates.[9] Another possibility, which does not preclude Mwase having learned some Latin at Overtoun, is that he gleaned some of his Latin from exposure to Roman Catholic sermons and or schools. In the course of discussing John Chilembwe's decision to send a request for assistance to the Germans in neighboring Tanganyika once the uprising was underway, Mwase speculates that Chilembwe could only have acted out of ignorance of conditions in German East Africa, and of the fact that their colonial administration and provision of schooling was even worse than that of the British. This occasions a digression on the inferiority of Catholic schools, with whose system of education Mwase claims to be familiar.[10] Of the twenty Latin phrases that occur in the Dialogue, two are ecclesiastical:

> p. 50 *Deusvobisum* [sic]

and

> p. 59 *Pace tua*

Mwase also seems to allude to Latin as the *lingua franca* of the Catholic Church when he apologizes, preemptively, in case his critique of the standard of education in Catholic schools in Nyasaland is interpreted as anti-Catholic sentiment: "I will [be] very sorry, if some of my remarks, will cause other people feel when reading them [that I was against the Roman Catholic religion], surely I did not mean it, if I meant it '*Ruat Coelum*' on me. As '*hominis est errare,*' the same may apply to me, for which may be kindly apologized."[11] It is difficult to pin down the precise logic in Mwase's use of Latin in this passage. The doubling of Latin tags might be a conciliatory gesture to appease any Roman Catholic readers, or a knowing joke that shows readers that Mwase can signify in Latin and that the Roman Catholic Church does not have a monopoly on the language, mixing a

---

[8] McCracken 1977:186. McCracken notes that classes in "rudimentary" Greek and Latin were taught by James Henderson outside of the regular school timetable.

[9] From the Institution's roll-book, McCracken has calculated that three hundred and fifty students graduated in the period between the Institution's foundation and 1915, with many more students (850) attending the Institution in this period but not completing their courses. McCracken 1977:188 with n71.

[10] Mwase 1967:64–65.

[11] Mwase 1967:65.

Emily Greenwood

phrase from legal Latin with a tag that derives from Cicero.[12] Mwase also uses the Ciceronian tag elsewhere, in the solecism *hominiest errar* (1967:114), also in a context where he offers a preemptive apology to his readers if they object to his account (this context is Mwase's commentary on conditions in prisons in Nyasaland).

A complete list of the Latin phrases that Mwase uses is as follows:[13]

> p. 3 *A Verbis Ad Verba* (From Words to Blows) [ND]
>
> p. 6 *?Lingua Fraula?* <*lingua franca*> [ND]
>
> p. 42 '*Acerrema Proximorum odia*.'[14] [ID]
>
> p. 42 He also told his army that through *Amor Patria*, and *Anirio et fide*, fight on, fight on! [ID][15]
>
> p. 48 'One great thing you must remember is that *Omnia Vincit amor* so for love [of] your own country and country men, I now encourage you to go and strike a blow and bravely die.' [DD]
>
> p. 49 this blow means '*non sibi sed patria*'[16] [DD]
>
> p. 49 Where you are going to find money, goods and other kind of wealth, does not matter what, do not touch such for '*Amor Patria*'[17] sake [DD]
>
> p. 49 ... But where ever your hand is going to lay on any kind of a weapon, take that, for it will help you in your struggle for the '*Amor Patria*'[18] [DD]
>
> p. 50 He bade them 'God's speed.' At last he prayed again and said '*Deus-vobiscum*'. [ID][19]

[12] Legal Latin: *fiat iustitia ruat caelum* (let justice be done though the heavens should fall); Cicero: *cuiusvis hominis est errare; nullius nisi insapientis perseverare in errore* (anyone can make a mistake, but only a fool persists in error, Cicero *Philippics* 12.5).

[13] I have used the following abbreviations to distinguish different levels of narrative: ND = narratorial discourse; ID = indirect discourse, paraphrased speech of John Chilembwe; and DD = direct discourse, reported speech of John Chilembwe. Rotberg preserves Mwase's use of capitalization and quotation marks, and I have reproduced it here.

[14] Rotberg supplies the correct Latin in an editorial note: *Acerrima proximorum odia*—the bitter hatred of their neighbors (Rotberg in Mwase 1967:42n19).

[15] Rotberg's editorial correction: "*Amor patriae*—'love of country.' *Anirio* probably is a typing mistake for *Animo*, which makes the phrase read: 'with spirit and devotion'" (Rotberg in Mwase 1967: 42n21).

[16] Rotberg's editorial correction: *Non sibi sed patriae* (Rotberg in Mwase 1967:49n3).

[17] See n16 above.

[18] See n16 above.

[19] Rotberg notes, "a baptist preacher would be unlikely to dismiss his flock with *Deus vobiscum* ('God be with you'). The Latin is probably Mwase's not Chilembwe's" (Rotberg in Mwase 1967:50n4).

p. 59 *Pace tua.* I wish to remark something. [ND]

p. 59 In my opinion, and if I were John, surely I could never communicated with the Germans nor the Portuguese in the aspect of '*Commune Corum*'. [ND][20]

p. 64 This is purely *Sine Odio*, but '*Pro bono publico*'. [ND]

p. 65 If I meant it '*Ruat Coelum*' on me. As '*hominis est errare*,' the same may apply to me. [ND]

p. 80 *Amor Patria*[21] [ND]

p. 95 Heading '*Felinis nullius*'[22]: who holds responsibility for a mulatto? [ND]

p. 114 but one thing should be remembered that '*hominiest errar*' [ND]

Turning to the Latin phrases that Mwase attributes to John Chilembwe in direct and indirect discourse, Rotberg plausibly reasons that Chilembwe is unlikely to have used Latin tags in his exhortatory speeches to his fellow conspirators:[23]

> The Latinisms are probably Mwase's gloss, particularly since he seems consciously to have striven for literary effects. Mwase presumably derived his knowledge of Latin from his education by missionaries at Livingstonia. The Latin phrases and aphorisms that appear in the remainder of the text are notably corrupt—in some cases almost indecipherable. Nevertheless, they reflect Mwase's love of the grand gesture, his desire to impress his readers with superior learning and, of course, an ability to turn to his own use the mannerisms and knowledge of white men.

A narratological approach supports Rotberg's judgment that the Latinisms belong to Mwase rather than Chilembwe.[24] The Latin tags occur at all levels of

---

[20] Rotberg's editorial note: "Reading *coram* for *corum*, this phrase probably means 'publicly or privately'" (Rotberg in Mwase 1967:59n2).

[21] See n16 above.

[22] Rotberg's editorial note: "'*Feelins Nullins*,' probably should be *filius nullius*, 'nobody's children'" (Rotberg in Mwase 1967:95n1). *Filius nullius* is used in legal Latin as a term for an illegitimate child.

[23] Rotberg in Mwase 1967:48n2. In his "Editor's Acknowledgments," Rotberg thanks the classicist Erich Gruen for assistance with translating the Latin in the typescript (Rotberg in Mwase 1967:v).

[24] We should not rule out the possibility that John Chilembwe had some grasp of Latin. Whether or not he received any instruction in Latin in the missionary schools which he attended in Nyasaland, when he attended Virginia Theological Seminary and College in Lynchburg, Virginia in 1897–1899/1890, the African American scholar and educator Gregory Willis Hayes was

discourse in the narrative: in direct speech in the mouth of John Chilembwe, in indirect speech as Mwase summarizes Chilembwe's deeds and actions, and in Mwase's own freestanding commentary on the significance of the uprising in Nyasaland's history.

It is notable that Mwase uses Latin at the head of the Dialogue, in the title of the first chapter: "*A Verbis ad Verba* (From Words to Blows)."[25] Mwase's gloss of the Latin indicates that he meant *A Verbis ad Verbera*: understanding *verbera* (neuter plural of *verber*, a blow), instead of *verba* (neuter plural of *verbum*, a word). This infelicity is typical of the use of Latin throughout the document, which is characterized by solecisms and grammatical errors that suggest phonetic spellings based on oral knowledge of Latin rather than a literate education. Nonetheless, it is striking that the first language that Mwase's reader encounters is Latin, and that he uses Latin to encapsulate the trajectory of the uprising. In Mwase's interpretation, the words of the American abolitionist John Brown and written accounts of Brown's action, inspired John Chilembwe's heroic action, imparting a clear logic to an uprising that hostile sources were inclined to depict as a violent massacre. In giving the uprising a narrative, Mwase also hints at the possibility that his own words might be a spur to some future action. The future-oriented quality of the narrative is apparent in the dialogue form chosen by Mwase, which is a dialogue for both contemporary and future readers. This proleptic aspect is seen most clearly on page 74, where Mwase gives Chilembwe the prize of ultimate heroism in the asymmetrical contest of anti-colonial struggle, expressed through the metaphor of striking an armed enemy with a maize stalk:

> Has he won it? Clearly so. John was the first and last man to attempt to strike a whiteman with a maize stalk in this country. I cannot, of course, state what will be the state of affairs, after a century from now. That I leave it with our great grandchildren and the present great grandchildren of whitemen to judge. ... Only John won such heroic.

In Mwase's presentation, it is as though John's actions are seeking an answer from future generations.

---

president of the College. Hayes had graduated from Oberlin College with a Major in Classical Studies in 1888 and was a noted opponent of the view that Negro colleges should only provide an industrial education ("Negro" was the term used at this time). Shepperson and Price 2000:113 speculate that Chilembwe might have been given special tuition by Hayes as part of a curriculum tailored to his needs and point out that a 1917 American government report on Negro education criticized the fact that there was "excessive time devoted to foreign languages" in the curriculum (Shepperson and Price 2000:114 and n100).

[25] The full title of the first chapter is "The Education on Chilembwe's Actions and Deeds: *A Verbis ad Verba* (From Words to Blows)" (Mwase 1967:3).

Given that Chilembwe's uprising was partially motivated as a protest against the conscription of Nyasaland subjects in the First World War, the repeated invocations of "*Amor Patria[e]*" are highly resonant.[26] This phrase occurs four times in Mwase's typescript, and the phrases "*Omnia Vincit Amor*" and "*non sibi sed patria[e]*" reinforce the same idea. Mwase's narrative is bi-temporal: looking back at the historical moment of the uprising in 1915 from the perspective of the early 1930s, Mwase is able to appropriate British patriotic discourse of the First World War, which frequently used Latin tags to articulate patriotic sentiments,[27] but for the articulation of an anti-colonial Nyasa patriotism. While Chilembwe probably did appeal to love of Nyasaland and Nyasa way of life, the use of Latin patriotic tags implies knowledge of hindsight to engage in ironic, anti-colonial classical exhortation.

Mwase's use of Latin is multi-layered and reflects the diffuse circulation of Latin in different cultures and institutions, but there also seems to be a coherent logic and purpose to the citation of Latin in the Dialogue. As with other writers who espouse national counter-narratives to British colonial rule in this period, Mwase has a clear sense of the cultural politics of language and the role that Latin can play in writing back to English.[28] His initial narratorial self-presentation is tactically self-effacing, calling attention to the imperfections in his command of English as an outsider in the language:[29]

> I am very sorry to express my deep regret to have recorded such in English, by which language, I am not origin, even not a good speaker of the language, but as the language is *?Lingua Fraula? <lingua franca>* in the Protectorate, I therefore venture to write my book in English. I call therefore on your assistance, you the speakers of a better tongue of the English language, to correct the errors, and to fill in the proper word instead, because I meant it. Certainly, the word which is wrongly recorded in [my book] I did not mean it, so the word correctly put in, I meant so.

In the midst of this apologetic gesture, Mwase includes the Latin phrase *lingua franca* to signal a grasp of idiom and a cosmopolitan education. He may also have

---

[26] The previous year, John Chilembwe had written a letter to the letter to the *Nyasaland Times*, which was published under the heading "The Voice of African Natives in the Present War." Shepperson and Price 2000:234–235 reproduce the text of Chilembwe's letter and date its publication in the *Nyasaland Times* to issue no. 48, published in November 1914.

[27] See Vandiver 2010 for a discussion of both the ironic and the non-ironic (i.e. conventionally patriotic) use of classical tags in British poetry of the First World War.

[28] See Greenwood 2010:112–185 for examples from the Anglophone Caribbean.

[29] Mwase 1967:6.

in mind the historical irony that as Malawian vernacular languages (Tonga and Chinyanja in Mwase's case) are to English, so was English once to Latin. Compare Kamuzu Banda's reflections on English in his unpublished prison memoirs (written in 1959), in which he uses the analogy of Latin *vis-à-vis* the vernacular languages of Europe to explain his desire to learn English as a young student in Nyasaland:[30]

> To acquire a working knowledge of the English language was becoming a real and most desirable achievement. English had become, when I grew up in Nyasaland, in particular, and in Central Africa, in general, in its own way, what Latin was in Europe in the Middle Ages—the most important, valuable and useful knowledge one could speak.

In his own narratorial commentary, Mwase's citation of Latin acts as a counterweight to English, redressing the straightforward axis of cultural imperialism through recourse to another, older civilization. Where Mwase attributes Latin phrases to John Chilembwe, presumably the intended effect is to place John Chilembwe on a global stage and to use Latin to present him as a world historical figure in a succession of heroic patriots. Mwase seems to have envisaged a double audience: the colonial authorities on the one hand, and fellow Nyasa subjects on the other. At several points in the Dialogue, he splits his audience, distinguishing white readers from Nyasa readers and discriminating between a Nyasa focalization and a colonial focalization.[31]

George Simeon Mwase's and Kamuzu Banda's uses of Classics bear comparison. The two men were rough contemporaries, with Mwase perhaps a decade older, and their respective careers intersect in interesting ways. Like Mwase, Banda's early education was through the Free Church of Scotland mission, and the two men were involved with the Malawi Congress Party in its early years.[32] Banda's uncle, Hanock Msokera Phiri, was a graduate of the Overtoun Institution, which he attended from 1903-1910. At the point at which he left Malawi for South Africa, prompted by failing his Standard Three Certificate due to a mistaken accusation of cheating, Banda was intending to apply to the Overtoun Institution. For all the solecisms on evidence in the Dialogue, Mwase domesticates Latin in the service of indigenous history in a way that Kamuzu Banda never attempted. With Banda's citation, quotation, and invocation of

---

[30] H. K. Banda Archive, Box 2, Folder 16, citing from page 208 of the typescript.
[31] See Rotberg in Mwase 1967:xl.
[32] In Banda's case, after starting at a mission school in Mtunthama, he progressed to a mission school at Chilanga where he completed his education up to Standard Three. Banda began his inaugural Founder's address for Kamuzu Academy, delivered on November 21st, 1981, by recounting his early mission education: H. K. Banda Archive, Box 2, Folder 5.

Latin, the focus was always on Latin as a foreign possession that was a mark of Western Civilization—a form of credentialing. Here we see the contradictoriness of Kamuzu Banda's Classics: using Classics to stake a claim to national selfhood, while at the same time branding Classics as Western and as white. In fact, in Banda's logic, it was his conception of the Classics as Western/European/white that led to its efficacy on the political stage, as it enabled his admission into a rarefied club and alienated him from his own people in the process. Mwase's *Dialogue* offers an alternative narrative of Classics in Malawi, representing Latin in the service of a national consciousness.[33]

Another example that challenges Banda's presumed monopoly on Classics is that of Aleke Banda, who co-founded the Malawi Congress Party (MCP) with Orton Chirwa in September 1959. Aleke Banda endorsed Kamuzu Banda to be the first head of the Malawi Congress Party; he was Secretary-General of the Malawi Congress Party and served in Banda's government as Minister of Development and Planning and Minister of Finance. Aleke Banda was dismissed from government in 1973 after open speculation in foreign media that he would succeed Banda. After a partial rapprochement, he was expelled from the Malawi Congress party in 1980 on grounds of breach of discipline and accusations over his alleged mismanagement of the parastatal corporation Press Holdings.[34] Aleke Banda was detained, without charge, in Mikuyu prison from 1980–1992.[35]

Aleke Banda was educated in Southern Rhodesia and was twenty-one years old when he co-founded the Malawi Congress Party. His crucial contribution to the emerging party was as the organizing secretary and editor of the *Malawi News*, which was—as its banner proclaimed—"the voice of the Malawi Congress Party." In January 1960, while Kamuzu Banda was imprisoned in Gwelo, Aleke Banda published an editorial in Vol. 2.1 of *Malawi News* entitled "The Monckton Commission: The Wooden Horse of Central Africa."[36] This was a bi-lingual pamphlet, with text in English followed by text in Chewa. In 1953, the British government imposed the unpopular Federation of Rhodesia, which brought Nyasaland and Northern Rhodesia into Federation with Southern Rhodesia.

---

[33] Banda's uncritical veneration of Greek and Roman Classics leads to deep ironies in Malawian classical receptions in the next generation, such as the poet Jack Mapanje's artful use of the myth of Antigone to criticize Banda's authoritarian regime, where the use of classical myth enables the criticism to go under the radar—see Greenwood 2016.

[34] See Baker 2001:321–322; and van Donge 2002:658 for discussion of the accusations of financial mismanagement.

[35] After the collapse of Kamuzu Banda's regime, Aleke Banda returned to politics. Among other positions, he had the portfolio of Minister of Agriculture in the government of Bakili Muluzi from 1997–2005.

[36] *Malawi News* pamphlet Vol. 2, No. 1, 2nd January 1960; the quotes below are from pp. 1–3 of the pamphlet. Source: H. K. Banda Archive, Box 5, Folder 21.

Emily Greenwood

The Nyasaland African Congress (a precursor to the Malawi Congress Party) led Nyasa opposition to the federation, which intensified in 1958 and 1959, culminating in the declaration of a State of Emergency in Nyasaland on March 3rd, 1959.[37] In 1960, the British government set up the Monckton Commission to review the state of the Federation of Rhodesia and Nyasaland, and its future viability. This is the context for Aleke Banda's editorial on the 2nd of January 1960, which presents the Monckton Commission as a Trojan horse, intended to put the unpopular federation on a permanent footing:

> Editorial "The Monckton Commission: The Wooden Horse of Central Africa"
>
> (p. 1) In 1960, Africans are more opposed to Federation than they were in 1953. It is because Sir Roy [Welensky] is aware of this, that he and Mr. [Harold] MacMillan invented a plan whereby they could lead the Africans into accepting the Federation permanently. This plan is the WOODEN HORSE OF CENTRAL AFRICA, which they disguise as the "Monckton Commission." A brief reference to the Wooden Horse of Troy will serve to illustrate the viciousness of the Wooden Horse of Central Africa.
>
> On pp. 1–2 (omitted here), Aleke Banda devotes six paragraphs to a précis of the myth of the Trojan horse in Greek mythology.
>
> (p. 2) The people of Malawi have a great deal to learn from this event. The Monckton Commission is a wooden horse – the wooden horse of Central Africa. Just as the people of Troy were cheated, the Settlers and the Government are cheating the African people all over the country to go and give evidence to the Monckton Commission which is coming to Central Africa in February this year.
>
> (p. 3) We are glad that OUR KAMUZU and all OUR CHIEFS who have the Welfare of their people at heart are going to boycott the Monckton Commission. We too, Men, Women, Boys, and Girls of Malawi, should not go to see this commission.
>
> Remember what happened to the people of Troy!!

Although Aleke Banda's use of Greek mythology here is not particularly sophisticated, it serves as an important reminder that, among educated Malawians in

---

[37] For a contemporary account of Nyasa resistance to the Federation and the response of the British government, see Stonehouse 1960:206–224.

this period, knowledge of ancient Greek and Roman history and mythology was certainly not the exclusive property of Kamuzu Banda.

Kamuzu Banda's Kamuzu Academy

While detained by the British Government in Gwelo, Southern Rhodesia (March 1959–April 1960), Banda formulated three dreams for the development of Nyasaland, which he subsequently referred to as his "Gwelo dreams." These comprised: the construction of the lakeshore road; moving the capital from Zomba to Lilongwe; and establishing the University of Malawi.[38] The creation of the Academy was an offshoot of the latter and rooted in a long-standing preoccupation with the educational needs of Nyasaland.[39]

As the quotation at the head of this chapter makes clear, any attempt to understand the conception of Kamuzu Academy and its influences must engage with the African American connection. Scholars of Malawian history have long been aware of the important role that American education played in the intellectual and political formation of John Chilembwe and Hastings Kamuzu Banda,[40] but there has been no study of the relationship between Banda's Kamuzu Academy and wider traditions of Black classicisms. The phrase "Black classicism" alludes to Michele Valerie Ronnick's coinage *classica Africana*, to highlight the fact that the African American study of the Classics had been ignored in Meyer Reinhold's influential study of the American classical tradition (so called *classica Americana*).[41] Although its sphere of reference was originally North American, the field of Black classicisms now encompasses the reception of classics in all Black national and transnational traditions and includes important studies of classical education in West Africa and South Africa.[42]

As with all scholarship on the thought of Kamuzu Banda, there are considerable methodological obstacles. Kamuzu Banda's self-fashioning was inventive,

---

[38] Munger 1983:259.

[39] Lwanda 1993:121 cites a letter that Banda wrote on June 14, 1946 to Arthur Creech Jones, British Under Secretary of State for the Colonies, complaining about provisions for education in Nyasaland and the fact that vocational training was allowed to crowd out pure academic study.

[40] Shepperson and Price 2000 (on Chilembwe); Shepperson 1960; Phiri 1982; and Ralston 1973, on the Black South African Alfred Bitini Xuma, who studied at the Tuskegee Institute, the University of Minnesota, Marquette University, and Northwestern University between 1914 and 1925.

[41] The phrase "black classicism," was theorized in and popularized by Rankine 2006. On the connection with Ronnick's coinage, see Rankine 2006:23–27. Ronnick first brought the phrase *classica Africana* to the wider attention of classicists in the US in 1996 when she organized a panel at the American Philological Association under this title (Ronnick 2005:334n10). See also Reinhold 1984.

[42] On Classics in West Africa, see Goff 2013; on classics in South Africa, see Lambert 2011; and Parker 2017.

and he edited his oral biography depending on the audience, revealing different aspects of his education, experience, and thought to suit the rhetorical occasion. This protean rhetorical character was in keeping with his style of personal rule, which had a strongly mythical dimension, based on a concerted program of image-making to cement his status as a suitable leader for the country in 1958.[43] A crucial biographical document in all of this—Banda's *Autobiography*—was never published and, although a typescript exists and can be read in the H. K. Banda archives at the University of Indiana, it was abandoned as a work in progress.[44]

Kamuzu Banda was in the habit of rehearsing the charter myth for Kamuzu Academy when he gave annual Founder's Day addresses at the school, and the texts of these speeches reveal both recurring themes and shifts in emphasis. At the opening speech for Kamuzu Academy, which Kamuzu Banda delivered on November 21st, 1981, he rehearsed the history of his own education before, in the last two pages of the typescript of the speech, forging a connection between his own experience and the goal of Kamuzu Academy.[45] Banda cites his previous record as a patron of education in the district of Kasungu:[46]

> When Rev. Hanock Msokera Phiri established the A. M. E. Church at Chilanga, he also established Mdabwi School at Linga. In fact, the Academy should not be regarded in isolation from Mdabwi School, which was established at my own expenses, because I wanted English to be taught. Now, the Academy must be considered as Mdabwi at a higher level. Mdabwi was established to teach English, which the Dutch Reformed Church were [sic] not doing, at least, to my satisfaction. The Academy is being established for the main purpose of teaching the Classics, the ancient world, ancient people, the world of Greece, Rome, if not Persia and Egypt; the Greeks and the Romans, if not the Persians and the Egyptians.

[43] A core elite who were active in the Nyasaland Congress (Kanyama Chiume, Henry Masauko Chipembere, and Dunduzu Chisiza), colluded in this mythmaking and then apparently tried to scale it back when Banda began to embody the myth so willingly. On the deliberate cultivation of a "personality cult" for Banda, see Short 1974:92, and Power 2010: 129–135.

[44] The copy of the *Autobiography* in the Banda Archive at Indiana University is complete with editorial post-it notes added by Dr. Donald Brody, whom Kamuzu Banda had appointed as his official biographer. The Archive (Box 2, folder 6) also contains correspondence between Kamuzu Banda and British publishers about the potential publication of his *Autobiography*: a December 18th, 1962 letter from the Publisher Rupert Hart-Davis Limited; and an 2nd April 1973 letter from Kamuzu Banda to Mr. Charles Clark, Managing Director, Hutchinson Publishing Group Limited.

[45] H. K. Banda Archive, Box 2, Folder 5.

[46] Quoting from pp. 19–20 of the typescript of this speech.

The primacy and urgency of education for self-improvement is a running topic in Kamuzu Banda's letters home from America to his uncle Rev. Hanock Msokera Phiri in Kasungu. In a letter that Kamuzu Banda wrote on October 8th, 1938,[47] addressed to Ernest C. Matako in Kasungu, he describes working with Chief Mwase and Reverend Hanock Msokera Phiri to provide two full bursaries to fund an education at the Overtoun Institution in Khondowe for the two cleverest boys in Kasungu.[48]

At one level, then, Banda conceived of the Academy as an extension of his support for education in Nyasaland/Malawi, inspired by his own transnational quest for education. This Malawian uplift through education was a deeply held conviction, but tensions arose from Banda's inflexible vision of the ideal curriculum and the cultural content of this education. Having portrayed Kamuzu Academy as a higher, more elite instantiation of the modest AME mission school at Mdabwi, Banda concluded his inaugural speech with a paean to ancient Greek and Roman history:[49]

> At the Academy, I repeat, the history of the ancient world and the ancient people will be taught, Persia, Egypt, Greece, Rome; the Persians, the Egyptians, the Greeks, the Romans. To an intelligent boy leaving the Academy after six years, he must know such names as Cyrus, Darius, Alexander the Great, Pericles, Demosthenes, then of course, Julius Caesar, Marcus Tullius Cicero, Pompey. I want a boy leaving the Academy to know these names, who these people were.
>
> To me, it is a prostitution of the phrase "higher education," when a boy or girl is allowed to leave the school with a kind of diploma, when (p. 21) he or she does not know the history of the ancient world, Persia, Egypt, Greece, Rome; when he or she does not know such names as Cyrus,

---

[47] At this point, Kamuzu Banda was in Edinburgh, having arrived from the US in August 1937, but had not yet applied to the Royal College to begin his studies for a British medical degree. See McCracken 2017 for a detailed chronology.

[48] Published in Morrow and McCracken 2012, quoting from p. 353: "I wrote Chief Mwase, as well as Rev Phiri to pick out the two most clever boys at Kasungu, to go to Khondowe as my personal bursaries. Please help the Chief and Rev. Phiri in choosing these boys. I want these boys to be chosen on the basis purely of merit rather than any thing else. In other words, they do not have to be related to me in any way whatever. All I want is that they must be the most clever boys at Kasungu. And I shall bear all their expenses at Khondowe, except clothing, which they must bring with them. If the experiment works, I shall increase the number to four. And I hope that others at Kasungu, who are economically able to do the same, will offer to help some other boys. For it is only in this way that we can help the country." For the significance of the Overtoun institute, see pp. 122–123 above. Short (1974:50–51) cites other examples of Banda sponsoring other students in Nyasaland and in Northern Rhodesia.

[49] Quoting from pp. 20–21 of the typescript of the speech.

Darius, Alexander the Great, Pericles, Demosthenes, Julius Caesar, Marcus Tullius Cicero, Pompey and Crassus, among others.

In short, then, the Academy is being established to teach the Classics at a Grammar School level. A boy or girl leaving the Academy must be able to prance and prank and say:

"Gallia est omnis divisa in partes tres, quarum unam incolunt Belgae, aliam Aquitani, tertiam qui ipsorum lingua Celtae, nostra Galli appellantur. ... , cum aut suis finibus eos prohibent aut ipsi in eorum finibus bellum gerunt."

[The Latin is quoted without a translation.]

It is instructive to compare this articulation of the mission and educational curriculum of Kamuzu Academy with the versions that Banda offered in two subsequent Founder's Addresses, in February 1982 and November 1984. Banda had ended his Founder's Day Address in 1981 by quoting the beginning of Caesar's Gallic Wars in Latin. The next year, in his Founder's Day address on 11 February 1982, Banda offered what he billed as a "Speech on Grammar."[50] This speech is remarkable for its recitation of basic Latin grammar. On page two of the typescript of the speech, Banda recalls his education in Latin at Wilberforce Academy and contrasts his previously restricted knowledge of grammatical cases in English with the more complicated case structure that he had to master in Latin:

But at Wilberforce, three other cases were taught, dative, ablative, vocative.

[...] when I was taught Latin, three other cases were taught ... for the study of both Latin and Greek, a good knowledge of cases is necessary.

In dwelling on Latin grammar, Banda's intention seems to have been twofold: to identify with the students who are currently studying Latin and to amuse them, and to perform his own credentials as a classically educated statesman. On page six of the typescript, he prefaces the declension of the Latin pronouns *ego, nos, tu,* and *vos* with the remark, "now, some of you are already studying Latin. Two years from now, you will be studying Greek. I take it for granted that you are already saying: *ego, me, mei, mihi, me* [et cetera]."[51] This grammatical interlude

---

[50] H. K. Banda Archive, Box 2, Folder 5.

[51] The declension of these pronouns spans pages 6–7 of the typescript. Compare Shepperson 1998:83, who recalls Banda's Inaugural Lecture at the ceremony for the opening of the University of Malawi in summer 1965: "His Inaugural Lecture is the most remarkable, indeed bizarre,

then segues into a discussion of the centrality of studying classics to an elite education, on the grounds that Latin was the vehicle for the dissemination of civilization in the modern world:

> These days, in Europe, even more, in America, classical education is not as popular as it used to be when I went overseas. When I was a student in America, topmost universities insisted on classical education. Latin and Greek were insisted on in the universities. [...] I think it is wrong for universities not to insist on Latin and Greek, particularly, Latin. To me, topmost universities, both in Europe and America, should insist on classical education. Lower type of universities may not worry about classical education. But topmost universities, such as Oxford, Cambridge, Edinburgh, Glasgow in Britain, and Harvard, Yale, Chicago in America, should teach Latin, Greek and the ancient world as a whole. These topmost universities are supposed to be fountains of knowledge at its best or highest level. Therefore, they should teach the ancient world, in all its aspects; history and languages, Greek and Roman history, Greek and Latin languages.

> What passes for European civilization is not, strictly speaking, European at all. Because what is called European civilization is supposed to have started in Mesopotamia, now Iraq. From there, it went to Persia, now Iran. From Persia, it went to Egypt. From Egypt, civilization went to Greece by way of (p. 9) Crete, that is, the island of Crete. So experts speak of Minoan and Mycenaean civilization; all this, on the island of Crete. And then, from the island of Crete, it went to the mainland of Greece, Athens, Sparta, Corinth, Ephesus.

> From Greece, civilization went to Rome in Italy. [...] From Rome, civilization went to France or Gallia, as Julius Caesar called it. And from France or Gallia, it went to Britain or Britannia, again, as Julius Caesar called Britain.

> It was the conquest of Gaul or Gallia by Julius Caesar that spread Roman rule or Roman power, not only over the greatest part of Europe, but also part of Africa, North Africa and even the Middle East.

---

academic occasion that I have ever attended. It consisted of a complete outline of English grammar!"

(p. 10) Since civilization was spread through this language all over Europe and parts of Africa and the Middle East, to me, for academic, cultural and historical reasons, topmost universities should teach Latin, Greek and the ancient world. To me, no one is highly educated if he or she does not know Latin, better still, both Latin and Greek. And this is why I want both Latin and Greek taught here. Boys and girls who come here, must know something about the ancient world, Greece, Rome, the Greeks, the Romans, Socrates, Plato, Aristotle, Solon, Demosthenes, Pericles, in Greece; and then, Gaius Julius Caesar, Marcus Tullius Cicero, Pompey and Crassus, in Rome or Italy.

[This list of names is repeated, verbatim, in the final paragraph of the speech.]

There are a number of striking features to this speech. In his inaugural Founder's Day address in November 1981, Banda had put forward an enlarged vision of ancient history, beginning with Mesopotamia, Persia, and Egypt, before the civilizations of ancient Greece and Rome. The speech in 1982 goes further, stating explicitly that, "What passes for European civilization is not, strictly speaking, European at all. Because what is called European civilization is supposed to have started in Mesopotamia, now Iraq. From there, it went to Persia, now Iran. From Persia, it went to Egypt." As Kenneth Goings and Eugene O'Connor have demonstrated, one way in which the intense focus on the study of Greek and Roman Classics was justified in Black colleges and universities in America was through an Afrocentric model of classical education—the insistence that the origins of these civilizations lay in Africa and were, therefore, as germane for African Americans as to other Americans.[52] The account of world history that Banda offers here is reminiscent of the civilizationist model of Afrocentrism espoused by Du Bois, which attempted to marry African cultural nationalism with a veneration for Western culture.[53]

Banda's emphasis on the longer civilizational durée of Greek and Roman civilization was undoubtedly influenced by this tradition, as he speaks and writes elsewhere of the influence of Abyssinianism, Garveyism, and Pan-Africanism on his intellectual formation, initially through the mission of the A. M. E. Church

[52] Goings and O'Connor 2010:523 and 525. See also Goings and O'Connor 2011, for the idea of "Black Athena before *Black Athena*."
[53] See Moses 2008:127: "Like their [referring to Du Bois and Garvey] predecessors in the movement, notably Blyden and Crummell, they tended to conceive of Africa's worth in terms of its relationship to Western symbols of civilization, such as city buildings, architectural monuments, written languages, and those regions of Africa associated with such accomplishments."

in South Africa.[54] But while Banda does not subscribe to a Eurocentric model of classical education, he does reproduce a hierarchical model of education, listing an exclusive group of universities in the United Kingdom and the US, and contrasting them with "lower" universities. This sits oddly with the beginning of the speech, in which Banda adopts a rhetoric of humility, playing down his educational accomplishments and adopting the pose of "a simple farmer, a simple G.P.":

> Experts define the word "grammar" in a number of ways, and not all of
> them define it exactly the same. I am not an expert, not even a teacher.
> I am a simple farmer, a simple G.P. or General Practitioner. As a simple
> farmer and simple practitioner, to me, the word "grammar" means
> correct use of words in expressing a thought, an idea, or an action.

With its blend of folk humility and mild anti-intellectualism on the one hand, and elitism on the other, this speech echoes the ambiguity of Banda's political persona, which played on a populist persona, using analogies from village life, while also reminding his audiences of his Western education and foreign credentials, through his speech (speaking English rather than Chichewa and using an interpreter), his dress, and his insistence on his Western sensibility.[55]

Two years later, in his Founder's Day address at Kamuzu Academy on 14 November 1984, Banda offered yet another framing narrative for the Academy, this time singling out Wilberforce Academy in Ohio, the high school which he attended between 1925 and 1928, as the primary inspiration for Kamuzu Academy:[56]

---

[54] On Banda's encounter with Garveyism, see Short 1974:18. In Banda's unpublished autobiography, he writes of his early consciousness of what he terms "Abyssinianism" through John Chilembwe's example and the influence of African American missionaries in Malawi. Banda was the Nyasaland delegate at the famous fifth pan-African Congress held on 15–21 October 1945 at Chorlton-on-Medlock Town Hall in Manchester. On Garvey's importance for Malawian nationalism, see p. 142 below.

[55] On Banda's English mannerisms upon his return to Nyasaland, see Short 1974:92, and on Banda's political rhetoric and self-presentation to crowds of Malawian villagers on the campaign trail, see Power 2010:132–134. Among his associates, Banda did not disguise his affinity and his estrangement from the Chewa culture of his upbringing, sometimes referring to the people of Nyasaland with hauteur and cultural condescension. Responding to a query about his marital status in a letter from Ernest Matako, a graduate of the Overtoun Institution who had taught Banda at Chilanga primary school, Banda replied to Matako in a letter dated 8 October 8 1938 (Morrow and McCracken 2012:351), "You will readily understand that no girl in Nyasaland now would be a real companion to me. [...] I still respect our women highly. But I have to admit the fact that our women are backward, and could not, by any means, make me the type of home to which my education, training and experience entitle me."

[56] H. K. Banda Archive, Box 2, Folder 6, quoting from pp. 10–11 of the typescript of the speech. In his first Founder's speech in November 1981, Banda briefly mentioned his education at Wilberforce

It was then [his return to Malawi in 1958], that I decided that after we became independent, and I was in a position to do so, I would establish a Grammar School of my own, on the model of the Wilberforce Academy in Ohio, in America, if not better. Because, as a high school student at Wilberforce Academy, I became interested in the Ancient World – Mesopotamia, now Iraq; Persia, now Iran; Greece, Rome, and then the Charlemagne Empire, in the Middle Ages [...] The Academy was established, essentially and primarily, for Classical education, a nursery for Classical scholars. By Classical scholars is meant students interested in the Ancient World—Mesopotamia, Persia, Greece, Rome; Cambyses, Cyrus, Darius in Persia; and then Socrates, Plato, Aristotle, among the teachers in Greece; Pericles and Demosthenes, among soldier statesmen, and Solon, among jurists. And then, Rome, of course, Julius Caesar, Cicero, Pompey, Crassus, among statesmen and politicians. [...] Any student who is not interested in Classical education must not come here. Any student who is interested only in Chemistry, Physics, and Biology must not come here. This is a wrong place for him or her.

Why the term Academy? Wilberforce Academy, Plato's Academy; not Edinburgh Academy. I did not know there was Edinburgh Academy.

I want to repeat what I have said before, that, only the best of teachers will be, and are, employed here. And, by the best of teachers, is meant only those teachers who, whatever their specialty of field in education, also had classical education in their school days, Latin and Greek.

After his introduction to ancient history at Wilberforce Academy, Banda subsequently studied ancient history at the University of Indiana and as part of his history major at the University of Chicago. Although the speech delivered in 1982 devoted some time to the importance of Latin grammar and language study, all three speeches emphasize ancient history, and a great-man theory of ancient history, at that. The rollcall of great statesmen, thinkers, and jurists offered in each speech is very similar (see Table 3, p. 139), but with greater elaboration in the speech delivered in 1984.

In the speech delivered in 1984, there is a strong emphasis on the tradition of Liberal Arts education, which Banda had encountered at the Universities of

---

Academy: H. K. Banda Archive, Box 2, Folder 5, quoting from pp. 15–16 of the typescript: "In December, 1925, then, I took my first set of examinations at Wilberforce. My subjects were English, Latin, Algebra, Spanish, History, Drawing, Music, and Vocational Training, Agriculture."

1981 Founders' Address	1982 Founder's Address	1984 Founder's Address
Cyrus	Socrates	Cambyses
Darius	Plato	Cyrus
Alexander the Great	Aristotle	Darius
Pericles	Solon	Socrates
Demosthenes	Demosthenes	Plato
Julius Caesar	Pericles	Aristotle
	Gaius Julius Caesar	Pericles
Crassus	Marcus Tullius Cicero	Demosthenes
	Pompey	Solon
	Crassus	Julius Caesar
		Cicero
		Pompey
		Crassus

Table 3: Statesmen, Thinkers, Jurists

Indiana and Chicago;[57] hence Banda rules out specialization in the sciences to the exclusion of a classical education. He had expressed his commitment to the liberal arts in many of his speeches, as exemplified in a lecture at Bunda College of Agriculture on March 29th, 1969:[58]

> When I was going through my educational career—starting from High School at Wilberforce, although I knew that I wanted to be a doctor, I

[57] In his application to the University of Chicago, dated April 12th, 1930 (12-4-30), Banda mentioned that he wanted to gain the best liberal education possible. Source H. K. Banda Archive, Box 2, Folder 13. Banda transferred to the University of Chicago from the University of Indiana and received his degree from Chicago in 1931.

[58] "The origin of the Word 'Chewa': A lecture given by his Excellency the Life President, Ngwazi Dr. H. Kamuzu Banda, at Banda college of Agriculture on 29th March 1969." H. K. Banda Archive Box 2, Folder 2, quoting from pp. 1–2 of the published speech.

did not want to be one of those doctors who limits himself or herself to pills and bottles. I wanted to know something outside my own profession. So I did not confine myself to medical sciences, when I went through my educational career, both at the University of Indiana and the University of Chicago.

As a matter of fact, I deliberately took my degree in a subject that had nothing to do with medicine. I told the Dean of the College of Arts and Sciences at the University of Indiana that I was going to be a doctor, but I did not want to take my first degree in medical or physical sciences of biological sciences. I wanted to take one in the social sciences and humanity—history, political science, some economics, sociology and then languages—Latin, Greek, English—of course, French.

In spite of the emphasis on the place of Classics in a Liberal Arts education in the 1984 Founder's Day address, there is no attempt in Banda's speeches to offer a detailed justification of the value of a classical education. Instead, a classical education is treated superficially, as the sign of an advanced, higher education, with the rote quotation of the beginning of Caesar's *Gallic Wars* introduced with the pronouncement, in the speech in 1981, "A boy or girl leaving the Academy must be able to prance and prank and say: ..."[59] Where the focus is on language, as in the Founder's Address in 1982, the approach is instrumental—as a means to correct expression and to read works in order to extract a knowledge of history. Banda appears never to have spoken or written about the value of Plato, Demosthenes, Cicero, or Caesar as works of literature.

His preoccupation with Caesar has more disquieting overtones. When asked whom he most admired during an interview with Alec Russel for the British newspaper the *Daily Telegraph* in 1995, Banda's response was Julius Caesar:[60]

As I rose to go, I asked in parting whom he most admired. There was not a moment's reflection. "Julius Caesar. He could be tough. He could be kind. But when he was tough, he was tough, ... oh yes." Again came the cackle, louder than before and more sinister.

Although Banda drew an analogy with Plato's Academy in the 1984 Founder's Day Speech delivered, the association was loose, and Banda never provided a coherent or detailed justification for the link. In the published program for the

---

[59] Quoted on p. 134 above.
[60] "Twilight days of a north London doctor," the *Daily Telegraph* 9 August 1995. H. K. Banda Archive, Box 1, Folder 2.

official opening of Kamuzu Academy on November 21st, 1981, the Academy was placed in the tradition of the *Akadêmia* in ancient Athens:[61]

> Kamuzu Academy is the newest of a long list of academies stretching back to the ancient Greek Academia—literally, a garden where thinkers and philosophers met to exchange ideas. The landscapers have seen to it that the garden aspect has not been overlooked—the quadrangle, surrounded by the Administration Building, Library, Teaching Blocks and Art and Music Rooms well illustrate this point.

The only direct quotation from Plato that I found in the archives was a passage from Plato's *Republic* which was included in a document that Cecilia Kadzamira, Banda's official hostess, faxed to Donald Brody on August 23, 1996, in the context of an appeal to Brody to help raise funds for student bursaries. These documents included a brief, chronological history of the Academy, a mission statement, an overview of the balance (total expenditure), and a selection of miscellaneous remarks about the Academy, including the following quotation from Plato:[62]

> Youth should dwall [*sic*] in a land of health, amid fair sights and which will meet the sense like a breeze, and insensibly draw the soul in childhood into harmony with the beauty of reason. (Plato)

Although no reference is provided, this quotation comes from Book 3 of Plato's *Republic* (401c4–d3) and is adapted from Benjamin Jowett's translation of this passage.[63] This passage occurs in Socrates' discussion with Glaucon about the strictures that they will place on poets, artists, architects, and other craftsmen in their ideal city Kallipolis, so that the Guardians (*hoi phylakes*) will dwell in an environment conducive to the pursuit of the supreme good. Coupled with the quotation from the Programme for the Academy's opening ceremony, the logic for the Platonic analogy seems to have been that Banda conceived of the Malawian scholars selected for the Academy as akin to the Guardian class— highly educated leaders who would direct the future life of the nation, and he

---

[61] Programme of the official opening of Kamuzu Academy by His Excellency the Life President Ngwazi Dr. H. Kamuzu Banda at Mtunthama in Kasungu District on Saturday, 21 November 1981. Source: H. K. Banda Archives, Box 7, Folder 12.

[62] This section is titled "Some Remarks about Kamuzu Academy."

[63] Vol. II of Jowett's *The Dialogues of Plato*, p. 225: "... then will our youth dwell in a land of health, amid fair sights and sounds, and beauty, the effluence of fair works will meet the sense like a breeze, and insensibly draw the soul even in childhood into harmony with the beauty of reason." ... ὁπόθεν ἂν αὐτοῖς ἀπὸ τῶν καλῶν ἔργων ἢ πρὸς ὄψιν ἢ πρὸς ἀκοήν τι προσβάλῃ, ὥσπερ αὔρα φέρουσα ἀπὸ χρηστῶν τόπων ὑγίειαν, καὶ εὐθὺς ἐκ παίδων λανθάνῃ εἰς ὁμοιότητά τε καὶ φιλίαν καὶ συμφωνίαν τῷ καλῷ λόγῳ ἄγουσα.

seems to have taken quite literally the emphasis in the *Republic* on the aesthetics of the built environment as a factor in the education of the Guardian-scholars.[64] In a widely-read article in *The New Yorker*, published in December 1991, Caroline Alexander suggested the analogy of Kamuzu Banda as Philosopher King, with the students of Academy as the Guardian class.[65] A general, uncritical Platonic influence is undeniable, but this influence needs to be understood in terms of modern mediating traditions. In the case of Kamuzu Academy, the most salient mediating tradition and institutional context is that of America's HBCU's (Historically Black Colleges and Universities), as suggested by Banda's mention of Wilberforce Academy as the primary model for Kamuzu Academy (pp. 137–138 above).

The HBCU Connection (The Influence of W. E. B. Du Bois and Booker T. Washington)

Pan-Africanism and African American thought were given pride of place in the official booklet published to commemorate Malawian Independence on 6 July 1964. The booklet begins with a verse epigraph from the Pan-African leader Marcus Garvey. [66] These verses reflect the decision of Malawi Congress Party to base Malawi's flag on the Pan-African Flag of Garvey's Universal Negro Improvement Association, altering the order of the colors on the flag and adding a red, rising sun. The booklet closes with the poem "Youth" by Langston Hughes, leading poet of the Harlem Renaissance, with its vision of Black emancipation as a new dawn.[67] Although it is not clear what role Banda played in the conception and design of the booklet, which would have been the work of several people, this

---

[64] See the description of the impressive grounds of Kamuzu Academy in Alexander 1991:81–82.

[65] Alexander 1991:88; earlier in the article, Alexander also suggests an analogy between Banda's conspicuous patronage of farmers in Malawi and Plato's myth of metals in the *Republic*, likening farmers to the bronze class and suggesting a conscious policy of educational culling. Alexander 1991:78–80.

[66] Booklet "A Portrait of Malawi." Published on the Occasion of Malawi Independence, 1964. The Government Printer, Zomba, pp. v–vi (quoting the first two stanzas of Garvey's "Battle Hymn of Africa"): "Africa's sun is rising beyond the horizon clear, / The day for us is dawning, for black men far and near; / Our God is in the front line, the heavenly battalion leads, / Onward make your banners shine, ye men of noble deeds. [new stanza.] There is a flag we love so well, / The red, the black and the green, / The greatest emblem tongues can tell, / The brightest ever seen." Source: H. K. Banda Archive, Box 6, Folder 16.

[67] Langston Hughes "Youth" in "A Portrait of Malawi," p.119: "We have tomorrow / Bright before us / Like a flame [new stanza.] Yesterday a night-gone thing, / A sundown name [new stanza] And dawn, / Broad arch above the road we came, / We march." This poem was first published in the magazine *Crisis* (August 1924), p. 163 with the title "Poem," and was also selected by Alain Locke for a special issue of *Survey Graphic* (Vol. 6, No. 6, March 1925), where it was published under the title "Youth." This famous issue formed the basis for Locke's *The New Negro* (1925).

clear dialogue with Black diasporic thought provides an apt lens for considering the influence of two prominent African American thinkers—W. E. B. Du Bois and Booker T. Washington—on Banda's prioritizing of the Classics in his educational ideals.

W. E. B. Du Bois

In the context of the history of Black education in America, the obvious analogy for Plato's class of Guardians is the concept of "the Talented Tenth," as developed by W. E. B. Du Bois.[68] An alumnus of Wilberforce Academy, which was the preparatory school for Wilberforce University, Banda was undoubtedly aware of W. E. B. Du Bois's importance as an educator, scholar, and prominent commentator on Negro education.[69] Subsequently, Banda and Du Bois were both present at the fifth Pan-African National Congress in Manchester in 1945, but seem not to have spoken on that occasion, or—if they did—the meeting seems not to have made an impression on Du Bois. The only correspondence between Banda and Du Bois that I have been able to find is in the W. E. B. Du Bois Papers at the University of Massachusetts, Amherst. In 1961 and 1962, Du Bois wrote to Banda asking for his assistance with the *Encyclopedia Africana*, which Du Bois was overseeing and editing.[70] In the letter dated 28 April 1961, Du Bois wrote "I had the pleasure of meeting you in Nigeria," referring to their meeting when they attended the celebrations for Nigerian Independence in October 1960.[71]

Du Bois himself came out of an existing African American tradition that saw mastery of the Classics as instrumental for social uplift and Black

---

[68] Du Bois 1903b. Gooding-Williams 2009:266n44 points out that the idea of a "Talented Tenth" originated with Henry Morehouse, citing Higginbotham 1993. For discussion of Du Bois's Platonism, see Gooding-Williams 2009:34 and 267n56, with a discussion of previous literature. See also Hawkins 2018 for another analogy between Du Bois and Plato (Hawkins focuses on analogies between Du Bois' metaphor of the veil and the allegory of the cave).

[69] Du Bois was Chair of Classics at Wilberforce University from 1894 to 1896. See Du Bois 2007:115–121 and Cook and Tatum 2010:100–101. Short 1974:26 has a very brief mention of Banda coming under the influence of Du Bois in America.

[70] Letter from W. E. B. Du Bois to Hastings K. Banda, April 28, 1961, and Letter from W. E. B. Du Bois to Hastings K. Banda, June 6, 1962, W. E. B. Du Bois Papers (MS 312). Special Collections and University Archives, University of Massachusetts Amherst Libraries.

[71] Banda and Du Bois might also have met at the First All African People's Congress held in Accra in 1958, had Du Bois not been prevented from attending due to illness. In the event, Shirley Graham, Du Bois's wife, read his address at the opening of the Congress on December 9, 1958. Du Bois' strong appeals to Communist solidarity and his criticisms of European missionaries are unlikely to have gone down well with Banda, who was in the audience (Banda and Kanyama Chiume attended the conference on behalf of Nyasaland). A version of the address is included in Du Bois' posthumously published *Autobiography*: Du Bois 2007:260–262.

leadership,[72] and it was Du Bois who came to typify this tradition in opposition to the industrial education championed by Booker T. Washington. But, although Kamuzu Academy bears little relation to Washington's Tuskegee Institute or to an industrial model of education, it was Washington whom Banda named as an explicit influence on his self-fashioning and thought. This ambivalence in Banda's thought—the pull of both Washington and Du Bois—makes it difficult to reconstruct the influence of Black education movements on the development of Kamuzu Academy.

As a Black African, Banda learned from African American thought, but did not collapse the cultural difference between African and Black American identities. This cultural separation, and the fact that Banda was already a self-determining adult when he enrolled at Wilberforce Academy, might explain why Banda did not adopt any one Black philosophy systematically, instead developing his own syncretic vision for Malawian education. He also avoided being cast as a "race man," to the point of earning contempt from other African leaders for his accommodationist stance towards the apartheid government in South Africa and the Portuguese colonial government in Mozambique. Although race was a contributing factor to the injustice and oppression of Malawi's experience of colonial government, Banda never played this up and repeatedly boasted about his good relations with whites and their respect for him.[73] Nonetheless, he did experience racism in America, and occasionally referred to it in his correspondence.

In a poignant letter to Dr. Grace Caufman, a former classmate at the University of Indiana, written on 3 June 1974, Banda expresses gratitude for the friendship extended by her and two other students—Prescott Nesbit and George Reeves—across the color line:[74]

As I can remember, we last saw each other in 1932, before I went to Meharry Medical College, and you were a medical student at the University of Indiana. That is over forty years ago now.

---

[72] See Goings and O'Connor 2005 and 2010; and Malamud 2016:10–51 on African Americans' fight for the right to have a classical education.

[73] Short 1974:61 quotes a speech that Sam K. K. Mwase delivered at a meeting of the Nyasaland Congress in March 1949, expressing the fear that Federation with Rhodesia would bring the introduction of the pass law to Nyasaland ("The pass law which we consider to be the Roman yoke, will be introduced in Nyasaland and we shall not be a free people on our own soil.") For segregated entrances for Africans in colonial Nyasaland (up until the 1950s) see Mwase 1967:92, with Rotberg n6.

[74] Letter from Hastings Kamuzu Banda to Dr. Grace Caufman, Cincinnati, 3 June 1974. H. K. Banda Archive, Box 1, Folder 2.

As you know, Dr. Caufman, I was the only African on the Campus, a Black boy from Africa, among strangers. True, there were on the Campus American Negroes. But I was an African, a Black African in a (p. 2) University which was predominantly white in composition though with a sprinkling of American Blacks.

As you know, in those days, white and Black did not mix, even in the North or East.

[...] Therefore, it took real courage on your part, Prescott Nesbit and George Reeves to befriend a Black boy, and a Black boy who was not an American citizen at that. For this reason, I will never forget you, Prescott Nesbit and George Reeves.

In his unpublished *Autobiography*, Banda recounts the pain and humiliation of being shunned in the dining hall and cafeteria at Indiana University, with students and faculty vacating tables when he joined them or else studiously ignoring him. But in the *Autobiography*, Banda also writes about the friendship and mentorship extended to him by the African American physician Dr. Walter Bailey and his own awkwardness as it dawned on him that his status as an African meant that he was exempted from some of the racism that Dr. Bailey encountered. In particular, when Dr. Bailey recounted tales of the racial abuse that local industrialists meted out to their African American employees, Banda learned not to mention that these same men were friendly towards him and helping to fund his education at the University of Indiana. Banda also apparently encountered the lethal race terror of Jim Crow in the form of a lynching in Tennessee.[75]

In spite of his experience of racism in America, Banda emphasized Pan-African anti-colonial resistance, rather than Black pride.[76] As a result, the focus on racial uplift in Du Bois's philosophy of education made these writings less assimilable for Banda, and by the time Banda had achieved power and was in a position to enact educational policies, Du Bois's vocal support for Communism presumably also made Banda less likely to invoke him. While propounding an unapologetically elitist model of education, Du Bois never lost sight of race

[75] Short 1974:25; Munger 1983:251. This incident may have been the lynching of seventeen-year-old Cordie Cheek of Maury County, TN in December 1933. See Russell 2010:171–172: having been released from prison after an allegation of rape was disproved, Cordie Cheek was abducted from Nashville, where he had gone to stay with an aunt near the campus of Fisk University, and brutally murdered by a lynch mob. Fisk University is located in Nashville, where Banda was studying at Meharry Medical College. I have not found any reference to this atrocity in Banda's own words.

[76] See Forster 1994:484 on Banda's ambivalence towards the socialist tenor of Pan-Africanism.

as a factor in determining the historic destiny of African Americans.[77] On the contrary, the racial factor was a key, extrinsic impetus for the quest for an elite education, in order to prove that African Americans were the equal of white Americans and could complete the most exacting curricula with distinction and, crucially, author their own distinguished, original works. There were other important factors too, not least the intrinsic value placed on fields of study that would equip African Americans for the leadership of the race, but race was omnipresent. As Du Bois wrote in an essay on "The Negro College," published in *The Crisis* in August 1933, "there can be no college for Negroes which is not a Negro College ... while ... many rightly aspire to a universal culture unhampered by limitations of race and culture, yet it must start on the earth where we sit and not in the skies where we aspire."[78] By contrast, Banda avoided any mention of race in the context of the Academy and, whereas Du Bois and other African American intellectuals had stressed the importance of teachers and role models from the African American community, Banda established policies that discriminated against Malawian and African teachers. In fact, Banda used Classics as a proxy for discriminating against Malawian and other African teachers, requiring that, whatever the subject of instruction, teachers should themselves have completed a classical education to a certain standard. When former students of Kamuzu Academy met this standard, the goalposts were shifted, adding the stipulation that teachers should be familiar with teaching in the British system.[79]

Nonetheless, Banda's passionate insistence on the centrality of Latin and Greek to the curriculum at Kamuzu Academy owes much to Du Bois, as does the aristocratic conception of this Academy that could only educate a tiny fraction of Malawi's students. In a speech that Du Bois delivered to the graduating class of Fisk University, his alma mater, in June 1898, Du Bois distinguished between the professional class of graduates—educated for skilled professions and to lead the Negro race—and the graduates of the "normal" schools who would fill vital but less skilled occupations. He then proceeded to summarize the skilled occupations (managerial, mercantile, professional, artistic, and academic) appropriate for Black "college men."[80]

In the famous essay "The Talented Tenth" (1903), Du Bois was even more explicit and completely unapologetic in formulating an elitist doctrine of Black education, arguing that the quickest route to uplift and improvement for

---

[77] See Dawson 2001:254 on racial pride in Du Bois's model of Black liberalism.
[78] Du Bois 1986:1010.
[79] See Lwanda 1993:182; and Alexander 1991:82.
[80] Du Bois 1986:833–834.

the race was via the "aristocracy of talent and character" represented by its "Talented Tenth":[81]

> All men cannot go to college but some men must; every isolated group
> or nation must have its yeast, must have for the talented few centers of
> training where men are not so mystified and befuddled by the hard and
> necessary toil of earning a living, as to have no aims higher than their
> bellies, and no God greater than Gold.

For Du Bois, this pyramidal educational scheme makes sociological and economic sense through an educational relay in which the educated elite instruct the rest of the race in the knowledge that they need to lead productive lives. As Michael Tratner puts it, "property or wealth is, in this sequence, the end-result of culture."[82] Du Bois wrote:[83]

> The college trained in Greek and Latin and mathematics, 2,000 men;
> and these men trained full 5,000 others in morals and manners, and
> they in turn taught thrift and alphabet to nine millions of men, who
> to-day hold $300,000,000 of property.

This utopian scheme is reminiscent of Plato's Kallipolis, but Du Bois' worldly economic calculations bring us closer to Banda's dream, since Banda was aiming to establish an actual school and had an existing *politeia* rather than a theoretical one.

Booker T. Washington

For the fulfilment of his educational dream, Banda was evidently inspired by Booker T. Washington's example and his famous Tuskegee Institute. Commentators have been quick to dismiss any connection because the Academy was clearly not founded on Washington's model of industrial education, but this is to miss deeper affinities. For all that Banda espoused a classical education reminiscent of Du Bois's philosophy of Negro education, he was not an intellectual and identified much more closely with Booker T. Washington's example as a charismatic leader and the founder of the Tuskegee Institute.[84]

The extent to which Banda was inspired by Washington is revealed in Banda's unpublished *Autobiography*. In a passage in which he reflects on his decision to

---

[81] Du Bois 1903b:46.
[82] Tratner 2001:188–189.
[83] Du Bois 1903b:47.
[84] It is presumably a coincidence that Kamuzu Academy was opened in the 100th anniversary year of the Tuskegee Institute, which opened on 4 July 1881.

study in America, Banda mentions the South African Charlotte Manye,[85] who was sponsored through Wilberforce University by Bishop Payne of the A. M. E. Church, as a major influence and source of inspiration for him, "in no way smaller than the story of Booker T. Washington": "The story of Charlotte Manye has always fascinated me. It has had influence on my life, in no way smaller than the story of Booker T. Washington or of Dr. Aggrey, himself."[86]

Even more interesting than Banda's overt reference to the influence of Booker T. Washington on his life is the pervasive, generic influence of Washington's *Up from Slavery* (1901) on Banda's *Autobiography*. In a seminal typological study of African American narrative, first published in 1979, Robert Burns Stepto identified the quest for freedom and literacy as "the pre-generic myth" for Afro-American culture and literature and analyzed how these twinned goals influenced the structure of slave narratives and their influence on subsequent Afro-American literature. In his study of different phases of narrative, Stepto demonstrated how slave narratives make use of authenticating documents to establish their veracity and authority, and then struggle to integrate these documents within the narrative structure (the "integrated narrative") and subsume them under their own authorial control (the "generic narrative"). Stepto has suggested that Booker T. Washington's *Up from Slavery* is an example of an authenticating narrative, where the authorial narrator has integrated and subsumed the testimony of others, and the slave narrative is itself used to authenticate a cultural myth. According to Stepto's interpretation, in Washington's case this myth was the Tuskegee Institute and Washington's philosophy of industrial education.

Banda's *Autobiography* was unfinished in the sense that Banda never completed the task of editing it for publication. The typescript contained in the Banda archives contains copious post-it notes added by Donald Brody, Banda's official biographer, in an attempt to establish a coherent narrative sequence for the different sections of the *Autobiography* (see n44 above). As a result, it is impossible to offer a thorough analysis of the structure of the narrative. Nonetheless, there are two key episodes where Washington's *Up from Slavery* is an obvious intertext, and these episodes alert the reader to its pervasive, generic influence on Banda's narrative.

---

[85]   Charlotte Mannya, later Charlotte Maxeke (1874–1931); Manye is Banda's spelling.
[86]   H. K. Banda Archive, Box 2, Folder 17, p. 84 of the typescript. For James Emman Kwegyir Aggrey (1875–1927) and his knowledge of Classics, see Goff 2013:135–138. Short 1974:18 and Munger 1983:249–250 describe the impression that Aggrey made on Banda when he lectured in South Africa in 1921.

Reflecting on his self-fashioning as a young man, Banda addresses the question of his chosen name, Hastings Kamuzu Banda:[87]

> To return to the name Hastings. No, it was not given to me by any missionary or anyone else. Not at all. It was given to me by me. I took fancy to the name. The hissing sound in it sounded particularly nice and pleasant to my ears. And so, I gave it me. I was in Johannesburg when I gave myself the name Hastings. It was long after my bush school days at Kasungu.

This act of self-naming, with its strong first-person enunciation, recalls the famous passage in *Up from Slavery* where Washington describes how he improvised his name in a schoolhouse in the Kanawha Valley in West Virginia:[88]

> When I heard the school-roll called, I noticed that all of the children had at least two names, and some of them indulged in what seemed to me the extravagance of having three. I was in deep perplexity, because I knew that the teacher would demand of me at least two names, and I had only one. By the time the occasion came for the enrolling of my name, an idea occurred to me which I thought would make me equal to the situation; and so, when the teacher asked me what my full name was, I calmly told him, "Booker Washington," as if I had been called by that name all my life; and by that name I have since been known. Later in my life I found that my mother had given me the name of "Booker Taliaferro" soon after I was born, but in some way that part of my name seemed to disappear ... but as soon as I found out about it I revived it, and made my full name "Booker Taliaferro Washington."

In Washington's autobiographical narrative, the scene of self-naming is both compensatory and self-affirming. The boy who lacks the right attire for school and whose mother improvises him a homespun hat, improvises a name when his single name falls short of convention—and as a providential sign of his ingenuity, he chooses a suitably historical name.[89] In Banda's case, the overwhelming emphasis is on self-sufficiency and self-determination, and the scene of self-naming becomes an act of autogenesis: "It was given to me by me. ... I took fancy ... I gave it me. ... I ... I gave myself." There is also a clear sense of upwards ascent, as Banda refers disparagingly to "my bush school days at

---

[87] H. K. Banda Archive, Box 2, Folder 14, p. 45 of the typescript.
[88] Washington 2010:22–23, 24.
[89] See Olney 1989:12–14 on the different devices that Washington used to link his life to that of the founding fathers.

Kasungu." Although ascent is no less important a theme and structuring device in Washington's narrative, Washington repeatedly takes his bearings from his humble beginnings.

The next section of Banda's *Autobiography* that bears traces of *Up from Slavery* is more elaborate and reveals the way in which this intertext mediates a larger tradition of African American literature in his narrative. The first two sentences of *Up from Slavery* are formulaic[90] within the tradition of slave autobiographies:[91]

> I was born a slave on a plantation in Franklin County, Virginia. I am not quite sure of the exact place or exact date of my birth, but at any rate I suspect I must have been born somewhere and at some time. As nearly as I have been able to learn, I was born near a cross-roads post-office called Hale's Ford, and the year was 1858 or 1859.

In particular, Washington evokes the beginning of Frederick Douglass's *Narrative*, claiming Douglass as exceptional ancestor and setting himself up as Douglass's successor.[92] It is this tradition, modelled by Washington, that Banda adapts for his own *Autobiography*. Unlike Washington and Douglass, Banda has a very clear sense of ancestry and the history of the Chewa people. Large sections of his *Autobiography* are dedicated to tales of his family, including his parents' court-ship and his birth. But although Banda had the benefit of a rich genealogical tradition, it was an oral one, so, in order to inscribe his account within a literary tradition, he borrowed that of African American literature[93] as his own kind of authenticating strategy:[94]

---

[90] As with the majority of extant slave autobiographies, *Up from Slavery* begins with Washington's birth in slavery. See Olney 1984 on repeated formulae in slave autobiographies.

[91] Washington 2010:1. See Onley 1989:11–12 on the "found felicity" of name of the county in which Washington was born and his artful decision to have the speaking name "Franklin" in the first sentence of his *Autobiography*.

[92] Douglass 2017:40–41: "I was born in Tuckahoe, near Hillsborough, and about twelve miles from Easton, in Talbot county, Maryland. I have no accurate knowledge of my age, never having seen any authentic record containing it. [...] The nearest estimate I can give makes me now between twenty-seven and twenty-eight years of age [...]." See Olney 1989 on Douglass as founding father for Washington.

[93] At the time at which Banda wrote his *Autobiography* (1959–1960), there was very little published Malawian literature. Banda had co-edited and translated a collection of essays by Malawian writers with the Rev. Thomas Cullen Young (Banda and Cullen Young 1946), but George Simeon Mwase's account of the Chilembwe uprising had yet to be published (it was published posthumously in 1967—see p. 122 above), and Aubrey Kachingwe's *No Easy Task*—the first novel by a Malawian novelist to be published—would not appear until 1965. See Currey 2008:258–9.

[94] H. K. Banda Archive, Box 2, folder 14, quoting from pp. 67–68 of the typescript. This section occurs within "Book V," but it is not clear if this is Banda's book division or Donald Brody's.

No one knows the hour, the date, the month and the year in which I was born. When I was born the Chewa, as all the Bantus in Central Africa, knew months in terms of moons. They also knew the year in terms of seasons, so many of which constituted *chaka*, a year. But of hours, days of the week, the week itself, and dates of the month, they knew nothing. In this respect, they were much more behind their cousins, the Akan of Ghana, ...

I do not know what I am, Kwame, Kojo, Kewku, Kwesi or Kofi.

But from the anonymity or obscurity of the date of my birth, I suffer a sense of neither humiliation nor disgrace. I am insulated from the shock of humiliation and disgrace by the knowledge that, in this respect, I am not alone. Many men, whose names have passed into history, never knew the hour, the date, the month and the year they were born. Some of the emperors in ancient Rome never knew the date they were born. In modern times, Booker Tariafaro Washington, founder of Tuskegee, did not. I am content to know that I exist. Since no one can deny my existence, certainly, not Sir Robert Armitage, Sir Roy Welensky, Sir Edgar Whitehead, and Mr. Lennox-Boyd. I, as Booker T. Washington, must have been born at some hour, on some date, in some [p. 68] month and in some year. For it was not a phantom, on whose arrest and detention these men, among others, consulted and took counsel among themselves. It was not a phantom that was hustled out of bed, in pyjamas, in the early hours of the morning, and bundled into H. M. Prison, Gwelo, on March 3, 1959. It was a living reality of human flesh and blood, in which, men in position of absolute power over the Africans, saw an obstacle, an alarming threat of danger to their continued enjoyment of power, and which, in their view, had to be removed, and removed at once, by means fair or foul.

Banda mentions Booker T. Washington not once but twice, as though to under-score the connection. This is canny literary citation as sociality ("I am not alone"). In the same way that slave autobiographies used authenticating documents and witnesses to establish the veracity of their accounts and to launch the narratives that would establish their existential claim as a being worthy of freedom, Banda uses the comparison with Washington for existential affirmation: "I, as Booker T. Washington, must have been born at some hour [...] ." What follows next is even more curious: "For it was not a phantom, on whose arrest and detention these men, among others, consulted and took counsel among themselves. It was not a phantom [...]." The tone is hard to gauge (humorous, sardonic, mocking, vaunting?), but the repetition of the phrase "it was not a phantom" is reminiscent of the Prologue to Ralph Ellison's *Invisible Man* (1952), in which the Black narrator-protagonist, Invisible, turns the laugh on the theme of racial invisibility by narrating an incident in which he beats up a white man with whom he had got into an altercation after accidentally bumping into him in the street, laughing that the man had not seen him through the veil of race: "He lay there, moaning on the asphalt; a man almost killed by a phantom."[95] Banda's roll-call of the colonial politicians whom he had stood up to (Sir Robert Armitage, Sir Roy Welensky, Sir Edgar Whitehead, and Mr. Lennox-Boyd) in negotiations over Nyasaland's political destiny recalls the agonistic squaring up of Ellison's Prologue; Banda's confrontations with these politicians were also across the color line.

There is very little metareflective commentary on the composition of the *Autobiography* in the typescript, but one such passage offers a brief insight into Banda's access to books while in prison and his affinity for biography. Recounting his journey to Johannesburg as a teenager, Banda quotes Thomas Jefferson's reflections on his own self-making:[96]

> And, in the words of Thomas Jefferson, I am tempted to say: When I recollect that at fourteen years of age, the whole care and direction of myself was thrown on myself entirely, without a relation or friend to guide me, and recollect the various sorts of bad company with which I associated from time to time, I am astonished I did not turn off with some of them, and become as worthless to society as they were.

Banda provides a citation in a footnote, indicating that the quotation comes from "Gilbert Chinard, Thomas Jefferson, p. 6," referring to Chinard's biography *Thomas Jefferson, the Apostle of Americanism* (1929). Later in the typescript, Banda refers back to this passage, revealing that American supporters had sent him Chinard's biography during his imprisonment:[97]

> I never allowed myself to be caught to the detriment of my goal and of my scheme in life. That was why I was so deeply impressed by the observations that Thomas Jefferson made, which I have quoted earlier on, when I read his biography here in Gwelo, where these lines are being written, sent by my American well-wishers and sympathizers.

---

[95] Ellison 1995:4–5.
[96] H. K. Banda Archive, Box 2, Folder 17; a note on this page identifies it as "3rd cord (p. 1)."
[97] H. K. Banda Archive, Box 2, folder 17, p. 69 [labelled as Bk 6, pages 177–217].

Once in power, as part of his didactic persona, Banda made a point of telling audiences how well-read he was and that he had an extensive library. At a lecture that Banda delivered at Bunda College of Agriculture on 29 March 1969, he told his audience, "If any of you went to my house now, either in Zomba or Blantyre, you would find hundreds upon hundreds of books, nothing to do with medicine. True, I have medical books but at the same time I have other kinds too."[98] In spite of Banda's self-presentation as a great reader, there are very few references to specific works in his papers. Ultimately, in the absence of more concrete evidence, it is not possible to prove that Banda was alluding to Ellison's novel with his joking existential proof "I am not a phantom," but the similarity—in a passage in which Banda cites Booker T. Washington—raises interesting questions about Banda as reader of more experimental African American literature.[99]

Washington is sometimes misrepresented as an opponent of classical education *tout court*, not least by W. E. B. Du Bois.[100] Instead, Washington's contention was rather that knowledge of Greek and Latin was being fetishized as a passport to a social and economic advancement that it could not possibly deliver for the majority of African Americans. However, Washington's framing of a model of industrial, vocational education in opposition to a more scholastic education did restrict opportunities for African Americans to obtain a liberal education. In expounding the case for an industrial education, Washington interweaves sardonic vignettes illustrating the valorization of learning Greek and Latin at the expense of a practical education:

> During the whole of the Reconstruction period two ideas were constantly agitating the minds of the coloured people, or, at least, the minds of a large part of the race. One of these was the craze for Greek and Latin learning, and the other was a desire to hold office. [...] The ambition to secure an education was most praiseworthy and encouraging. The idea, however, was too prevalent that, as soon as one secured a little education, in some unexplainable way he would be free from most of the hardships of the world, and, at any rate, could live without manual labour. There was a further feeling that a knowledge, however

[98] A lecture given by his Excellency the Life President, Ngwazi Dr. H. Kamuzu Banda, at Bunda college of Agriculture on 29 March 1969. H. K. Banda Archive, Box 2, Folder 2, p. 2 of the typescript. This lecture is also cited on p. 139 above.

[99] Booker T. Washington's model of education is a target of satire in the early chapters of *Invisible Man*; Ellison had attended the Tuskegee Institute from 1933–1936.

[100] Du Bois's strongest criticism of Washington was contained in the third chapter of *The Souls of Black Folk*, "Of Mr. Booker T. Washington and Others" (Du Bois 1903a:41–59).

little, of the Greek and Latin languages, would make one a very superior human being, something bordering almost on the supernatural.[101]

At Hampton the student was constantly making the effort through the industries to help himself, and that very effort was of immense value in character-building. The students at the other school seemed to be less self-dependent. They seemed to give more attention to mere outward appearances. In a word, they did not appear to me to be beginning at the bottom, on a real, solid foundation, to the extent that they were at Hampton. They knew more about Latin and Greek when they left school, but they seemed to know less about life and its conditions as they would meet it in their homes.[102]

It was also interesting to note how many big books some of them had studied, and how many high-sounding subjects some of them claimed to have mastered. The bigger the book and the longer the name of the subject, the prouder they felt of their accomplishment. Some had studied Latin, and one or two Greek. This they thought entitled them to special distinction.[103]

In fact, one of the saddest things I saw during the month of travel which I have described was a young man, who had attended some high school, sitting down in a one-room cabin, with grease on his clothing, filth all around him, and weeds in the yard and garden, engaged in studying a French grammar.[104]

[O]ne man may go into a community prepared to supply the people there with an analysis of Greek sentences. The community may not at that time be prepared for, or feel the need of, Greek analysis, but it may feel its need of bricks and houses and wagons.[105]

Washington's commonsensical critique of a classical curriculum was overshadowed by accusations of accommodationism and for appearing, under the guise of a romantic vision of self-help, to be encouraging African Americans to be

---

[101] Washington 2010:56.

[102] Washington 2010:61. Here Washington contrasts the practical education that he received at the Hampton Normal and Agricultural Institute in Virginia with the education he received at the more academically elite Wayland Theological Seminary in Washington, DC.

[103] Washington is commenting on public school teachers who entered Tuskegee when it opened so that they could gain a formal qualification.

[104] Washington 2010:84–85. To this, Du Bois retorted, "One wonders what Socrates and St. Francis of Assisi would say to this" (Du Bois 1903a:43).

[105] Washington 2010:108.

content with their place in society, as articulated in the Atlanta Exposition Address of September 1895: "No race can prosper till it learns that there is as much dignity in tilling a field as in writing a poem. It is at the bottom of life that we must begin, not at the top."[106] As William Andrews has pointed out, Washington's anti-intellectual and anti-literary stance dissembles the extent to which he himself was a man of words and a man made by words. In Andrews's interpretation, Washington's pragmatism and "Tuskegee realism" were themselves a literary effect, with *Up from Slavery* as a manifesto of realism, where realism is, itself, an authenticating strategy aimed at shoring up Washington's plausibility and the veracity of his mission.

Up from Slavery is both the biography of a man and an institution, and the reputation of both the man and the institution are mutually implicated. The character of Washington's life lends authority to the ethos and mission of the Tuskegee Institute (not to mention his fundraising efforts for Tuskegee),[107] and in turn the Institute gives purpose and kudos to Washington.[108] There are parallels here for the way in which Banda seems to have viewed Kamuzu Academy as his supreme work. Banda never addresses Washington's wariness of a classical education, and it is perhaps telling that, in forging an explicit comparison between Kamuzu Academy and Wilberforce Academy, he chose an HBCU feeder school that was well known for providing an education in which Classics was central to the curriculum. But something of Washington's commitment to a practical education comes across in Banda's rhetoric. In Banda's thought, there was an enduring contradiction between his sincere, lived commitment to a Western education and his consciousness, by virtue of the African education of his upbringing, that this education was by no means universal. This might explain why, even in those passages and moments where Banda professes the supremacy of Western education, there is a lingering suggestion of colonial mimicry, of advantageous role-playing. We see Banda wrestling with this dichotomy in the *Autobiography* (my emphasis):[109]

---

[106] Washington 2010:153. See Dawson 2001:283–287 on "The Legacy of Booker T. Washington."

[107] See Norrell's Afterword in Washington 2010:232: "*Up from Slavery* functioned as a fund-raising tool for Tuskegee Institute, a book-length grant proposal to anyone with philanthropic instincts and ability to help black education."

[108] See Stepto 1991:35.

[109] H. K. Banda Archive, Box 2, Folder 15, quoting from pp. 137–138 of the typescript. [An editorial note identifies this section of the typescript as belonging to "Book 10."] Banda offered a rather different presentation of his dual educational inheritance when delivering a Chubb lecture on "Nyasaland's Struggle for Freedom and Independence" at Yale University on April 17, 1961. On that occasion he described himself as "belong[ing] to the West" by birth: "But as everyone knows, by birth, religious and educational upbringing, political status, I belong to the West. I was born in Nyasaland, educated in a mission school, accepted Christianity for my religion, and all this in a country which was still is under British protection. As a boy I spent years in

Of me, it may be said with truth, that I have had two kinds of education, the African kind and the European or Western kind. The African kind, the Chewa one, to be specific, was, essentially, a practical kind of education, as befitted a child of the soil and country side. I was born in it. From it, there was no escape for me. It was no effort for me to acquire my Chewa kind of education.

(p. 138) It was different with the European or Western kind of my education. I was not born in it. It was an effort to acquire it. And it was all by accident that I came by it or that I acquired it. There was no plan or design in or about my acquiring the European or Western kind of my education. Neither my parents nor my grandparents knew anything about education in the European or Western sense. If I am the educated man I am supposed to be now, it is purely an accident that I am. I merely stumbled on or into European kind of education. It was not to learn or acquire knowledge that I first went to school. *It was to dance the European dance or to play the European game.* To the people at Kasungu, in my childhood, *school was considered or taken to be European dance or European game or sport.*

This striking language is repeated in a later section of the *Autobiography*, where the incantatory repetition underscores how widespread and deeply held this skeptical, amused attitude to European education was (my emphasis):[110]

It was *to dance European dance or to play European game* that I first went to the bush school at Mtunthama. No higher purpose than *to dance a European dance or to play European game* propelled me to the bush school at Chinyama's village in Mtunthama area.

The school ceased to be a place where *to dance a European dance or a place where to play a European game.* And teaching ceased to be *a European dance or a European game.* It became a career, a vocation or a calling. I developed a strong ambition to become a teacher, a great teacher, a great Christian teacher, as Lameck Manda was.

---

this country, as a student, where political, social and economic ideas of the West, apart from the physical and biological sciences were hammered into whatever brain I possessed, during my student days, both in the High School and in the Universities. And all through my life I have moved in the orbit of the Western World." H. K. Banda Archive, Box 2, Folder 1, quoting from p. 32 of the typescript of the speech.

[110] H. K. Banda Archive, Box 2, Folder 16, quoting from p. 204 of the typescript.

By the end of this passage, Banda has apparently resolved the tension between skeptical mimicry of European letters and earnest vocation, but the language of mimicry recurs in (of all places) his Inaugural Founder's Address at Kamuzu Academy in November 1981. In a passage quoted on p. 134 above, as Banda approaches the peroration of his speech, he introduces the Latin quotation from the beginning of Caesar's *De Bello Gallico* with the curious phrase "prance and prank": "In short, then, the Academy is being established to teach the Classics at a Grammar School level. A boy or girl leaving the Academy must be able to prance and prank and say [...]," as though an instrumentalist attitude to the performative benefits of a classical education takes over. When considering the influence of America's HBCUs on Kamuzu Academy, it is important to underscore the point made above about Banda's shifting (re)presentation of his education at Wilberforce Academy. In other rhetorical contexts (i.e. not Founder's Day addresses at Kamuzu Academy), he chose to emphasize the importance of the agricultural education that he received at Wilberforce and it is perhaps in this respect that he is an heir to Washington.[111]

Conclusion

The harshest criticisms of Kamuzu Academy under Banda were directed not at its curriculum, but at its funding. Banda and his inner circle were always adamant that Kamuzu Academy was his private gift to the nation, ensuring that future generations of Malawian youth had the opportunity to attain a world-class education without having to travel overseas, as he had done.[112] As his personal gift, the logic went, he was free to prescribe the curriculum, design, and ethos of the school. But it was not his personal gift by any objective budgetary reckoning, and it is in the financing of the Academy that Banda's dream diverged wildly and exponentially both from Du Bois's model of the Talented Tenth and from Washington's Tuskegee Institute, which was financed by Washington's unremitting fundraising.

The construction of the Academy cost roughly sixteen million Kwacha and was funded by Press Holdings, a parastatal company in which Banda owned 99.98% of the shares. Basing his calculations on DevPol II figures and World Bank

---

[111] See Pryor 1990:62, 66n20 on Banda recounting how he was taught to plough at Wilberforce Academy.

[112] The programme for the official opening of Kamuzu Academy contained the following wording, "The Academy is a personal gift of HIS EXCELLENCY to the people. "Only by undertaking the full cost of the school will I be able to ensure that the buildings are of the highest standard," he said. And the Academy we see today is the result." H. K. Banda Archive, Box 7, Folder 12: Programme of the official opening of Kamuzu Academy by His Excellency the Life President Ngwazi Dr. H. Kamuzu Banda at Mtunthama in Kasungu District on Saturday, 21 November 1981.

figures,[113] John Lwanda offers the following analysis of how the Academy was funded:[114]

> The building of the 16 million pound [*sic* kwacha] Academy had been started in 1978 and was due to be completed in 1981. By then Dr Banda's Press Holdings which was supposed to fund it was in dire financial straits and owed K54 million to the two Malawi Commercial banks and K54 million to ADMARC. The financing of the Academy was therefore informally passed on to the Ministry of Education and school fees were raised in 1982 by 50% for grades 1–5 and 25% for grades 6–8. After the financial restructuring, Press still owed K40 million to ADMARC and was still in no position to the finance the Academy. It was at this stage in 1984 that the financial running of the Academy was formally retained by the Ministry of Education. [...] The total education development budget for 1977 to 1980 was 17,497,000 Kwacha. This should be contrasted with the 16,000,000 used to build the Academy.

Once the Academy was constructed, its annual operational costs allegedly constituted roughly 40% of the entire annual budget for the Ministry of Education.[115] The appropriation of roughly 40% of Malawi's annual educational budget, to fund this one school, which could only cater to 360 students, effectively rendered it an Academy for the Talented 0.03%.[116] Du Bois's fraction was

[113] *Statement of Development Policies, 1987–1996 (DevPol II)* was a publication released by the Government of Malawi in 1988 summarizing the economic philosophy that would guide policymaking in the ensuing decade, with supporting data.

[114] Lwanda 1993:178–179. Phillips 1998:219–221 offers an insight into this fiscal restructuring, undertaken in collaboration with the World Bank and the IMF. In the 1980s Henry Phillips served as an employee of Standard Bank, which had a 20% shareholding and a management agreement with the National Bank: "Solving the problem of the principal parastatal Press Holdings, in which Banda had a vested interest, was not so easy. Although it was in receipt of substantial income from the marketing operations of its subsidiaries, it had run up a massive debt and was insolvent. ... Restructuring was achieved, with the help of the World Bank, by transferring its shares into a trust for the benefit of the people of Malawi. Its indebtedness was taken over by the government and converted into a long-term loan. To compensate Banda for the loss of the substantial income from his shareholding (he had been the founder member of the original Press Corporation, which had taken over his farms), the trust was to pay him an annual income of a million Kwacha" (Phillips 1998:221).

[115] See Lwanda 1993:178 with n84, citing an "unattributable source." Lwanda describes this figure as "an open secret both in Malawi educational and financial circles."

[116] The figure of 0.03% is arrived at by expressing the number of students who attended Kamuzu Academy in a given year (1987–1988) as a percentage of the total number of children who were in primary school in Malawi at the time, according to government statistics (1,202,836 pupils). However, since this figure only represents 47% of the total number of pupils of primary school age in Malawi at the time (2,884,498 pupils), the real figure should be the "The Talented 0.01%." Statistics taken from Lwanda 1993:177.

also criticized, with David Levering Lewis quipping, "A far more accurate characterization would have been the Talented Hundredth."[117] In the case of Malawi, the devastating reality was that, "by the end of Banda's rule [i.e. by 1993] only 3.4% of the pupils finishing primary school could proceed to secondary school, and of those finishing secondary school, only about 20% (or 1% of age group) proceeded to Higher Education."[118] A further irony of the analogy between the Du Boisian ideal of The Talented Tenth and Banda's Academy is that Banda's autocratic style of government and his removal of any political opposition meant that a large proportion of the Malawian intelligentsia and professional classes went into exile, and, thus, one could speak of Banda's policies contributing to "The Removal of the Talented Tenth."[119]

Banda was not the sole author or framer of the Academy; but for the most part, the deliberations about the Academy and how exactly Banda's close associates had a hand in shaping the school are shrouded in obscurity. Henry Phillips records that Banda had sent some of his ministers on a fact-finding mission to study the phenomenon of the British boarding school: "To achieve the kind of institution he had in mind, he sent a few of his inner circle, including John Tembo, to England and Scotland to discover how public boarding schools functioned."[120] When Banda's associates articulated his vision of the school, they emphasized its role in training Malawian professionals. The fact that Banda never published an account of his vision for the Academy and its educational mission means that it will always be open to conflicting interpretations, but the ways in which he adapted the tradition of Classics in African American thought are an important part of the story.

---

[117] Lewis 1993:290.

[118] Lwanda 1993:178.

[119] Lwanda 1993:180 reports, "it has been estimated that there were about 5,000 economically and politically 'useful' exiles in the late seventies. By the end of 1992 this figure was nearer 8,000." See also Mapanje 2002:186.

[120] Phillips 1998: 219.

4

A Mini-SWOT Analysis of the Classics Program, Chancellor College

Steve Nyamilandu

THIS CHAPTER BORROWS FROM the business world the concept of the SWOT (Strengths, Weaknesses, Opportunities, and Threats) analysis in an attempt to highlight the historical opportunities, limitations, and challenges that the Classics Department at Chancellor College has encountered.

Strengths

This section details the Department's positive attributes, as well as how others perceive it.

- Since inception, the Department has enjoyed a dedicated staff. Beginning with pioneer Dr. Caroline Alexander and, despite the fact that the Department has been understaffed, all of those who have taught after her have done so with dedication.

- Our students come from secondary schools all over Malawi. Because students from a variety of backgrounds are studying Classics for the first time, we do not recruit entirely from secondary schools or seminaries that teach either Classics broadly, or Latin only, as is the case with some Catholic seminaries.

- As a department, we encourage one another to give additional assistance to students in the form of tutorials and extra classes, focusing especially on struggling students. We realize that the bulk of our students have their first acquaintance with Classics at the university level and that, therefore, they necessitate more attention.

- Although we have relatively few Classics graduates on the job market, the few that there are speak highly of the Department to the external community.

Weaknesses

Let us now explore our areas for growth, as well as how others view the Department.

- Unlike students in other departments, most of the students who join the Department are discovering Classics for the first time.

- Historically, the Department has had very limited resources for staff development—although there has recently been some improvement, as the administration now endeavors to send staff for further training. Due to budgetary restrictions, the preferred countries are those within the African region, particularly South African universities. Delays may occur between a staff member seeking the opportunity for postgraduate study and the ability to enroll in the chosen program: this was the case with Dr. Thokozani Kunkeyani and, more recently, with Mrs. Esela Munthali.

- The Department's staff retention is poor. We have lost the few Malawian-trained staff for a variety of reasons. The first Malawian Staff Associate, Mr. Eric Ning'ang'a, could not stay long after returning from studying in Germany: he went into the mainstream civil service—and was appointed in January 2020 as Deputy Director (tax audit and investigations) at the Malawi Revenue Authority. Mrs. Eltrudis Katemba stayed in the UK after completing her MA studies at Durham University with her husband, whose career is in the British Army. A few years ago, we lost Dr. Thoko Kunkeyani, who took an early retirement to join the Department of Education at the Malawi Adventist University. Toward the end of November 2019, Mrs. Esela Munthali resigned. Thus, staff turnover has been a large problem.

- Unlike other departments, which run extra income-generating programs and deposit these funds into their departmental accounts, the Classics Department does not have its own account to run its own academic business. Instead, we heavily rely on the single main College account, which is often constrained.

- For some years, and due to understaffing, the Department has experienced high staff workloads. To circumvent this problem, the authorities allow us to hire part-time demonstrators who have not yet obtained their postgraduate degrees.

- We have failed to adequately market our courses to communities outside the University of Malawi, especially secondary schools.

Opportunities

I now turn to places for growth and how the Classics Department can capitalize on these.

- Owing to general population growth and the increase of secondary schools in Malawi, there is huge demand for the limited number of available slots at tertiary institutions—to such an extent that many who qualify for the University are still not selected. At the time of writing this (in 2021), we have been informed that the number of admitted BA Humanities students will double. Therefore, there is a high prospect of enrolling many students within the generic BA degree, and we believe that Classics will have its share.

- Although a reasonable number of Malawian students are interested in Classics during their first and second years, we do not have many majors. This is likely because most of our students are drawn from the Education cohort, and they are not allowed to take Classics courses beyond their second year in college. We still have cases of Education students who plead to take our courses beyond Year Two, and, as a Department, Classics does not have a problem allowing such students to continue, but it is the Education Faculty, and its rigid course map, that does not accommodate them. Understandably, the Education Faculty (School of Education) adheres to the Malawi Ministry of Education policy to train would-be teachers only in courses that are reflected in the secondary school curriculum. In 2018, the Junior Certificate of Education (JCE) was temporarily removed as part of the national examination, but it was reinstated after a general outcry. We hope the seminaries, which have in the past offered Latin up to JCE level, will continue to have students sit for JCE Latin exams.

- We can use technological advances to increase our registration numbers. As the College gradually improves its bandwidth, we shall reap the gains. Nowadays, students have access to Google Classroom, where lecturers can set up assignments and readings, but this system has problems: first, Wi-Fi bandwidth (Google Classroom runs slowly, if at all, on the network); and the students are inexperienced, particularly those in Year One and from rural secondary schools, with computers.

Threats

This section details some of the threats to the Department, including from competitor institutions and internal restructuring.

Ever since the advent of democracy in Malawi in 1994, we have seen the rise of private universities, many of which we are now in serious competition with. The competition is twofold: we are competing against numerous university programs, but competing for the attention of the same pool of secondary school leavers. These new universities have programs that respond to current challenges such as climate change, gender issues, human resource in the industries and many more. Although this may not appear to be a threat to the Classics Department, because these universities do not have Classics programs that compete with ours, it may mean we are not a big threat to them on the job market. In the past, there was only the University of Malawi with its five constituent colleges: Bunda College of Agriculture (now LUANAR, the Lilongwe University of Agriculture and Natural Resources), Kamuzu College of Nursing, Polytechnic, Chancellor College, and the College of Medicine. However, now Malawi has recently-founded universities such as the University of Mzuzu, Livingstonia University, Catholic University, Daughters of Mary Immaculate (DMI) University in Mangochi, Blantyre International University, Skyway University, Adventist University, and the Malawi University of Science and Technology—to name only a few.

Our public perception is not particularly appealing. First, it was tainted by its association with the autocrat Dr. Hastings Banda, the first President of Malawi, and some, thus, still see the Department as a relic institution. However, the good news is that most of our current students were either born after Dr. Banda or were too young to witness his rule, as Dr. Banda died in 1997. To that end, Knight rightly observed:[1]

> At Chancellor College, Classics as an institution remains secure for the moment, despite the popular association with Banda's dictatorship and notwithstanding the temptation of government to curtail university spending. The imperative of democratic transparency prevents such political meddling.

Second, however, many of the parents and guardians of new recruits are not familiar with Classics and so cannot advise prospective enrollees from a well-informed standpoint.

---

[1] Knight 1997:6–10.

Because the government subventions given to public institutions, which mostly cover salaries, keep dwindling, we are encouraged to raise additional funds through various Income Generating Activities (IGAs). As mentioned above, the Classics Department does not have its own account, nor extracurricular income-generating programs, making the shrinking subventions a cause for concern.

The biggest threat to Classics, depending upon how the Department reacts, is restructuring—not of a single department but of the college as a whole. I, therefore, present below our history of restructuring, as well as how we have historically responded.

Restructuring (Largely a Threat)

"The attack that Classics is remote, irrelevant, and useless is part of the tendency of our modern materialistic society to believe that nothing is worth having if you cannot sell it for more than it cost. Before long it will be argued that all education is useless."[2]

On several occasions the Department of Classics and the Faculty of Humanities in general have fought attempts to restructure departments arbitrarily. Realizing that restructuring did not threaten the existence of Classics alone, but rather the Faculty of Humanities as a whole, the faculty responded in 2008 to the Chancellor College Restructuring Committee by raising twenty-two arguments.[3] For the present purpose, I will restate only seven pertinent ones:

- The faculty said it was convinced that the real aim of academic restructuring as presented in the document was not to enhance the efficiency of services and quality of programs as claimed, but rather to save costs. The faculty believed that Chancellor College should not compromise the academic integrity of the Humanities for the sake of cost-saving.

- The faculty observed that, for a long time, efforts had been made to merge departments in the Faculty of Humanities. Members, therefore, felt that they were victims of a materialist conservative ideology that is opposed to a liberal arts education.

- There had been efforts to merge departments such as English, French, African Languages, and Linguistics and Classics, among others, and the faculty wondered why the same was not happening to the Faculty of Science—especially the Departments of Chemistry, Biology, and Physics, which have a lot in common. There is, for example, in the

---

[2] Chapman 1985:2.
[3] "Response of the Faculty of Humanities Addressed to Chairman of College Restructuring Committee" 2008.

secondary schools, either General Science, which includes all these subjects, or there is Physical Science, which combines Physics with Chemistry. At the University, these subjects are separate for purposes of greater specialization. Why should it be assumed that the principle of specialization does not apply to disciplines in the Humanities?

What synergies would there be among literatures in different languages—such as Greek, Latin, French, Chichewa, and English—if the subjects were lumped together in the then-proposed literature department? Literature in any language is a product of its specific language and can only be accessed through that language. Therefore, mastery of the language is a prerequisite for appreciation of its literature, much as the appreciation of literature reflects mastery of its language. The linguists in the four departments were really specialists only in their specific languages—that is, French, English, Greek, Latin, and Bantu languages. They might have certain minimal theoretical similarities, but the languages to which they apply the theories are remarkably different from one another. The literature specialists only share the name "literature" with specialists from other sections; the literatures they teach are as different as the languages in which they are expressed. Therefore, there would be no meaningful synergy among the specialists in both linguistics and literature because of the different languages involved.

- Restructuring as proposed in the College Restructuring Committee document should be spear-headed by departments and specialists in the disciplines concerned. The approach taken by the report was top-down and heavy-handed, which was a contradiction of participatory governance. The restructuring proposals should originate from departments, and proceed via faculties until they reached Senate, not vice versa. The College Restructuring Committee should ensure that everybody owned the process of restructuring.

- Faculty observed that the actual benefits to be realized from the restructuring process were not clearly stated in the document. Those mentioned were in the form of general statements without supporting data. A situational analysis would provide some of that data. References to costs given in the document merely reinscribed the cliché language of anybody talking about organizational change. Phrases such as "enhance quality," "relevance," and "effectiveness of delivery," among others, were repeatedly mentioned but not explained, as should have been done in a situational analysis. These were issues that could not be taken lightly; they required the involvement of subject specialists.

- The faculty noticed that the Committee on Restructuring did not carry out a comprehensive literature review on why several departments in the Faculty of Humanities were created, and they advised the Committee to make a comprehensive literature review to assist the restructuring process in terms of historical background. This review would be part of the situational analysis referred to above.

Following the repeal in 2019 of the University of Malawi Act 1965 by the Malawi Parliament, the constituent Colleges, as of 4 May 2021, were delinked—this is the term of art here—and are now stand-alone universities. The erstwhile Polytechnic is now the Malawi University of Business and Applied Sciences, and the Medical School and Kamuzu College of Nursing are now combined as the Kamuzu University of Health Sciences. Chancellor College has chosen to maintain the name of the University of Malawi. The new Act does not use the term "Faculties": it speaks of "Schools." A transition task force has seen the appointments of new Councils for the new universities, but change has been slow to take shape—particularly given the pandemic conditions that we have faced since 2020. As things stand at the moment of finalizing this book in August 2021, the new Council has completed its orientation and is understood to be about to appoint an Acting Vice Chancellor and Acting Registrar, who will hold office while substantive holders of these appointments are recruited through an interview process.

In the interim, the Department of Classics still exists. During the delinking process, proposals have come forward for change, including a proposal to bring together the Departments of Philosophy, Theology, and Classics. It may be noted that the combination of these three departments would be similar to the scenario at the University of Zimbabwe, where they have a Department of Theology, Classics, and Philosophy. It is also worth noting that Professor R. Joseph Hoffmann, who in 1997 became the first full-rank Professor of Classics of at the University of Malawi, later participated in the restructuring of that department in Zimbabwe. This Hoffmannesque structure may be what awaits us here, but such an outcome remains uncertain. Both the Theology and Religious Studies Department (TRS) and the Philosophy Department have already shown marked reluctance to be merged with Classics. TRS wants to remain as a stand-alone Department, as does Philosophy.

When guidelines for establishing a department were laid out by the Delinking Steering Committee at an early stage in the delinking process, they were as follows:

- A Department should have a defined theme or academic discipline in line with the School to which it belongs;

- A Department should have a minimum of ten modules worth at least three credit hours (twelve credits) each per year (except where necessity overrules);
- A Department should have at least one postgraduate program;
- A Department should have at least ten suitably qualified full-time academic staff members;
- A Department should have at least five members of staff with a doctoral degree in a relevant field or discipline; and
- A Department should have at least one Associate Professor, who will give academic leadership in the Department.

In the case of Classics, we are presently able to satisfy only the first two guidelines. We have never been in a position to offer graduate education in Classics, and the numbers of staff do not meet the scale expected in the guidelines. No one can tell, however, whether a Vice-Chancellor, once appointed, will think it incumbent on him or her to follow the course of action advocated by the Delinking Steering Committee.

In a situation in which no one can predict with confidence whether the future will bring growth or decline in student numbers and funding, any department called on to amalgamate could rightly fear that staff establishment may not expand as might otherwise have been hoped.

Let us now take stock of challenges in general, although inevitably some challenges may appear to overlap with threats. We realize that our challenges are not unique to us and that other departments have relatively similar ones. But here are some of the challenges we have encountered all along, most of which date back to the time the Department was established.

Challenges Stated by Students

I administered an open-ended questionnaire soliciting the challenges Classics students face with the results revealing that they face challenges at all levels. They, for example, decried the lack of teaching and learning resources; they referred to teaching and learning difficulties; they argued that there is a need for syllabus evaluation to include interesting topics and relevant issues; and they spoke also of the need for student attachments (internships) to different organizations during vacations.

Lack of resources, both human and material, has been a perennial problem for Classics, and, realizing that at no point will the resources suffice, the challenge remains for those teaching Classics to be innovative and to teach well within the limited resources without compromising standards. With regard to student attachments, Chancellor College, as a training institution in conjunction with both public and private sectors, should institutionalize them (as is done in other universities) so as to enhance the balance between theory (as conducted in the classroom, specifically in our Archaeology and Art course) and practice in the field.

Challenges Facing the Department of Classics as Documented by Teaching Staff Earlier in the History of the Department

Challenges go back to the time when the Department was first established. Prof. Joseph Hoffmann, the Head of Classics, summarized, in 1998, the challenges in a controversial memo to the Dean of Humanities, entitled "The Status of Classics within Chancellor College":[4]

> The Department has no majors, a decreasing intake of students interested in the ancient languages, and makes a minimal contribution to minor subject-studies in BAH and BEd Hum. It is unlikely for four reasons, that the Department will attract greater numbers in future: (a) the virtual discontinuation of Latin teaching in secondary schools and minor seminaries in Malawi; (b) lack of A level Latin and Ancient History candidates in secondary schools, including Kamuzu Academy; (c) the increasingly pragmatic focus of entering students, who associate Classics with the study of irrelevant and "dead" civilizations; (d) the lack of interdepartmental co-ordination, especially notable in content overlaps between Classics 110 [Greek and Roman Politics and Society] and History 200b [Ancient History offered by the History department] [...] and certain philosophy courses, and in the apparent lack of philological interest in Greek studies in the Department of Theology and Religious Studies—from which the department once derived two-thirds of its enrolment in language courses. [...] It cannot be overlooked that Classics, as taught at present in its "language/literature-based" form, is of decreasing importance and widely perceived to be irrelevant to the educational and social needs of Malawi. The intake in core (ancient language) courses in 1998 was fewer than eight students. The Department relies heavily on expatriate staff (the total of the establishment of three lecturers), most of whose time is spent teaching three or fewer students in a tutorial mode.

Indeed, it can be argued that some of the challenges Hoffmann writes about have persisted, but others have changed. For example, except for 2012–2013, when

---

4 Hoffmann 1998.

Classics registered a total of forty-nine students for Greek and Latin combined, few to none want to study the ancient languages: in the 2019–2020 academic year, we had a total of six students registered—four in Greek, and two in Latin. Although Latin was discontinued in Government secondary schools due to a lack of teachers, it persists in some seminaries, where it is taught up to JCE level and to reasonable numbers (on average, 230 sit for JCE per year). However, most potential Latin and Greek students from Kamuzu Academy do not register for Classics when they enter the University.

Hoffmann was candid in writing what he called "the increasingly pragmatic focus of entering students, who associate Classics with the study of irrelevant and 'dead' civilizations," and asserting that "Classics as taught at present in its 'language/literature-based' form, is of decreasing importance and widely perceived to be irrelevant to the educational and social needs of Malawi." That was indeed the situation in 1998.

The problem of the lack of interdepartmental coordination cited in Hoffmann's memo persists. It is interesting to note that, in 1985, Caroline Alexander decried the lack of serious interdepartmental coordination with disciplines that had overlapping spheres of interest. To that end, Alexander candidly lamented:[5]

> Over the years I have given several guest lectures on Greek tragedy for the English department, but apart from this, attempts to establish interdepartmental links with this department have failed. This has been particularly disappointing in view of the fact that there are so many natural points of interaction between the two disciplines: epic, heroic poetry, drama, literary criticism to name but a few. Our request for a joint meeting between Classics and English was denied by the latter.

Concurring with Caroline Alexander, it is, indeed, interesting to note that Classics has, in some ways, contributed to the teaching/understanding of other Chancellor College subjects, as the following list of our course offerings and other cognate disciplines would indicate, and yet the interdepartmental links are not utilized:

- Greek and Roman History, Politics and Society (History/Political Science)
- Historiography (History)
- Greek and Roman Mythology and African folklore (English and any literature)

---

5   Alexander 1985.

- Greek and Roman Drama in Translation (Fine and Performing Arts)
- Classics in Translation (English)
- Latin and Greek Linguistics (Linguistics)
- Ancient Greek and Roman religion (Theology and Religious Studies)
- Word Origins (Linguistics, English, Law, some scientific terminologies)
- Archaeology, Greek and Roman Art and Architecture (History, Social Sciences, Fine Art, etc.).

Staffing

Another significant challenge is related to staffing. The Classics Department at Chancellor College has never had stable staffing levels—for it has relied heavily on expatriate staff who have proven difficult to recruit due to our terms of employment, in particular the uncompetitive salaries.[6] In fact, in 1997, given the circumstances on the ground, Dr. Henri de Marcellus was compelled to recommend that, as a contingency plan, Classics merge with other departments based on lack of expatriate staff. This staffing crisis prompted student rumors that the Department had been unsuccessful in its recruitment efforts and would probably close—intending that Classics majors be diverted to cognate fields.

A lack of funding to conduct a comprehensive curriculum review of the Classics program has been a perennial problem, to such an extent that whatever review was conducted in the past was not comprehensive enough—a comprehensive review would require a much more robust review process, including stakeholders' consultative meetings at different levels. However, there have been various attempts to come up with new courses or bring new perspectives to courses during the times of: Caroline Alexander (1982–1985); Maryse Waegeman (1988–1993); Thomas Knight (1993–1996); Joseph Hoffmann (1997–1998); and Cybelle Greenlaw (2007), who is credited with the creation of the Gender course, and the Women Philosophers course.

The range of courses started to widen during the tenure of Dr. Maryse Waegeman and Jozef De Kuyper (1988–1993). Dr. John Dubbey, who was appointed Vice-Chancellor in 1987, comments with satisfaction on their appointment in his book, as having brought the combination of skills he felt was needed for Classics teaching in Chancellor College.[7] In the Waegeman years, the department had three complete undergraduate courses—from Year One to Year Four. Latin and Greek went as far as Year Four. The Classical Civilisation stream had

---

[6] De Marcellus 1995.
[7] Dubbey 1994:153.

a more general course, shared with the History Department under the banner of Ancient History, but taught by Classics. The course attracted large numbers, since all History students were compelled to take it during Year One. A course on Greek and Roman Art and Architecture was also introduced. Waegeman and De Kuyper were part of the editorial team which, in 1987, launched the *Journal of Humanities*—then used for journal exchanges as hard copies within and outside Africa. Now, however, it is an open-access journal—still Zomba-based, but international in scope.[8] Before returning to Belgium, Waegeman was promoted to the rank of Associate Professor.

Jozef De Kuyper introduced a new course in Year Three, entitled "Introduction to Computational Research." That was a unique innovation for Classics and attracted so many students that numbers had to be trimmed so they could, using borrowed computers, fit into the Mathematical Sciences computer laboratory. Because this was the early nineties, that course afforded many Humanities students the opportunity to touch a computer for the first time. However, the course was shelved because it could not run on the resources from another department belonging to a different faculty altogether. In fact, in the view of those in the Mathematical Sciences Department, the Classics Department was scrambling for resources that were not ours. The communication below from Jozef De Kuyper addressed to the Chairman of Computer Lab Committee is clear evidence of the antagonisms that existed:[9]

Dear Sir,

It is with great concern that I have taken cognizance of your decision to withdraw one (!) computer, actually used for the E-mail project, allegedly to serve the students better. The suggestion that each department should acquire its own modem (with or without the computer involved?) cannot be taken seriously and is unrealistic. Your decision will increase the international isolation of Chancellor College. I have also been surprised by the timing of a long weekend, at least two days before any student can be expected to be back at work. However, it is exactly one day before the elections in Malawi: pure coincidence?

During the period of Dr. Thomas Knight (1993–1996), course offerings were expanded, including the introduction of: English Word Origins and Word Power,

---

[8] African Journals Online.

[9] De Kuyper 1994. Political considerations, as this letter hints, have never been far from the surface. The election referred to was the one in which President Kamuzu Banda was defeated and President Bakili Muluzi elected for the first time.

which I took over and developed further; Greek and Roman Mythology; and Ancient Greek and Roman Religion and Magic.

Further expansion of courses was also carried out during the tenure of Prof. Joseph Hoffmann, Edward Jenner, and Dr. Michael Chappell, including Roman Law, the Black Athena Controversy, and Greek Lyric Poetry. The curriculum, however, was not completely revised. Furthermore, it is important to note that, as much as course offerings were expanded, they eventually disappeared when their originators left, as most courses were devised to suit the expertise of the course lecturers. In general, the number of appropriately-trained teaching staff has been inadequate, and the Department has been forced to rely heavily on part-time teaching staff instead.

For a long time, the Department has been unable to buy neither up-to-date texts for the offered courses nor equipment for teaching and learning. Caroline Alexander managed to source books from the University of Zimbabwe, other book donations, and—through a stringent book budget—managed even to source a few other texts. During her tenure, however, there were not as many students as now. In their time, Maryse Waegeman and Jozef De Kuyper sought to resource the Department through their Flemish funding organization called VVOB. Paul McKechnie and Mark Usher have also given some books to the Department, and so too did Thomas Knight, who sourced books from the USA after pleading our cause in the *American Classical Newsletter*. As the situation still stands, we are failing to buy up-to-date academic books for our courses. Students used to receive a book allowance, and there used to be a Malawi Book Service bookshop on campus. However, the bookshop has closed, and the allowance—received only by a minority these days—is now only enough to buy a little stationery. It appears, too, that the College Library does not prioritize books for Classics, but mostly for Social Sciences and Sciences.

The lack of office space has been a perennial problem. It is, nowadays, not strange to find three staff members sharing an office that was designed for a single member. I do recall that, in 1995, when I first joined the staff, I shared a tiny cubicle with my three colleagues. We were placed far from our Department (some 200 meters away) in the Geography Department cubicles. I still recall the animosities that existed then: the Head of Geography did not want us to occupy space in his Department, and the situation was made worse by the fact that we were, in fact, from a naughty Department, because this was not long after President Banda lost the 1993 referendum and the 1994 presidential election.

Lack of office space is worse for part-time staff, who operate from outside the campus. As we grow, however, and as new structures keep arising, we hope the office problem will be eased. At the moment, the World Bank and the African Development bank are funding the building of new facilities for the promotion of STEM subjects. We just hope that as our colleagues move into their new science structures, some of us will move into their vacated spaces.

This may also solve the problem of classroom space. With the rise of student numbers, and particularly in the Classical Civilisation courses during Years One and Two, we have found that the teaching spaces they used to allocate our courses no longer accommodate our new numbers. We hope that this will also be addressed through the construction of new lecture theatres under the HEST (Higher Education Science and Technology) project.

Moving Forward

English language problems, as well as basic writing skills, are a big challenge for some of our learners—particularly those who have just joined the College. We realize this is a carry-over problem from their primary and secondary schooling, where English standards have decreased. Similarly, Dr. Thomas Knight remarked that

> ... there is the problem of language: English is a second or a third language for all of them, and the quality of English instruction in the country has begun to decline. At the practical level, one must routinely gloss common English words, metaphors, and idioms. The English translation of a literary work can sometimes prove to be itself a foreign text requiring careful interpretation.[10]

Another challenge, with which we are happy to assist, concerns the teaching of diverse learners. Classics registers eight to ten students each year, many who use braille. We also have several learners with hearing differences. "Inclusive Education" demands that all learners, regardless of any differences, be taught together with the rest and treated equally. However, while many with visual differences choose to take a Classical Civilisation course over a classical language, we lack Classics texts in braille. The affected students record the lecture and rely on their colleagues for notes and discussions after classes. Things are better now that the Special Needs Section of the College has a computer that can, if given soft copies, decode into braille or even voice. It is only relatively recently that the Department has begun to teach visually different students.

In the case of language teaching, it has always remained a challenge to teach those who have already studied Latin and Greek for four to six years together with real beginners—since currently there is no provision for advanced learners to be placed in Year Two or Year Three, as was previously possible. For example,

---

[10] Knight 1997:8.

while I started Classics from Year One (selected from Dedza Secondary School[11]) I did four years, but my two colleagues, Thoko Kunkeyani (now Dr.) and Eltrudis Katemba, only joined me at Year Three, because there was that provision/intervention under the three-term system which then existed. I reckon it would be difficult to implement a similar provision now because of the Credits and Credit hours under the current semester system.

Acknowledging that partnerships and collaborations are important for universities, we have tried to initiate partnerships with other universities, but were unable to find support. A case in point is the University of Vermont through Prof. Mark Usher: we tried to set up a student exchange program, but it flopped due to a lack of support on our end. It is quite frustrating when there is too much bureaucracy involved.

The ability to further our own studies has also been a challenge; none among us local Malawian staff has, with rare exception, had the opportunity to advance our degrees: Mr. Chikondi Medson, a new recruit (2019), already had an MA scholarship at the time he was employed; Steve Nyamilandu managed to complete his first MA after working for five years (joined in February 1994 and graduated in April 1999); Eltrudis left for MA studies at Durham in 1997–1998, but never returned upon completion; and Thoko Kunkeyani completed hers after a couple of years.

Opportunities for pursuing PhD degrees are also not readily available. Thoko went to do her PhD at the University of Western Cape in South Africa, funded by Chancellor College. Steve was supervised jointly by his home university (University of Malawi) and the School of Classics at St. Andrews University, as part of a cotutelle arrangement between the two—Steve's study included two spells at the School of Classics in St. Andrews, where, amongst other things, he was able to research the important contribution to Malawian Classics made by the late Professor Robert Ogilvie. It was, furthermore, at the School of Classics (popularly known as Swallowgate) and under the supervision of Professor Roger Rees that Steve had the opportunity to meet the ageing Professor Emeritus Adrian Gratwick, a contemporary of the late Professor Robert Ogilvie. In conversation with Steve, Gratwick said, "If you are to publish, don't publish for quantity but for quality."

---

[11] This school was renowned for producing the so called "rebels" in the eyes of Dr. Banda. This is one of the oldest high schools, built during colonial era. The school's initial Latin motto was *lux in tenebris* ("Light in Darkness"), but, later, though before Independence, it was changed to *sapere aude* ("Dare to be Wise", Horace *Epistles* 1.2.40). "Light in Darkness" (in English) was the motto beneath the first heraldic achievement of British Central Africa, adopted in about 1894, and in the coat of arms granted for the Nyasaland Protectorate in 1914, the motto "Light in Darkness" was translated into Latin: *lux in tenebris* (De Vries 2009). My Latin teacher in Dedza, Mr. Damiano Chikwawa, told us that the school's motto was changed in proleptic recognition of leaving the darkness of colonial times behind.

Concluding Remarks

I will conclude on a positive note, as I have never been a pessimist. Fortunately, amidst the challenges and threats, the Classics Department, as of writing this, still exists, and should there be any form of restructuring, it has always been our plea that such restructuring maintain the integrity of our discipline. We assert that since the establishment of our Department, we have maintained the identity of an educating force, whose value is out of proportion to the moderate cost of funding us.

And now, Classics needs to capitalize on its strengths and opportunities, so as to counter the threats and challenges.

5

Teaching Greek Language and Literature in Malawi

The Risks and Rewards

MICHAEL CHAPPELL

I FIRST ARRIVED IN MALAWI in March 1998, to take up a post as Lecturer in the Department of Classics at Chancellor College in Zomba. I knew little of what to expect from the country itself or from the University and its Classics Department. I had applied for the job after seeing it advertised in the *Times Higher Education Supplement*, and, since accepting the offer, had been reading what I could about Malawi and its history. Another new Classics lecturer, the late Edward Jenner from New Zealand, arrived on the same flight, and we were met at Chileka airport by our Head of Department, Professor Joseph Hoffmann. The other staff of the Department were two Malawian lecturers: Steve Nyamilandu and Thokozani Kunkeyani (both now have PhDs, though only Steve remains at Chancellor College).

The prominence of expatriate lecturers was typical of the Department's history up to that point.[1] Zomba, though the colonial capital, remains a small town, known for its greenery and attractive colonial buildings on the lower slopes of Zomba mountain.

Often compared to an Indian hill station, it was an attractive place for the colonial British and offered a peaceful location for the new college campus when the political capital moved to Lilongwe (though Parliament continued to meet in Zomba until 1994).

Dr. Banda, who was a Classics enthusiast, advocated the establishment of the Department at Chancellor College. His enthusiasm was also evident when he opened his own school, Kamuzu Academy, in 1981. Then, in 1982, Caroline Alexander arrived in Zomba to begin her tenure, although she initially taught

---

[1] For a useful account of the Department's history, see Jenner 2001.

Figure 9. Chancellor College and Zomba, with Zomba Mountain behind.
Photograph by Blackwell Manda, reproduced by permission.

Classics in the Department of Philosophy; she later wrote a lively and insightful account of her time at Chancellor College in a piece published in the *New Yorker*.[2] Professor Alexander worked hard to provide texts for the department, establishing links with other universities in the region and reaching out to Malawi's expatriate Greek community, who generously responded with donations. Ogilvie had envisaged a department focused more on Latin than Greek, as Latin was, at that time, taught in around twenty secondary schools. This vision is still reflected in the Department's textbooks: the shelves of our offices are lined with (largely unused) school texts of Horace or Ovid and books of Latin unseens, while the books on Greek language and literature are few and far between.

Professor Alexander left once the Department was established, and, over the next few years, it was, to varying degrees of success, staffed with mainly short-term expatriates. The most significant to the Department's development were the Belgian couple Maryse Waegeman and Jozef De Kuyper, who stayed from 1988 to 1993. The Belgian government generously paid their salaries over this period and donated books to the Department. It was Waegeman and De Kuyper who created the course structure that continues largely to this day. They envisaged three main "cycles": one each for students studying Greek and

[2] Alexander 1991.

Latin and one for Classical Civilization.[3] The number of students studying the ancient languages has always been small, and, as in other parts of the world, it is the Classical Civilization courses that are more popular and that have enabled the Department to survive. Chancellor College has four-year degrees, and the cycle developed by Waegeman and De Kuyper was Ancient History in the first year, Classics in Translation in the second, Ancient Philosophy in the third, and Art and Archaeology in the fourth.

The arrival, in 1998, of Edward Jenner and myself was the result of a successful recruitment drive by Professor Hoffman and his predecessor as Head, Dr. Henri de Marcellus, after a period when the Department was short-staffed. Although three young Malawians were recruited to teach in 1994, one—Eltrudis Nthete—left in 1996 to obtain an M.A. in England and never returned. The others—Steve Nyamilandu and Thokozani Kasakula (née Kunkeyani)—were not full Lecturers in 1998, though Nyamilandu achieved this status in 1999 after completing his M.A. Hoffmann, whose main expertise is in early Christian history and theology, developed plans for restructuring Classics, but, in 1998, left for a better paid teaching post at Kamuzu Academy, at which time I took over as Head of Department, remaining in the post until my departure in 2001. Edward Jenner and I shared an expertise in early Greek literature, although I also specialized in Homer.

The main courses I taught upon arrival were a third-year course on Greek literature in translation and a second-year course on mythology and epic. I also taught advanced Latin to two students from Kamuzu Academy, who, although they were first years, had already taken several years of Latin and Greek and so could not enroll as beginners. In the course of my three years, I also taught Greek and Roman religion and developed new courses on the (then recent) *Black Athena* controversy and Afrocentric views of Classics (semester 1), and the history of classical North Africa (semester 2).

Since returning to Chancellor College in 2013, my teaching areas have been similar, although the course on Afrocentrism and North Africa lapsed after I left in 2001 and has not been revived. Currently, I teach courses on mythology, epic, and religion, and some first- and second-year Greek language courses.

In 1998, I inherited the Ancient Epic course from Professor Hoffmann, and the epics studied at that time were the Book of Genesis, the epic of Gilgamesh, and the Homeric epics. Genesis was originally Hoffmann's choice, reflecting both his own religious interests and those of many of the students. In Malawi, various types of biblical fundamentalism are common, making it an interesting challenge to teach Genesis as literature and mythology. In the class, we studied

---

[3] De Kuyper 1993.

mythical elements, especially of the creation story, and I suggested that these stories were never intended to be true in a historical sense, and that to read them as such is a misunderstanding of the type of stories they are. If the students had objections to this, they largely kept them to themselves (as Malawian students often do). One interesting reaction came when I moved to teaching the epic of Gilgamesh. When we read the famous account of the flood told by the Noah-figure Utnapishtim, whom Gilgamesh visits in his quest for immortality, we noted the many similarities to the biblical story. A student, who was a strict biblical Christian, asked me after class if the flood story in Gilgamesh was older than that in Genesis. I said that it was, and, after a pause, he said, "So the story of Noah is just a human story."

Since 2013, I have been teaching a similar course on epic, but without Genesis, and with the addition of the West African *Epic of Sunjata*. Adding the African epic is a natural move for a course on epic in an African country, and the students find the comparisons between the different epic traditions interesting. In exams or assignments, I have asked students which aspects of the Sunjata epic they see as distinctively African, and they point to features such as the prominence of magic and spirits (and absence of the personalized gods prominent in the Near Eastern and Greek epics), as well as polygamy and the importance of having children, especially male heirs. All three epics studied appeal to the students in different ways. Though critics today usually avoid talking of the universal appeal of great literature, it is true that these epics seem capable of resonating with people from different cultures and traditions. The epic of Gilgamesh seems to have a particularly powerful impact, with its themes of friendship and loss, death and the search for immortality, and its exciting story. When I returned to Chancellor College in 2013, one of my former students, now a Lecturer, said immediately upon seeing me, "I remember you teaching us the epic of Gilgamesh." More recently, two male students told me they had nicknamed each other Gilgamesh and Enkidu (I did not ask who was which).

Postcolonial commentators have noted that there are some aspects of the study of Classics that can resonate more with many African societies than with modern Westerners, despite the subject's association with the canonical Western tradition. Two such areas are oral epic and traditional poetry, which are still living traditions in many parts of Africa. Though Malawi does not have any tradition which would correspond with standard definitions of epic, oral and traditional performances are familiar.

When we begin this course by looking at what epic is and its possible definitions, I consider the debate about whether there is such a thing as African epic useful for approaching the topic. The denial that there is epic in Africa was most famously stated by Ruth Finnegan, who based her denial on formal criteria.[4] Today it is generally accepted that there are African epics, notably the *Epic of Sunjata* and the *Mwindo Epic* from the Congo,[5] but the debate raises interesting questions about the nature and definition of epic: is it a purely Western construct based largely on Homer, or a useful category for much more widespread traditional poems?[6] Should Africans care if they have something called epic, and are they just trying to fit their own traditions into an alien framework? Such debates have helped clarify the nature of epic: the research on Homer's orality led to a broader interest in oral epics around the world, and these in turn have helped scholars gain more understanding of Homeric poetry.

Over the last few years, my colleagues and I have been trying to incorporate more postcolonial elements into our courses. Since the year 2000, there has been a rapid growth in research on Classics and postcolonialism, linked to the rise in the importance of reception studies in the field of classical literature.[7] As Classics, central to the educational curriculum imposed on colonized nations, was one of the most colonial of subjects, it has correspondingly featured strongly in postcolonial writing that often seeks to appropriate or subvert classical works. As the most canonical of all western Classics, Homer has featured prominently, especially in postcolonial literature. This has been helped by the dual identity of Homer that developed in the twentieth century, as pointed to by various scholars: Homer has his traditional role in the western literary tradition as the ancestor of written epics such as those of Vergil, Tasso, and Milton—but thanks to the studies of Parry and Lord, he is also categorized alongside traditional oral poets from around the world. Thus, Homer can move easily from the Western canon to the more contemporary concept of "world literature."[8] With its varied cast of characters and different locations, themes of journeying and returns, the search for identity, and encounters with monsters and descent to the underworld, the *Odyssey* has, from antiquity to today, constantly lent itself to different adaptations, re-imaginings, and reinterpretations.[9] This is also true for postcolonial authors, who have made various uses of the *Odyssey*, some of which I discuss with students in my courses on epic and Greek literature.

Among postcolonial responses to Homeric epic, two important writers are the Caribbean poets Aimé Césaire and Nobel Laureate Derek Walcott.[10] Césaire

---

[4] Finnegan 1970:108.
[5] Cf. Biebuyck 1969 and Bulman 1997.
[6] For discussion of the "African epic" debate, with further bibliography, see Farrell 1999:275–279; Graziosi 2007:125–130.
[7] See e.g. Goff 2005; Hardwick and Gillespie 2007.
[8] Graziosi and Greenwood 2007:4, 28.
[9] See Hall 2008 and, on postcolonial responses, McConnell 2013.
[10] For good discussion of the relationship of Walcott and Césaire to Homer, see McConnell 2013, especially chapters 1 and 3.

came from Martinique and gained an advanced French education by studying at the *École normale supérieure* in Paris in the 1930s,[11] where he first developed radical anti-colonial ideas and propounded the influential concept of *Négritude*. His most powerful attack on colonialism came in the 1950 essay *Discours sur le colonialisme*, which argues against any civilizing aspect of colonialism, stressing its barbarity and the ways it dehumanizes both the colonizers and the colonized. Such ideas are also present in his 1939 long-form poem *Cahier d'un retour au pays natal*, written when he was about to return to Martinique from Europe. The title suggests a common postcolonial problem for the Westernized literary intellectual trying to return to his home, but also points to an interaction with Homer's *Odyssey*: the canonical return home in Western culture. Justine McConnell argues that "themes of return, *katabasis*, displacement, heroism, oppression and imperialism all contribute to the formation of *Cahier*'s relationship with the *Odyssey*."[12]

In one episode of the *Cahier*, Césaire depicts his encounter with an ugly, poverty-stricken Black man on a Paris tram. When some white women giggle at this "comical and ugly figure," the narrator smiles with them, betraying his race with what he describes as cowardly complicity. The Black man on the tram is described as enormously tall, with an eye socket hollowed by poverty, and has often been interpreted as a reference to the Odyssean Cyclops.[13] Césaire, as the one who is struggling to return to his native land and who views the "Cyclops" figure as a bestial other, is Odysseus in the poem. However, as the Black victim of colonialism, he also identifies with the Black Cyclops. The episode is the climax of a central section in the poem that Gregson Davis compares to an Odyssean *katabasis*: a psychological depth into the depths of self-loathing that is necessary before the positive affirmations of *Négritude* in the poem's concluding sections.[14] Hall suggests the passage is the root of what has become a well-known postcolonial reading of the famous episode in the *Odyssey*, viewing the Cyclops sympathetically as a victim defending himself against the proto-colonist Odysseus, who enters his home without permission and steals his produce.[15] This is an interesting example to teach and discuss with students, as it illustrates a typical strategy of postcolonial reading: taking the viewpoint of characters who have traditionally been marginalized or demonized in the interpretation of the text. In this case, the postcolonial reading is the reversal of many readings, in which

[11]   See Davis 1997.
[12]   McConnell 2013:63.
[13]   Césaire 1983:68–9; discussion in McConnell 2013:39–70.
[14]   Davis 1997 42–46; 2007.
[15]   Hall 2008.

Odysseus was identified with European colonizers and explorers, and the Cyclops with the brutish cannibals they believed they would meet in exotic places.[16]

Walcott's long (epic?) poem *Omeros* interacts with Homer in complex ways and provides good examples for teaching students about the different possible postcolonial treatments of a canonical Western classic such as Homer.[17] Walcott exhibits a typical postcolonial ambivalence towards Homer, both appropriating it in his own work, and subverting it by giving heroic Homeric names to local fishermen and depicting Homer as either a poor blind man called Seven Seas, or a vagrant on a London bench. With major characters called Achille, Hector, and Helen, the poem obviously seems to interact with the *Iliad*, yet it is the *Odyssey*'s influence that pervades the poem more deeply. It is filled with passages about the sea, sailing, voyages, and islands, and its structure is Odyssean: it begins on St. Lucia, then describes the poet's explorations of the world before his difficult return to his home island, where the closing books are set.[18]

Walcott himself has said of his classical education:[19]

> It's the greatest bequest the Empire made. Those who sneer at what they call an awe of tradition forget how old the West Indian experience is. I think that precisely because of their limitations our early education must have ranked with the best in the world. The grounding was rigid—Latin, Greek, and the essential masterpieces, but there was this elation of discovery. Shakespeare, Marlowe, Horace, Vergil—these writers weren't jaded but immediate experiences. The atmosphere was competitive, creative. It was cruel, but it created our literature.

This is a classic example of how many postcolonial writers have used their education in Western Classics to appropriate those Classics in their own writing, rather than simply rejecting them as alien. As with the controversy about African epic, discussions of the genre of *Omeros* have helped clarify the nature of epic. While Homerists and Eurocentric writers tend to classify it as an epic, postcolonial writers, including the author himself, have been less comfortable with this classification.[20] Joseph Farrell suggested that some postcolonial critics have been "embarrassed by the possibility that *Omeros* might be taken for an epic, and hence as a 'white man's poem,'" but he argues that this rests on a misunderstanding of epic, which is in fact a worldwide phenomenon and not a

[16] On the postcolonial Cyclops see McConnell 2013:1–38 and Hall 2008: ch. 7. Hall's chapter is an excellent survey of different treatments of and responses to the Cyclops figure.
[17] Walcott 1990.
[18] On Walcott and the *Odyssey*, see McConnell 2013.
[19] Hamner 1993:50.
[20] On this issue, see Burkitt 2007.

white man's genre. All of these issues are fruitful to grapple with when teaching a course on epic in an African university.

John Djisenu lists several "cross-cultural bonds" between Greece and Africa.[21] Among these are the existence and use of myths, polytheism (in parts of Africa), belief in curses, and fatalism. Focusing especially on drama, Djisenu points to[22] the use of spectacle, where ancient Greek dramas employ music, rhythm, dance or movements, and ritualistic elements. You will find that these features are comparable, and indeed compatible, with the holistic theatre concept of Africa where one finds an integrated approach to the use of music, dance, and drama.

Though he is talking especially about West African drama, his remarks are relevant to other areas of Africa too.[23] As with oral poetic traditions, this is one of the areas in which African students can appreciate the classical world more easily than many Westerners, who often have a text-based approach to ancient plays (though less nowadays than they used to). The celebrated Nigerian writer Wole Soyinka has said of his encounter with ancient Greek drama that,

> I remember my shock as a student of literature and drama when I read that drama originated in Greece. What is this? I couldn't quite deal with it. What are they talking about? I never heard my grandfather talk about Greeks invading Yorubaland. I couldn't understand. I've lived from childhood with drama.[24]

This is one advantage of the Classics for postcolonial writers: they can attempt to bypass the Western classical tradition and encounter Greek or Roman texts directly, showing us that these texts need not be viewed as the possession of white Europeans, but as part of a broader world literature. Walcott too speaks of an affinity between the Caribbean and the ancient Aegean, writing that "In maps the Caribbean dreams of the Aegean, and the Aegean of reversible seas."[25] Thus, in the realm of literature, the geographical and chronological gaps between the cultures are erased, and Caribbean or African writings can influence Homer or Sophocles, and vice versa. Teaching and studying Classics in an African country such as Malawi can lead students to make comparisons and see their own culture differently, but it also helps a Western lecturer, such as myself, to see familiar classical texts in new and unfamiliar ways.

---

[21] Djisenu 2007.
[22] Djisenu 2007.
[23] For Malawi, see Kerr 1987.
[24] Appiah 1988:782.
[25] Walcott 1997:62.

For such reasons, in the Department's course on Greek literature in translation, we have focused a great deal on Greek tragedy. As noted, the combination of masks, poetry, music, and dance is one that is easily understandable by Malawian students, though it is important to point out differences as well as similarities in the way these elements were used in the ancient Greek context. Greek tragedy's ability to be adapted and speak to audiences in many different cultures and contexts is familiar. One reason for this is its use of mythical material, which can be more easily applied to distinct situations than can historically-bound drama. The late twentieth and early twenty-first centuries have seen a rise in the number of performances or adaptations of Greek dramas in many parts of the world; just as the ancient dramatists used heroic myth to reflect on fifth-century Athenian issues, modern writers have used the plays to comment on issues such as feminism and gender, the nature of sexuality, war and its victims, political oppression and slavery, and racism and ethnic conflict.[26] In Africa, since the 1960s, many playwrights have turned to Greek drama to address the issues of their newly independent states.[27] This is particularly prominent in West Africa (especially Nigeria), perhaps because of its own strong dramatic traditions, as noted above in the quote from Wole Soyinka, although South Africa has also produced important examples, usually relating the dramas to the country's history of political and racial tensions.

In this context, some Greek dramas are obvious choices for teaching because of their adaptability to many situations and because there are good African adaptations to discuss and compare with the Greek originals. Sophocles' *Antigone* has probably been applied to more political situations than any other Greek tragedy, with its heroine usually seen as a protester against political oppression.[28] Important African versions include Fugard, Kani, and Ntshona's *The Island*[29] and Femi Osofisan's *Tègònni: An African Antigone*.[30] Osofisan's *Tègònni*[31] is set in late nineteenth-century Nigeria and tells the story of a Yoruba princess who buries her brother's body, although this had been forbidden by the local British governor Lt. Gen. Carter-Ross. On one level, the play is an obvious attack on imperialism, and Carter-Ross is almost a parody of a jingoistic racist imperialist. However, like many of the African adaptations, it is more than just

---

[26] On Greek drama and postcolonialism, see e.g. Hardwick 2004.
[27] On African adaptations of Greek tragedy, see Wetmore 2002, Budelmann 2004, Goff and Simpson 2007, and many of the chapters in Hardwick and Gillespie 2007.
[28] Goff 2007:41.
[29] Fugard, Koni, and Ntshona 1974.
[30] Osofisan 1994.
[31] On *Tègònni*, see Goff 2007.

a protest against colonialism, as it is also concerned with the problems of the postcolonial state. Osofisan himself writes in an introduction to the play:[32]

> my concern is also to look at the problem of political freedom against the background of the present turmoil in Nigeria—my country— where various military governments have continued for decades now to thwart the people's desire for democracy, happiness, and good government.

The Island, which depicts two prisoners on Robben Island preparing and performing a version of *Antigone,* was first performed in Cape Town in 1973, and clearly relates Sophocles' play to protests against apartheid. The play was inspired by real performances of *Antigone* that had taken place on Robben Island, including one in which Nelson Mandela played the role of Creon (interesting that he played the controlling ruler rather than the heroic protestor).[33] *The Island* was also performed at Chancellor College in 1980, as were some other plays by Fugard: *Sizwe Bansi is Dead*[34] and *The Blood Knot.*[35] In Malawi, the play was used as a covert criticism of Banda's regime, showing again the adaptability to different political situations of both *Antigone* and Fugard's play.[36] In Malawi in the 1970s and 1980s, "to sidestep censorship many university writers turned to historical myths, folktales and proverbs as a covert means of offering political commentary,"[37] just as Greek dramatists preferred to use myths to comment on contemporary issues indirectly. Another Malawian writer who has used the play to criticize Dr Banda is the poet Jack Mapanje, the most famous writer imprisoned by Banda. Mapanje was Head of the English Department at Chancellor College when he was imprisoned in 1987 for over three years.[38] One of the poems he wrote while imprisoned is "No, Creon, there's no virtue in howling," which uses Creon's grief for the deaths of his kin, that he himself caused, to reproach Banda for his treatment of his own people, in particular the murder of four MPs in 1983, whom he denied traditional burial rites.[39]

---

[32] Osofisan 1999 is critical of postcolonialism because it looks to the past and is still focused on the Western colonizers, whereas it is more urgent for Africans to address the current problems of their own societies. He states that his main target audience is Nigerian and African rather than Western.

[33] Mandela 1994:541. He comments on Creon, "His inflexibility and blindness ill become a leader, for a leader must temper justice with mercy."

[34] Fugard, Koni, and Ntshona 1974.

[35] Fugard 1974.

[36] Kerr 1987; Chisiza 2017.

[37] Chisiza 2017; on this topic see also Magalasi 2012.

[38] See his memoir, Mapanje 2011.

[39] In Mapanje 1993. For analysis of his use of *Antigone* in this poem, see Greenwood 2016.

Modern versions of *Antigone*, as noted above, tend to focus on Antigone as a martyr for principle standing up to a dictator. Sophocles' original play is more nuanced in its depiction of Creon and Antigone, even though the gods eventually declare Creon to be in the wrong. Antigone seems at times too stubborn, even determined to die, while Creon in the first part of the play puts forward reasonable arguments about the need for everybody to follow the laws of the state. Fifth-century Athenians, for whom participation in state affairs was very important, would have sympathized with this view. However, as the play goes on, Creon reveals himself to be more of a dictator, who states that "the city is the king's—that's the law!" to which his son Haemon replies, "What a splendid king you'd make of a desert island!"[40] These issues make the play good fodder for discussion with students: while most sympathize more with Antigone, there are always some students who support Creon. Issues of the state's laws versus laws of religion or conscience, and of dictatorship versus democracy, have resonance in Malawi. I have heard a few debates between Chancellor College lecturers or students as to whether democracy or benign dictatorship is the best form of government for African countries. Gender roles are another always relevant issue raised in the play. Antigone acts more boldly than would have been thought appropriate for a well-born Athenian young woman, and one of Creon's main fears is that he does not want to be beaten by a woman.

Euripides' *Bacchae* is another play I have taught at Chancellor College, and it is one that students usually enjoy and have strong reactions to. Apart from the play's obvious tragic power, Malawian students often find the Dionysiac religion as portrayed in the play fascinating and relate it to the various types of Pentecostal-style religion which are common in Malawi. Students generally have strong opinions either for or against this type of religion, just as Euripides' play can be interpreted as either sympathetic to or criticizing ecstatic worship of Dionysus. Again, there is an important African version: Wole Soyinka's *The Bacchae of Euripides: A Communion Rite*.[41] The title reveals the author's interest in communal ritual, of receiving the god into oneself and the importance of sacrifice. Indeed, the sacrifice of a scapegoat is a theme Soyinka emphasizes more than Euripides, though ritualistic interpretations of the *Bacchae* have sometimes seen Pentheus' death in this way. Soyinka also emphasizes the theme of slavery and liberation, using a chorus of slaves with a Black leader. Dionysus is linked with the Yoruba god Ogun, and there is a mixture throughout the play of Greek, Yoruba, and Christian languages and rituals.

---

[40] *Antigone* 738–739 (trans. Fagles 1982).
[41] Soyinka 1973.

The title of Ola Rotimi's adaptation of Sophocles' *Oedipus Rex*, *The Gods are not to Blame*,[42] shows an interest in the questions of fate and free will that have often preoccupied interpreters of Sophocles' play. The question of free will and divine responsibility is one that I raise with students in this and other texts, starting with Homer. Most students here tend to take the view that the gods *are* to blame, but the topic is one that leads to interesting discussions. Greek and Yoruba myth and religion share an interest in oracles and destiny, but the Yoruba concept seems to be more open to the idea that destiny can be reversed or avoided. In his play, Rotimi makes it clear that his lead character Odewale is ultimately responsible for his actions, and that his irascible character helps bring about his tragic fate. Rotimi has also pointed to another meaning of the title: that European powers and colonizers are not solely responsible for all of Nigeria's civil wars and ethnic strife (the play was first produced in 1968, during the Biafran war in Nigeria).

"Myth, however profound and symbolic, is not necessarily a coherent dramatic picture of the actions of living men and women. If it is to succeed on stage, the dramatist must give it human depth." This could be a comment on ancient Greek drama but is, in fact, from a discussion by Anthony Nazombe of Steve Chimombo's well-known play *The Rainmaker*,[43] first performed in 1975 at Chancellor College's open-air Chirunga theatre (long defunct, alas).[44] In fact, Nazombe argues that the play is not fully successful in this respect, though powerful in its handling of traditional myths and religious themes. The play is a version of the story of Mbona, who is an important hero in Malawian traditions and is revered at shrines, especially in the southernmost area of Malawi.[45] Though there are variant versions of the story, in all of them, he succeeds in bringing rain where a senior chief or religious figurehead has failed, before fleeing from persecution and eventually being killed. According to the most popular story, his head was buried at Khulubvi in the Nsanje region, the most important shrine of Mbona, where offerings are traditionally made, especially in times of drought and pestilence. Chimombo links the story to the historically important Central Region shrine of Msinja and its prophetess Makewana (whose female attendants, the Matsano, act as a chorus in the play), as well as to the creation myth of Kaphirintiwa.

Like many African plays, *The Rainmaker* also makes use of traditional masks and dances, notably those of the *Nyau* cult who perform in the play's finale. The play was created partly in response to a conference at which Matthew

[42] Rotimi 1971.
[43] Chimombo 1978.
[44] Nazombe 1987; on the first performance, see Kerr 1987:120f.
[45] For Mbona, see Rangeley 1953, Schoffeleers 1980, and Mazomb 1987.

Schoffeleers noted the protodramatic characteristics of *Nyau* performances and encouraged their use in creating distinctively Malawian drama. Chimombo's use of Malawian myth in many of his poems and plays was a way of reflecting on contemporary issues indirectly and allegorically, as many Malawian writers had to at a time when literature was strictly controlled and censored by Dr Banda's regime. David Kerr writes that "in *The Rainmaker*, it is not difficult to see that a seventeenth-century conflict between a young prophet, Mbona, and an older tyrant, Kamundi, served as a screen for youthful Malawian frustration with the gerontocratic rule of Kamuzu Banda."[46]

We can see that African writers have found Greek tragedy, as well as their own myths, fruitful in various ways for reflecting on issues relevant to them; and, in the same way, comparison of the original Greek plays and their African adaptations is useful for looking at these issues with students, and helping them to see that Greek drama and Greek mythology are not just museum pieces but continue to be used by writers and thinkers in Africa and elsewhere. The mythology course I teach in the Department is naturally one that lends itself to comparative discussion. Though the core of the course is ancient mythology, I compare it wherever possible with African myths and discuss the nature of mythology and the different theories of its origins and function. Creation-myths are especially good for comparative discussion. In the course, we look at comparisons between Hesiod's *Theogony* and Near Eastern and Egyptian myths, and also consider the wide variety of African creation-myths. Students are usually aware of local myths about the origin of humans and animals and about how death came into the world, which they compare with the story of Pandora in Hesiod.

The most prominent Malawian creation myth is the Chewa tradition of Kaphirintiwa, where God descended in a rainstorm together with the first man and woman and all the animals. Later, the rock there hardened and preserved their footprints, which can still be seen (a typical etiological myth).[47] The site in the Dzalanyama mountains, just on the Mozambique side of the border with Malawi, is an ancient sacred place which people still visit, though the shrine in the neighboring forest of Kasitu moved down to Msinja in central Malawi in the fourteenth or fifteenth century. As is common in creation stories, the story also tells of the origins of death and the separation between God and humans. Originally, they lived together in harmony, but one day the man invented fire by playing with two sticks. As the fire spread, the animals ran away into the forest, and *Chiuta* ascended to the skies on a spider's thread, declaring that

---

[46] Kerr 2004:289. On Chimombo's poetry and his use of myth, see his entry in Roscoe 2008:94–97.
[47] A good collection of Malawian myths is Schoffeleers and Roscoe 1985.

henceforth humans must die. As in Hesiod, fire here is ambivalent, enabling the development of human culture but also bringing about the end of the age of prelapsarian harmony.

A feature of Greek mythology is its focus on heroes and the large number of prominent individual heroes. In the mythology course, naturally, we discuss heroes a fair amount, and look at the standard patterns of a hero's life story, which are found in Greek myths as in the stories of many heroes from around the world. As part of one assignment, I usually ask the students to name a hero from outside the classical world who fits some of these patterns, and Mbona is always a popular choice (as is the West African Sunjata, whose story we study in the course on epic poetry).[48] Like most heroes, he comes from the family of a king or chief but is disregarded early in life. In Mbona's case, the chief is his maternal uncle, but he is not valued because he has no known father. When the chief fails to produce rain by his dance, his nephews—his likely successors— make the attempt but also fail. Mbona is overlooked and only summoned to try as a last resort. When he is successful, instead of honoring him, the chief plots to kill him, and, like many heroes, he has to flee his original home. Heroes often return later and become king, but Mbona fits another category of hero: those who become martyrs or are sacrificed. Like many Greek heroes, his cult grows up at the place where he was killed or his body is buried: offerings are made to him and his spirit is still believed to have power to help, especially in averting drought and disease.

Greek and Roman religion is currently taught as a fourth-year course, which means the class is generally small, and I have had many interesting discussions with them. As noted, many students are enthusiastic Christians and almost all have some religious faith, so the topic of ancient religion is one they find interesting, and they enjoy finding possible parallels with Christianity or Islam, as well as differences and things they disapprove of. It is also interesting to encourage them to make comparisons with traditional Malawian religions and beliefs. Last year, I mentioned that owls could be bad omens for the Romans and sometimes foretell death, and the class said it was very similar in Malawi. One student said in class discussion that he believed it was true because when he was a child, he saw an owl on the roof of a neighbor's house, and soon after there was a death in that house.

Divination and spirit mediums are a good area for comparisons between ancient Greek and African religions. An important Malawian example is the prophetess and rainmaker Makewana, based at Msinja, whom I compare to

---

[48] See n36 above.

the Pythia at Delphi in my teaching.[49] Makewana means "mother of children," signifying mother of all—and, like Pythia, it is a title that is aligned with the role rather than the name of an individual. Like the Pythia, she was subject to various rules and taboos, such as not cutting her hair or wearing white clothes (both of which might stop the rains). There might be gaps between Makewanas after one's death, until another woman appeared at Msinja who had the gift of inspired prophecy and could answer a set of secret questions. There is a contrast here with the Pythia, who was supposed to be an ordinary woman with no special talents—this was understood as proof that it was only by the god's power that she was able to prophesy. As she was seen as the wife of God, Makewana was not allowed to marry or have sex, except at the conclusion of girls' initiation rites, when she would sleep with a man called Kamundi Mbewe, who represented a snake, to ensure the fertility of the young women. Pythias also had to be celibate during their term of office, though it is disputed whether the Pythia was seen as the wife of the god Apollo, or whether his possession of her had a sexual meaning.[50] The role of the snake is interesting, and snakes are often linked with the earth and prophecy, though at Delphi, the snake was linked with the oracle of Earth believed to have preceded Apollo's, and was killed by Apollo himself. Just as the Pythia would bathe in the spring Castalia before prophesying,[51] Makewana washed in a sacred pool before the rainmaking ceremony.

The discussion of Makewana and the Pythia is an interesting one for students because of the important religious roles given to these women in largely patriarchal societies. Gender issues are naturally something that concern students in Malawi, and there are many campaigns to promote awareness of them. Performance poetry is quite popular in Malawi, and at the events I have attended, gender problems and gender-based violence have been easily the most popular subject; this is another area we try to highlight in our courses.

There is—or, until recently, there was—a course on women in the ancient world, but I also look at gender issues in my courses on mythology, religion, and literature. Of course, attitudes here are not always the same as those of contemporary Western students. In my literature class last year, we read Semonides' uncomplimentary poem comparing types of women to animals, and the male students agreed that it was a very accurate portrait of women—naturally, the women disagreed. One highly intelligent female student, who took my

---

[49] For a comparison of Makewana and the Pythia, see Munthali 2015. This was published on the website of Makewana's Daughters, a group founded at Chancellor College in 2014 to promote and provide a forum for women's writing in Malawi (https://makewana.org/). On Makewana, see further Rangeley 1952, Van Breugel 2001, and Smith 2005. For the Pythia, a standard account is Parke and Wormell 1956; see also Johnston 2008.

[50] On this question, see Johnston 2008:40–44.

[51] Parke and Wormell 1956:26–27.

mythology class a couple of years ago, used to complain that the course was misogynistic, though I replied that it was the myths that were misogynistic, rather than the course. I was also unconvinced by her claims that I might be corrupting the morals of students by teaching them about the love affairs of the gods, though she was right to challenge me after one lecture about Zeus' lovers for not using the word "rape." I had not consciously avoided doing so, but since then, I have introduced into the course discussion of the issue of rape and the gods. In recent examination papers, one student, while answering a question about the nature of the Olympian gods, wrote bluntly, "the Olympian gods were rapists."

In this chapter, I have discussed examples of parallels between Greek and African myths and religious practices, but it is controversial how useful such comparisons are. In anthropology the comparative method has been largely unfashionable since the middle of the last century. Comparative methods are criticised for focusing only on similarities while ignoring differences, and for excessive generalisations—to many, it seems better to focus on the specific details of a particular culture and not to take them out of context, as comparisons tend to do. Postmodernism is also suspicious of comparisons, preferring as it does to avoid broad generalisations and look at uniqueness, difference, and marginality. Some postcolonial critics argue that there is a danger in many postcolonial comparisons of imposing European criteria and categories on the non-Western.[52]

Comparative mythology has its roots in nineteenth century developments: the success of comparative methods in biological evolution and Indo-European philology, as well as the increasing availability of data from the different peoples encountered in colonial empires.[53] The most famous comparatist of the late nineteenth and early twentieth century was Sir James Frazer, whose monumental work *The Golden Bough* utilised comparisons of myths and rituals from societies throughout the world.[54] His promiscuous comparisons and eagerness to find similarities, even where they are not readily apparent, helped bring such methods into disrepute with later anthropologists. However, in recent times, there have been defences of the comparative method in mythology and religion. Robert Segal argues that both comparativism and particularism can be fruitful modes of inquiry: comparative studies need not seek to rank things in a hierarchy or evolutionary framework (as Frazer and others did), but can instead focus on differences as well as similarities.[55] The growth in recent work

[52] Young 2013.
[53] For overviews of comparative mythology, see Csapo 2005 and Clark 2012:97-110.
[54] A good, abridged edition is Frazer 1994.
[55] Segal 2001.

on postcolonial Classics discussed in this chapter rests on comparativism of different kinds, and its practitioners are generally wary of the pitfalls of this, and the need to be sensitive to the differences between cultures as well as their similarities.

Within Classics, comparative mythology has focused largely on either Indo-European or Near-Eastern analogues, as these are the most plausible. In the case of Indo-European comparisons, the relationships follow the genetic model—just as comparative philology has demonstrated that Indo-European languages share a common ancestry, and so, the theory claims, it should be possible to find cultural and ideological similarities among the speakers of these languages. The French scholar Georges Dumézil influentially argued that there was an original Indo-European ideology which divided society into three main functions, concerned respectively with sovereignty, war, and fertility. However, such comparisons are less precise than those of philology, and attempts to find examples of this trifunctional ideology in Greek myth have met with mixed success.[56] The Near Eastern connections, in contrast, are an example of the diffusion of myths between neighbouring areas. Especially convincing comparisons are those of the succession myth of Hesiod's *Theogony* with similar myths about creation and the early gods told by Mesopotamian people, Hittites, Hurrians, and others.[57]

So, shared descent and diffusion are two possible answers to the question of why stories found in different cultures and different parts of the world can be remarkably similar. Sometimes these explanations are less plausible, especially in the case of widely separated cultures such as ancient Greek and Malawian; and a third explanation of such similarities is psychological, based on the idea that all humans think in similar ways. Perhaps the most influential of such theories is Jung's idea of the collective unconscious and the "archetypes," universal symbols, and themes that derive from it. These can be found in dreams as well as myth, and examples of the type of archetype found in myth would be the mother, the child, the trickster, the hero, and others.[58] I have discussed above how the Malawian myths of Mbona fit the typical patterns of a hero's life seen also in the stories of Greek heroes, such as Perseus and Heracles. An influential popular discussion of such theories is Joseph Campbell's *The Hero with a Thousand Faces*, which is said to have influenced George Lucas' use of classic mythic archetypes in the *Star Wars* saga.[59] For Campbell and his followers, the

---

[56] A good summary and discussion of Dumézil's theories is Littleton 1966. On Indo-European comparisons see also Puhvel 1987 and West 2007.
[57] Walcott 1966, West 1997, and Haubold 2013.
[58] Jung 1998.
[59] Campbell 1949. For an introduction to Campbell's ideas, see Segal 1987.

comparison of myths from around the world is more than just an intellectual exercise: it can teach us about the universal truths embodied in the myths and help us understand ourselves more fully. Hero myths can inspire us in our own quest for self-fulfilment.

In summarizing his discussion of comparative methods in the study of Greek myth, Matthew Clark sensibly comments, "There can be no methodological objection to generalization; without generalization scholarship could never move beyond the mere collection of facts."[60] He concludes that, as classicists, we should study the role of Greek myths within the culture and society of ancient Greece, yet at the same time not lose sight of the general themes they share with myths from other cultures. In teaching mythology in Malawi, I hope to use both these approaches. I try to teach myths within their ancient Greek context and, at the same time, make comparisons with Malawian and other African myths where appropriate (of course, these myths also need to be looked at within their own cultural context). Naturally, I begin this course with a discussion of the nature of mythology and attempts at defining it, and this necessitates generalizing: assuming that stories from different places have enough in common that they can all be said to belong to the category of mythology.

Specific areas where I usually adduce comparisons in my teaching are creation myths and hero stories. Creation myths are fruitful for comparison as they are found worldwide and often have similarities. As I have noted, the Greek creation myths of Hesiod are the best material for comparison with Near Eastern myths; in the course, we look at these comparisons before also looking at various African creation myths, and their similarities and differences to the other ancient stories. Hero myths are also an obvious area for comparison, and, for that reason, a favorite of comparatists such as Campbell. After we have looked at some specific Greek heroes and at the Malawian Mbona, I usually give the students an assignment to find some other heroes from different cultures whose stories follow the same patterns. In looking at these comparisons, students can become more aware of what is unique in their own myths and what is similar to those of other cultures. They can see for instance that it is possible to understand Mbona in the context of Malawian history and culture and as one instantiation of the widespread concept 'hero.'

Writing this discussion of comparative mythology has also made me aware that I could do more in terms of encouraging students to think about why the stories of different cultures have such similarities and what they think of the different theories of common descent, diffusion, or shared human psychology. At the same time, there is a need to stress the importance of looking at Malawian

---

[60] Clark 2012:109.

myths and religious practices within their specific context of Malawian society and history. More broadly, in teaching Classics in Malawi, it is important to be aware of teaching Classics in a specifically Malawian context, and that Classics within Malawi has its own particular history. This is commonly linked to Dr Banda, but, in fact, goes back further to the teaching of Latin in the first schools set up by missionaries.

These are some of the experiences I have had teaching Classics at Chancellor College, and some of the ways in which my colleagues and I have been trying to develop our teaching to suit the Malawian context and contemporary developments in the field. We also offer Greek and Latin language courses, though currently only a handful of students are taking these. In the past, it was hoped that there would be students majoring in language-based courses as well as those studying Classics in translation, but, in the last few years, this has not happened. Almost all the language students are from the Education Faculty, and, even if they wish to (which some have), the Faculty does not permit them to take Latin or Greek beyond Year Two because these subjects are taught in too few schools. At present, the number of language students is dwindling, so the future of the Greek and Latin courses is doubtful. For Greek, a possibility is teaching New Testament Greek to Theology students, but so far it has not been possible to arrange this kind of cooperation, although one year I did take over teaching some New Testament Greek students temporarily, as their lecturer was unwell.

There are various threats to the future of the Department, though currently, apart from the language classes, we have a healthy number of students. At the moment, we have three full-time staff members and two part-time, but this should increase to four full-time, as we are advertising for a replacement for Esela Munthali, who left at the end of 2019 after ten years in the Department. As I noted earlier, for many years, the Department was reliant on expatriate lecturers who were frequently short-term, and the goal was always to develop a Department staffed largely by Malawian classicists. This has proved difficult to achieve, however. The most successful recruit has been Dr. Steve Nyamilandu, who has been the backbone of the Department for the last twenty years, and without whom it would not have survived. Dr. Thokozani Kunkeyani did complete a PhD in South Africa, but left the university soon after her return to Malawi; as I have said, Esela Munthali left recently. There is a young Malawian lecturer, Chikondi Medson, who is an alumnus of Kamuzu Academy and recently returned from studying at the University of Kentucky. His main expertise is in Greek and Latin teaching, though, unfortunately, there may not be much scope for this in future, and he may have to focus on teaching more general Classics courses. Caroline Alexander states that, in her time at Chancellor College, one quarter of the lecturers were white expatriates. By the time I arrived in 1998, this number was greatly reduced, but there were still ten to fifteen expatriate staff in the College. But the university stopped advertising internationally soon after the year 2000, and, currently, I am one of only two white expatriates. Since Ted Jenner and I left in 2001, there have been no long-term expatriates in the Department apart from returnees: Jenner returned for another two years from 2005–2007, and I returned in 2013, though the University was initially reluctant to offer me a post, and it only came about because of the persistence of Dr. Nyamilandu.

Currently, the University of Malawi is going through a process of "delinking," meaning that the university's separate colleges are becoming autonomous universities. As the oldest and largest constituent college, Chancellor College will take the name "University of Malawi." As a result of this, there are plans for the restructuring of faculties and departments, and the plan is for the departments in the current Faculty of Humanities to be merged into larger schools. Classics may end up in a school with Philosophy and Theology (similar to the arrangement in the University of Zimbabwe) or in a school of Languages and Literature. Of course, given the broad nature of the subject, arguments can be made for linking Classics with many different subjects (and this is also an argument in favor of keeping up the study of Classics within the faculty). There are also suggestions that the Department should be abolished, and its lecturers reassigned to other departments.

These discussions are not new. When Professor Ogilvie wrote his original report, he countered a suggestion from a then-professor of History at Chancellor College that Classical Studies should be taught within a number of existing departments: ancient history within history, literature within the English Department, and so on. Ogilvie emphasized that Classics is a unity; ancient literature, for instance, cannot be understood without reference to its historical, social, and cultural context. During and just before my first period of employment in Malawi, these issues emerged again. In 1997, Professor Hoffmann wrote a paper on the future of Classics at the University, responding to proposals of restructuring. Hoffmann also argued against the parceling out of the elements of Classics to different departments, and envisaged the development of Classics into a broader department of Cultural Studies. When I became Head after Hoffmann's departure, I also wrote a paper on "Classics and restructuring issues," arguing in favor of keeping Classics as a unified Department even if it was combined with one or more other departments (as is now proposed again). In the year 2000, it was decided that Classics should merge with the Department of English, and I was reluctantly elected Head of this new combined department. I then went to the UK on leave for several weeks, and when I returned, found that this plan had been quietly shelved, and the departments were again independent (to the relief of lecturers from both departments). It seems that this time around, the merging into larger schools will happen. Thus, we can hope that Classics will remain intact within such a school rather than being whittled away.

There have always been voices in the university hostile to Classics. In part, this arises from the kind of views that classicists face around the world: that ours is no longer a subject relevant to the modern world. In Africa, there is also the issue that Classics is especially seen as a Western subject, and one formerly used to justify an imperialist hegemony. There is a more specific objection in Malawi, which is that the Department was purely set up on the wishes of Dr Banda, and even today, many still see it as closely linked with him.

Hopefully, I have shown some small examples in this chapter of how Classics can still be relevant in Chancellor College and other African universities, and some of the risks and rewards of teaching Classics in this context. I have also tried to show the directions in which we have been developing our courses recently, in line with developments worldwide in the study of Classics. The work done in the areas of reception and postcolonial Classics shows how Classics in twenty-first century Africa need not be seen as an imposing of Western canons, but can be a fruitful way of looking at the relationships between colonial and postcolonial cultures. Classics also need no longer be seen as a Western possession but as part of world literature, and I have mentioned in this paper some ways in which ancient Greek and Roman culture can be closer to and understood more easily by Africans than modern Westerners.

6

Not in Kansas Anymore

Cybelle Greenlaw

Although I've called Kansas home for many years, my journey to Malawi began in a small town near Tacoma, WA, called Fredrickson, where my family owned the remaining twelve acres of an old homestead granted to my father's great-great-grandfather in the 1800s. For as long as I can remember, we had a menagerie: goats, pheasants, guinea fowl, peacocks, parrots, barn cats, dogs, ducks, geese, and many others. In 1984, my mother realized that what she really wanted—and had always wanted—was a primate sanctuary. We immediately began converting our empty guest house to a monkey house and obtained a federal permit to take in former research and zoo animals. Our first monkey was a young pig-tailed macaque (*macaca nemestrina*) called Tony. That led to a specialization in baboons and macaques, and our numbers grew to over a dozen within a few years. My mother was delighted, but I was less enthusiastic. It hadn't occurred to me that my teenage years outside of high school would revolve around building and cleaning cages and digging and maintaining drainage ditches. When I had the opportunity to spend my last year of high school in New Zealand, I took it. It was a nice break. When I got back, there were even more monkeys, more work, a family crisis, and a new outside threat to our little sanctuary: Boeing had purchased the land behind our property for a new 777 wing plant, and the ground water quickly became contaminated and unsafe to drink. My mother and I started looking for a way out.

Over the years, my mother developed a long-distance friendship with a woman in Kansas City, who shared her love of non-human primates. Although we had never met in person, we knew her well through the many home videos and letters she sent us. In early 1992, it turned out she was having a crisis of her own. Her eldest daughter had been murdered, and she needed money for a funeral. She asked if we would be interested in buying a house from her for the bargain price of $3,000. I flew down to Kansas City to check it out. As one would expect, it was in rough shape. However, my mother and I had become fairly skilled at home repair over the years, and so I bought the house, and my mother and the monkeys soon followed. We obtained a local permit to keep the monkeys we had and agreed not to take in any additional primates. Once enough repairs had been made, and my mother had the new primate area somewhat under control, I decided I'd probably better do something with my life and enrolled in a local university, majoring in French and Classics. I thought I'd be able to leave the monkey business behind, but then, in my third year as an undergraduate, I was introduced to the blue monkeys of Thera, and I knew there would never be any way out.

After graduating from the University of Missouri-Kansas City, I started looking for graduate programs in Europe and ended up in Ireland, first in an MA program at University College Dublin, then, after a brief period of teaching in Paris, in a PhD program at Trinity College Dublin. Under the supervision of Dr. Christine Morris, I wrote my thesis on the iconography and cultural significance of monkeys in five ancient Mediterranean civilizations. During my studies, I had the opportunity to work in several museums in Ireland and the UK. Museology seemed like a good career move, and on completion of my thesis, I was awarded a Des Lee Fellowship in Museum Studies from the University of Missouri-St. Louis with a curatorial internship in Ancient and Islamic Art at the Saint Louis Art Museum. After a year of provenance research taught me that the number of looted objects in American museums was staggering, I became disillusioned with the work and concerned that I was contributing to the destruction of the world's cultural heritage. I quit, and returned to Kansas City without a plan.

After months of applying for every academic job that seemed even remotely suitable, one of my good friends in Dublin forwarded an advertisement for a lectureship in Classics at Chancellor College, University of Malawi. The posting expanded on the natural beauty of Zomba and its diverse wildlife, including baboons and other monkeys that occasionally wandered into town. He sent it as joke, thinking it was a scam. Much to his horror, I applied and got the job.

In the months prior to leaving, I tried to find out as much as I could about the country, but very few sources were available. I exchanged several emails with Steve Nyamilandu to learn about the Department, the materials available, and anything else that might be relevant. When I suggested several possible courses I could teach, Steve seemed interested in all of them and requested a syllabus for each, which I was happy to supply. When I inquired about available books, Steve asked that I bring as many as possible. I was also informed that most visiting instructors hired a housekeeper and that Loudon Umi Gama would be a good choice.

Although I was excited about the prospect of going to Malawi, certain issues had me rather concerned about the legitimacy of the offer. The first was Chancellor College's website, which had images of the Great Hall, as well as several images of wealthy-looking international students. It was, to be blunt, a little dodgy. I would later learn that these images had been borrowed from the websites of American Ivy League universities. Secondly, the semester was supposed to start in late January 2007, but Steve informed me that there were ongoing student protests that could lead to delays. He assured me, however, that the University would pay for my airfare as soon as possible. After several weeks without news, he suggested I buy my own plane ticket and just show up. Although I considered this, my inner skeptic predicted too many negative outcomes, and I wasn't sure I could afford the airfare. I decided to wait. By early March, the Department had my ticket, and I arrived a few days later with five large boxes of books.

When Steve met me at the airport, he had our Department secretary with him, as well as Mr. Gama. We stopped at a couple of places in Blantyre to buy household items and have lunch. I remember it was a fried chicken fast-food type restaurant, and my Malawian hosts were a little surprised by the fact that I don't eat meat. We still had a good conversation, and I enjoyed the opportunity to ask dozens of questions about life in Malawi. As we continued to Zomba, we drove past field after field of maize—it almost seemed like a tropical version of Iowa. At one point, when we stopped the car to see baboons crossing the road, I got out to take a picture, prompting many more to come running out of the field. Unfortunately, as I learned, they are considered a pest to the farmers, so when humans stop to look at them, they run. Still, it was a magnificent sight and a marvelous introduction to the country.

Once in Zomba, I was taken to the house provided by the University, which was an attractive, two-bedroom, brick bungalow. Like almost all houses in Zomba, the floor was made of concrete. It was sparsely decorated but clean and orderly. The front garden was filled with colorful flowers and attracted a wide variety of animals including giant magpies, small brightly colored birds, geckos and other lizards, snakes, and giant mantises. I loved the place immediately and felt rather ashamed for suspecting that the advertisement might not have been legitimate.

Despite the natural beauty of the place, evidence of ugly colonialism soon became apparent: for example, behind the house was another small brick building called "the boys' quarters," which was to be Gama's residence in town, which he shared with the gardener he had selected for me. I soon realized many people referred to their housekeepers, gardeners, and night guards as "boys."

This seemed quite disturbing to me, as Mr. Gama was in his fifties and had a daughter my age. Shortly after I moved in, he lent me a book on the Chichewa language that was essentially comprised of a list of commands and insults. I remember seeing phrases such as "You're doing this wrong!" and "This place is filthy!"

The day after I arrived, Steve took me to Chancellor College to make introductions and show me around. The students seemed surprised that I was a young woman, but they were very friendly and welcoming. I also met one of the people who would be most helpful to me: our assistant who did all the photocopying and gofer work for the Department. We walked around the campus and made our way to the Library, a dimly lit building, in which a faint musty odor permeated the air. Walking through the Classics section, I noted that the most recent books dated from 1983. Pages had been cut out of some of the volumes, and specks of mold were visible on the fore-edges of the books. A few of the archaeological books bordered on pseudo-science. I noticed one by John Luce on Atlantis.[1] Luce was a professor emeritus at my old alma mater, Trinity College Dublin, and a highly gifted classicist—but his ideas on the lost continent were not considered his most convincing work. Perhaps the most surprising part of the Library, for me, was the American Corner, which was a brightly lit, modern section of the Library with new computers and an impressive collection of recent books on American government and history. I learned that this was a gift from the American Embassy. The Librarian informed me that this was a way for the Library to raise money, as students were charged the equivalent of $1.00 per hour for internet use. I noticed, however, that it was devoid of students, which made me question its value, but I didn't have time to give it much thought. That was a Friday. Monday, I started teaching.

I was asked to teach two classes: Ancient Philosophy for third year students and Greco-Roman Archaeology for fourth years. I soon discovered that electricity was not available in many of the classrooms, because people stole the copper wiring to sell. In fact, only the Great Hall was always in good repair, because the President of Malawi visited Chancellor College once a year for the televised graduation ceremony, so the Great Hall had to be well maintained. I also discovered that, although I had been assigned a room with electricity for my archaeology class, no projector was available for PowerPoint presentations. I was informed that the Department used to have one, but that it had been appropriated by a retired faculty member, and no one really wanted to report the issue.

---

[1]   Luce 1969.

Despite the technical difficulties, teaching the archaeology class was a genuine pleasure. I got around the lack of projector by holding up my laptop and passing it around the class so that students could examine the details more closely. Of course, this meant the number of topics discussed in each lesson was slightly limited—but it was gratifying to see the students discuss the images and point out details to one another. They were particularly impressed by images of *tholos* tombs that were still intact after more than 3,000 years. When I told them I had taken some the photographs myself, they were amazed. I remember one saying, "This is real? You can visit this place, Mycenae, and see these tombs? They aren't reconstructions?" It was an interesting moment because it illustrated just how abstract the study of Classics was for many of them. It prompted me to ask whether they knew where Greece was. Most did not. I brought in a map the next day, and we talked about how classical culture spread through the Mediterranean and even reached North Africa. That fact seemed particularly surprising to them, as most did not realize the Greeks and Romans had any connection to the African continent at all.

When we reached the archaic period, I first showed them images of *kouroi* and *korai* statues as we know them, and then I held up an image of a brightly painted reconstruction of a *kore*. There was a collective gasp followed by shouts of "Beautiful!" It was a wonderful reaction that the ancient artists would have appreciated—and presented a strong contrast to the common reaction among Western viewers to reject the original, colorful versions as garish.

One minor—and rather surprising—problem I encountered was that I had to remind some of the students not to circle images on my laptop with their pens. I soon learned that many students didn't have their own laptops, and most had never owned or even read an entire book. I let a student borrow one, and she returned it in poor shape: page after page filled with underlining and notes in permanent ink. When I expressed disappointment at the treatment of the book and asked why she did that, she just looked confused and said, "I was studying it." I began to understand why the books in the Library were in such poor condition: the students couldn't afford to photocopy, and they thought cutting chapters out of books gave them an edge in class. I tried to explain that it just wasn't polite to borrow a book and write in it, especially since I had to photocopy several pages for my class. More confused looks. I gave up and let it slide.

I should mention at this point that I probably broke all kinds of copyright rules while teaching in Malawi. Since the students had limited access to books, I asked our assistant to photocopy full chapters from the books I brought for both the archaeology and philosophy classes each week. It was an obscene amount of paper, and I felt ashamed of all the work she did for me. However, I just couldn't wrap my mind around the idea that university students had never read an entire book. That was something I couldn't let slide. The level of education they received was perhaps on par with an American high school in an underfunded district, and I hoped to give them something a little more challenging. When we were a few weeks in, I asked them to write a two-page essay and insisted that they type it. Most did, but they also told me that it was extremely expensive for them. The students who didn't have a laptop had to work in the American Corner, and they were charged $1.00 per hour, which was more than many Malawians made in a day. I realized I put them in the position of going without food in order to complete an assignment. I never asked them to type anything again.

This brings us back to the American Corner. A few weeks after my arrival, I was told an American foreign service officer would be visiting Chancellor College to talk about the embassy's gift to the Library, and I was asked to attend on behalf of the Department. The FSO was a young man, who had clearly written his speech on the ride over. It was a disjointed talk in which he posed the question, "Why libraries?" He then answered his own question by explaining that from the very beginning, America had libraries: "They were built by our German and English ancestors." He paused and looked around the audience, "Oh, and there were some Africans there, too." It made very little sense, and I wondered if he understood that he was referencing slavery. Fortunately, the speech was brief, and the gathered faculty politely smiled and applauded. We spoke afterwards. I mentioned that the American Corner was cost prohibitive for our students and asked what the purpose was if they couldn't afford to type their papers. He said it was a way for the Library to raise funds, and he hoped it would be an attractive resource for American tourists. That seemed rather odd to me, since I hadn't encountered any American tourists around the university, or even in Zomba for that matter. This was to be the first of many questionable foreign aid projects I would encounter in Malawi.

For now, I'll return to my role in the Department of Classics, which comprised three faculty members: Steve Nyamilandu, Thokozani Kasakula (née Kunkeyani), and myself. It was my understanding that although few majored in Classics, almost all Humanities students could choose a course from Classics as one of the options within the Faculty. That meant we had to offer courses for approximately 450 students. Steve had told me in confidence that there had been some controversy concerning the management of departmental funds and that Thoko, who had been serving as Deputy Head of Department, had been asked to step down. A few days later, I met with Steve and Thoko, and without mentioning any details, they both informed me that I should serve as the new Deputy Head of Department, since Thoko no longer wanted the position. Thoko then suggested we have a faculty retreat by Lake Malawi, and we all agreed that would be a good way to get to know one another, discuss departmental needs, and develop a plan for the year.

In preparation for the retreat, Steve asked me how much money we should request from the Dean. I, of course, did not have a good sense of the cost of living, so I suggested he request slightly more than we needed and that we could just refund the rest afterwards. He agreed, and the request was approved. A few days later, we were given a large stack of kwacha to divide three ways. When we got to Lake Malawi, we spent a little time sightseeing and looking at the carvings and trinkets. Steve and Thoko bought a few and asked if I saw any I liked. I said the carvings were beautiful, but I was going to wait a while. Eventually, we went to a local restaurant for lunch, and a waiter came over to take our order. Thoko tilted her head at the waiter and said, "You look like my father." She told him her father's name, and the waiter smiled, "Yes, he's my father, too." "I thought so," she said. Like many Malawian men, her father had multiple families, and some were more privileged than others. When we finished our meal, Thoko gave the waiter extra money, and we left.

The next day, we held our departmental meeting. I learned that Greek and Latin were no longer taught at the University, and that the languages were rarely taught in schools. Much had changed since Banda's time, they told me. The first President had insisted on the creation of a Classics Department as critical to the respectability of the University. Sadly, long-term funding for its continued development had not been arranged. Compared to other departments, Classics was underfunded, and the two permanent faculty members were overburdened, tasked with offering classes to hundreds of students seeking a general degree in Humanities. By contrast, the French Department had five permanent faculty members, and fewer than thirty students.

Given the pressure to offer classes to so many students who weren't majoring in Classics, we decided to hold off on offering language classes. However, we did discuss it as part of a future project to create an actual Classics degree. I hope that becomes a reality one day. Despite the fact that English is the official language, few Malawians speak it fluently. Even at the University, many students struggle with comprehension. Because so many English words have Greek or Latin roots, studying classical languages can greatly expand a student's vocabulary and help them understand parts of speech. That would give them an advantage in all their other classes.

As the day progressed, Steve and Thoko told me about some of the issues the College had had with previous visiting lecturers: for example, a young man who was too shy to work there and whose excuse for leaving was that he couldn't handle all the young girls looking at him. I suspect there was more to the story, but that was all they knew. A recently departed expat lecturer apparently had no such problem. Steve told me he was very charming and a real ladies' man. "Oh, you would have liked him so much!" Steve told me. "He had affairs with several students." "Oh, that's very much frowned upon in the States," I said. "We fire people for things like that."

This led to a discussion of gender roles in Malawi. I was told many of the young women at the University had their education funded by "sugar daddies" and that it was simply accepted as normal. Perhaps as a result, they didn't see anything strange about the behavior of the expat lecturer and even seemed to admire him for it. I, on the other hand, felt a bit ill. Still, it was a productive discussion, and I learned quite a bit about the challenges the College faced.

As we prepared to return to Zomba, my colleagues remained concerned that I hadn't purchased any souvenirs. I decided to come clean and admit that I was waiting for my first paycheck before I made any unnecessary purchases. I didn't exactly fit the stereotype of the rich American. They looked confused. "But," Thoko said, "we gave you all that cash. What are you saving it for?" "Uhhh, you mean the cash we took for necessary expenses? I've been writing down the cost of every meal I purchased, and I'm going to hand in my receipts with the remaining cash. It's not for souvenirs is it?" Steve and Thoko laughed. "Yes, it's like a bonus … If you try to return it, the secretary will keep it for herself. You keep it. It's a bonus. We work hard." Now, this was a development I had not anticipated, and I was in no way comfortable with keeping the money. I thought about Thoko's newly found half-brother and realized she probably had a number of other relatives who depended on her generosity. I handed most of the money over to her, because I couldn't bring myself to keep it and I knew that trying to return my portion would put my colleagues in an awkward position. Thoko was confused, but Steve urged her to take it. I still felt conflicted, but it seemed the best solution.

Back in Zomba, I got on with teaching. The philosophy students were just as much fun as the archaeology students. All were very attentive and interested in the subject. Perhaps luckily, some of the ideas weren't entirely new to them. Many had already taken an introductory class from the Philosophy Department that touched upon the early Greek philosophers. However, it became clear from class discussions that the readings I assigned were a bit beyond their level of English. I started asking them to read sections aloud, and we discussed what they meant. I also found that the students liked to work together outside of class, which often led to identical responses on essay questions. I got the impression that most of their other instructors simply expected them to repeat what they learned in class; I wanted them to think for themselves a little more. We spent time looking at examples of logical arguments, and I tried to make a game of naming the logical fallacy in common situations and statements. To encourage critical thinking, I usually added a bonus hypothetical question or two to weekly quizzes. I remember that one, in particular, proved very confusing for them:

> In an otherwise wealthy country, there is one poor region. Many people are out of work, the roads and buildings are in bad condition, and a few people are close to starvation. The local leaders petition the government for food banks so the people can eat. Once the food banks are established, the leaders consider the problem solved. Do you agree? If not, what would you recommend?

Most students correctly saw that the food banks represented a short-term solution that didn't address the root causes of the region's problems. Some suggested that work programs were needed to fix the roads and buildings so that people had enough money to buy food. Interestingly, all those who suggested work programs also said that the food banks were unnecessary. Other students were convinced it was a trick question. A wealthy country, they argued, could not have a poor region. I was rather surprised by these responses, so we discussed the question in class the next day. First, I asked the students what would happen to the starving people if they were offered jobs instead of being given food. They said they would be able to buy food after they worked. I asked how soon the people should get paid. Most said two weeks to a month. Then I asked how long starving people would be able to work on roads and buildings before they died. This got some confused looks. They hadn't thought about the effect of hard labor on hungry people. I asked if food banks or some other means of getting food to the people might be necessary before they were asked to work. A few nodded, so we agreed that a short-term solution was needed to prevent starvation and that a long-term solution was needed so people could continue to feed themselves. I then asked if the lack of employment was necessarily the only cause of starvation. There was a long silence. Finally, someone said, "Dr. Greenlaw, actually none of this makes sense. The problem said it was 'an otherwise wealthy country.' There is no starvation or unemployment in a wealthy country. It has to be a trick."

I asked the students if they considered the United States to be a wealthy country. Everyone immediately and emphatically agreed. "Well," I asked, "Did you hear about Hurricane Katrina?" It had happened only two years before, and most of the students said that they had heard something about it. I asked if they knew that many people were too poor to escape the flood, and that some couldn't even afford a bus ticket out of New Orleans. I explained how hundreds of people drowned, and thousands of others had to seek shelter in the Superdome, where they were trapped for several days with no plumbing, limited power, and insufficient supplies. Diabetics ran out of insulin and collapsed in shock. After the evacuation, most of the survivors were left with nothing. Over a million people were displaced by Katrina. Some were able to relocate to other states, but many could not. Thousands of shabby, temporary trailers were set up for those that remained, and many people continued to live in poverty long after the flood waters receded. The students were shocked. It never occurred to them that poverty could exist in America or that the wellbeing of so many people could be ignored in a wealthy country. I found this fascinating, particularly because the gap between wealthy Malawians and poor villagers was so pronounced.

Towards the end of the semester, I became curious to see if another subject might encourage even more class discussion. I asked the students if they would prefer to continue studying philosophy into the Roman period or whether they would be more interested in a class on gender in the ancient world. The vote for gender was almost unanimous. I was delighted with the response and glad for the few weeks between semesters to select some readings and have copies made. I was also glad for the chance to visit more of the country and spend time with new friends.

Two of my new friends volunteered with a nonprofit called IFESH (International Foundation for Education and Self-Help). As far as I know, the orga-nization is no longer active—its website (http://www.ifesh.org) is unavailable at the time of writing this—but at the time, it operated in approximately ten African countries. The volunteers served in a variety of ways and were paid a monthly stipend that was slightly higher than my salary at Chancellor College. Ted, who had been a professor at an American university, was placed in the Mathematics Department at Chancellor College and had the office above mine. His house mate, Jeff, worked with younger children and taught at one of the village schools. Through them, I was introduced to Emma Gondwe, sister of Esela Munthali, who worked for WESM (the Wildlife and Environmental Society of Malawi). One of the first WESM events we attended was the screening of Al Gore's film *An Inconvenient Truth*.[2] Although the event was intended for expats and wealthier Malawians, I invited Mr. Gama because I thought he might enjoy seeing a film and visiting a nice house, situated above the mosquito line. I remember that we walked over together in the dark, and I was quite glad to have him with me.

Zomba is a wonderful place for stargazing because there is virtually no light pollution, but walking to another house at night can be a little scary for someone accustomed to paved sidewalks and streetlamps. I'm not sure Mr. Gama knew what to make of the evening, but he seemed to enjoy being a part of it, as the expats were all kind to him and made him feel welcome, although I noticed

[2] Guggenheim 2006.

the wealthy Malawians gave a me a bit an eyeroll for bringing him. The film itself received mixed reviews. My American friends thought it was great and had excellent suggestions, while the many Scandinavians present considered it rather sad that Americans needed such a rudimentary introduction to climate change. They weren't wrong. And much to my relief, the Scandinavians kindly gave me and Mr. Gama a ride back home.

Of course, I was most eager to see the wildlife, particularly the baboons and vervet monkeys. I had learned that one could just find a spot to sit in the botanical gardens and observe dozens of lovely vervets, many of which were young mothers holding their little infants to their breasts. However, the baboons didn't visit town as frequently, and Mr. Gama told me I would have to walk up Zomba Plateau to see them. He was worried that I wouldn't be able to make it—the ascent is relatively steep—but I told him I enjoyed walking. I'd recently purchased a cell phone for him, which he used to call me about an hour into the walk to make sure I was okay.

It took me about an hour and half to reach the top. Along the way, I encountered several yellow baboon families, including young ones that hid in the bushes, screeching and throwing things at me. It was delightful! I also encountered young children who surrounded me and yelled, "Candy, *Azungu*! Candy!" Unfortunately, I didn't have any, so I gave them a few kwacha instead and made a mental note to buy candy before making another trip. I also observed women chopping huge stacks of wood, some with infants strapped to their backs while they worked, and men walking down the plateau with wood stacked high on their bicycles. Their strength was truly remarkable. By contrast, I met a wealthier young Malawian coming back down the plateau. He smiled at me and yelled, "I didn't make it to the top. It's too hot, and I'm tired. Good luck! Enjoy your walk!"

At the top of the plateau, there was a nice hotel with a bar and restaurant. I decided a cup of tea was in order, so I sat down by a window. I remember watching a baboon stealing sugar packets from a cart while the hotel staff cleaned the rooms. After a few minutes, an older Scottish couple asked to join me, and I learned that the man, Rex, was also a visiting lecturer at Chanco, and that his wife, Judy, had been wanting to return to Malawi for many years. She told me she had worked in Zomba back in the 1970s, remarking that times had changed. Back then, the dress code for women was very strict, and she laughed about being arrested for wearing trousers instead of a dress. When they realized I'd walked up the plateau, they offered to drive me back down. Along the way, they commented on how much the plateau had changed and pointed out areas of deforestation. We exchanged phone numbers and met up often in the following months. That was one of the things I liked most about Malawi—accidental meetings that quickly turned into friendships.

A few days later, Mr. Gama asked if I would like to visit his friends and family in the surrounding villages. I was eager to meet them and asked if we could go the next day. He said that wouldn't give him time to let them know we were coming and that they would be disappointed not to prepare food for me. I understood that would mean every household killed a chicken, and, as a longtime vegetarian, I really didn't want that to happen. I insisted a surprise visit would be better. He didn't tell me all the places we would visit, but I had a feeling that there might be some projects he wanted me to support. I ran to the bank and took out some cash for the following day.

We first arrived at a primary school, where children were playing outside. They all knew him, and we were quickly surrounded. Mr. Gama gave a few kwacha to the little ones in his family, and I started going through my pockets for small change. Our presence caused a stir: the Principal came marching out to ask why we were causing such a disruption. I apologized and tried to explain that Mr. Gama wanted me to meet his nieces and nephews. He saw that we were giving them coins and asked if we had enough for all the others. Already embarrassed that I didn't have enough small change (or candy), I offered to make a donation to the school instead. He gave me a skeptical look and asked, "How much?" I handed him the equivalent of $20.00, and the entire crowd cheered. The Principal insisted on escorting me to his office to write me a receipt. He said the students had been learning to write in the dirt and that he would use the money to buy notebooks. I wondered if any of my own students had learned to read and write this way, but I suspected most village children never got the opportunity to study at university.

As we walked, we encountered a disabled man from Mr. Gama's village. He gave the man a few kwacha, and we walked on. Mr. Gama told me that man was unable to work because he had been badly burned as a child and lost an arm. "Is there no work he can do?" I asked. Mr. Gama said, "No, of course not! He only has one arm!" I said that in other countries, people could get prosthetics if they lost an arm or a leg; it didn't have to be the end of everything. He looked a bit sad and said, "Well, you come from a special country. Here he can't work."

We continued on to visit Mr. Gama's extended family in several other villages. There were, indeed, multiple projects in need of support, and I was happy to be able to contribute a little to each of them. I was also exceptionally glad that it had been a surprise visit because every family lamented the fact that they hadn't killed a chicken for me. When we arrived at Mr. Gama's house, he introduced me to his wife, daughter, and many other dependents. He was very proud of his home, which was still under construction. It was partially open to the elements, and every weekend he would come back and add a few lines of mud brick to the front wall. He was also very proud of his little herd of goats and encouraged me to feed them some leaves. On the way back, he told me, "I only have one wife, you know. Some men have more than one, but that's not good." I agreed.

In anticipation of the second semester, I became particularly attentive to conversations and local news articles that touched on traditional gender roles in Malawi, and hoped to incorporate relevant examples in the class on gender in antiquity, which turned out to be the most entertaining I ever had at Chancellor College, and the students were more engaged than I could have anticipated. We began reading about goddesses and other mythological heroines to get an idea of the roles women were expected to perform in ancient Greek culture. The students found much that was familiar, particularly in the myths of Zeus' many infidelities and Hera's angry retaliation against powerless human women. A few weeks into the class, I came across an article in the *Saturday Nation* about Patricia Kaliati, who was serving as Minister of Culture and Education in Bingu wa Mutharika's government. The article reported that Kaliati had allegedly hired a group of men to kidnap and sexually abuse her maid, because she believed the woman had had an affair with her husband:[3]

> Ngala, 33, who once worked for the Blantyre-based women rights lawyer Seodi White, claims the group took her to Nkando (the minister's home) where Kaliati allegedly stripped the victim and the minister asked the men to lay with her as punishment for going out with Mr. Kaliati.

When asked about the alleged assault, the report said that Kaliati responded, "Wasn't she caught with my husband? Go and ask her if she wasn't found with him." I was filled with disgust, but I was curious to see how the students would react.

I brought the article in and asked, if the allegations were true, did Minister Kaliati remind them of any particular mythological woman? The students yelled, "Hera!" To my surprise, many of them found the article hilarious. I asked if they thought it was funny that the maid had been raped by a group of men. One of the young women said, "That's what powerful people do, Dr. Greenlaw." "Hmmm," I said. "How do you think the maid feels, though? That must have been a terrifying, traumatic experience for her." Another student spoke up, "Oh don't worry. Poor people are used to that. It's okay." Other students nodded in agreement. "Well," I said, "that seems like a pretty terrible thing to be used to. You don't think poor people care what happens to them?" The consensus was

---

[3]   Chandilanga 2007.

that there was no way to be sure, but poor villagers really should be used to misery because they didn't know any better.

Interestingly, I came across a recent book by Ann Swidler and Susan Cotts Watkins that cites the same 2007 article about Kaliati. They write of the awkward contradiction of elite Malawian women who adopt the rhetoric of global feminism and outwardly support the empowerment of women, and yet are willing to turn violent against another woman to protect their marriage. They note that Kaliati was widely celebrated for appealing to abused girls to report those who hurt them, even in cases of incest, and to mothers to not protect husbands who abused their daughters. As a former teacher, Kaliati encouraged girls to stay in school and avoid early marriage. If the allegations were well-founded, however, it seemed that when it came to her own husband's infidelity, the blame was placed entirely on the maid.[4] It seems both wealthy and poor Malawians tend to view certain women as "seductresses" and despise them as threats to virtuous wives.

Another reading I selected for the class was Apollodoros' *Against Neaira*. The story of the freedwoman Neaira haunted me for weeks after I first read it as an undergraduate. For those who aren't familiar with the text, it represents the prosecution speeches delivered by Apollodoros and his kinsman, Theomnestos, against the former *hetaera* and companion of their rival, Stephanos, the true target of the case. Although we have only one side of the case and no way of knowing whether Neaira was acquitted or condemned, I've always thought it must have been horrible for her—a woman then in her fifties or sixties—forced to listen to all the sordid details of her past, unable to defend herself. I had expected the women in the class to be sympathetic to her as well. I was wrong. Most of the students, especially the women, got hung up on Hipparchos' testimony that Neaira had two lovers, and that they paid her owner, Nikarete, to buy her for their own use.[5] "She should have just had one man," they insisted. "Well," I argued, "she was a slave, raised from childhood to be a courtesan. Did she really have the luxury of choice?" They considered this. "Well, maybe not, but she should have found a way to be with only one man." They simply could not muster any empathy for Neaira.

When we got to Medea, on the other hand, the women's views contrasted quite sharply with those of the men. They didn't have much sympathy for the likes of Jason, who callously tossed aside the granddaughter of Helios. The young men understood the story differently. This seemed a reasonable time to ask the students how they felt about the idea of a man having multiple wives or families.

---

[4] Swidler and Cotts Watkins 2017:144–146.
[5] [Demosthenes] 59 *Against Neaira* 29–32.

Should the feelings of the first wife and the children from that marriage be taken into consideration? Here, most of the men said it was completely acceptable for a man to find another woman and added the twist that it was even more understandable if the wife was pregnant. Women behaved irrationally in that condition, they argued, and men had needs that a pregnant woman couldn't satisfy. There were exclamations of outrage from the women in the class.

One young man was especially eager to tell me that men couldn't possibly empathize with the feelings of women. "How could we know what women feel, Dr. Greenlaw? We aren't women. We have nothing in common with them. So why worry about their feelings when understanding them is impossible? That's why it's okay for men to go to other women when a wife is pregnant." "Oh," I said, "in a sense it's impossible for one person to completely understand the feelings of another, but we can try to put ourselves in the place of another from time to time. Tell me, how would you feel if your wife or girlfriend felt justified in being unfaithful to you." "Now why would she do that?" he asked. "What's my crime, Dr. Greenlaw?"

"We're not talking about crimes, here, are we?" was my answer. "Pregnancy isn't a crime, but a medical condition. Let's say you had a medical condition. Something caused you to experience impotence, and you couldn't satisfy your wife for an extended period of time. By your reasoning, would she not be justified in leaving you for another man who could?" "Oh, no!" he exclaimed. "I think she should try to understand ..." This admission was greeted by uproarious laughter from the other students, both male and female. As the class ended, I saw a group of young women stomping off together and one of them yelling, "I never want to date a man from this place ever!"

As the semester progressed, I gained more friends from the ever-changing expat community. Jeff and Ted introduced me to a woman from Arkansas, Fleur, who had received a grant from the Clinton Library to promote democracy in Malawi. She was only staying for two months, and believed she had a plan that could not fail. She had printed dozens of two-page bibliographies of books on democracy (all in English) and planned to distribute them to children and their parents through local schools. Once the people read these books, they were sure to become empowered and start exercising their basic rights. Despite her somewhat misguided zeal and poorly concealed contempt for Northerners like me, we became relatively good friends. Fleur was in her early sixties and, despite frequent references to her childhood poverty, was clearly attached to comforts that can only be described as upper middle class. She rented a big house that was far more elegant than any I have ever lived in, and she had hired a driver to be at her beck and call for the duration of her stay. Like many expats, Fleur found it difficult to deal with long, dark nights without television or other forms of entertainment. Even reading could be difficult with blackouts that lasted for hours, so she was in desperate need of friendship and often invited me on day trips.

Shortly before the Fourth of July, Fleur called and asked if I would like to go the American Embassy's Independence Day celebration. I agreed, and was rather curious to meet the ambassador. I looked up the event, which actually took place 3 July. It seemed to be an informal gathering for the Peace Corps volunteers to cut loose and meet some of the other expats. On the morning of the event, her driver picked me up and drove me to her house. Fleur looked me up and down and asked what I was going to wear. "Well, since I didn't bring a change of clothes, I thought I'd just stick with the blouse and dress pants that I have on." "Oh, no," she said, shaking her head. "There are going to be dignitaries there, and you are not wearing a suit." "Well," I said, "I'll risk it. I mean, I'd be pretty surprised if all the Peace Corps volunteers show up in tuxedos." Fleur sighed wearily. "Well, that can't be helped. I guess I won't wear a suit, either then. But I will wear a jacket. There will be dignitaries!"

When we arrived at the Embassy, we were greeted by a large contingent of Peace Corps volunteers in cutoff jeans and well-worn T-shirts, a smattering of expats in khakis and short-sleeved shirts, and Ambassador Eastham himself in casual dress. I resisted the urge to say, "I told you so." As it turned out, the real Independence Day party with dignitaries was to be held the following day, and Fleur was miffed not to have been invited. Eastham was a personable man, who, despite having worked on the African continent for over thirty years, had never bothered to learn an African language. Indeed, I got the impression he rarely ventured far from the Embassy compound. Fleur had convinced him to visit a school with her, and that was his first and only visit to a Malawian school. In my view, his general lack of interest in the country to which he was assigned also explained the mindset of the protocol officer who visited Chancellor College earlier in the year: his cluelessness seemed to spring from a general lack of curiosity about the host culture.

A few weeks later, Fleur invited me on weekend trip to Lilongwe. At the end of the day, we sat in our room chatting. She was having some difficulty with her project. "I just don't understand it," she said. "I'm following a method that was highly successful in some of the poorest countries in South America." "Um, well, we're not in South America.," I said. "Well, I know. That's why I gave them bibliographies of books in English." "Okay, Fleur. You've been here a few weeks now. You must have noticed most people don't speak English." "It's the official language," she countered. "They're supposed to." "Uh, but they don't. And in case you hadn't noticed, we just purchased a couple of lousy paperback novels for $30.00 each out of desperation for light reading. That's a month's salary for a housekeeper. Think about it. You're handing out bibliographies of academic books in English. There's no way the average Malawian would be able to access any of those."

Fleur thought for a moment. Then she said, "So you're saying I should give them a list of articles to read on the internet?" I shook my head, "Fleur, the internet costs a dollar an hour at an internet café, and many people in villages don't even have electricity. You're asking them to choose between food and reading an article on a subject that doesn't matter much to them. If you want them to care, just work with someone who could make some flyers in Chichewa and don't make them do a lot of crazy research." Fleur gave a skeptical look. "I know you're just here to teach, but if you could do one thing for the people here, what would it be?" I thought of the man from Mr. Gama's village who was forced to beg because he had only one arm. "Prosthetics," I said. "Have you noticed the many amputees around Zomba? It's like a death sentence for many of them." "No, it's not. My brother lost his arm and he's fine. And besides that, I haven't seen a single amputee the whole time I've been here." I was ready to end the conversation. "Okay, Fleur. Poor in Arkansas isn't the same as poor in Malawi. Tell you what, next time you go to the grocery store in town, just look down."

A week later, Fleur told me she had been to the grocery store and that there were indeed several amputees begging outside the door. "I just can't take it all in," she said. "I get overwhelmed." Life in Malawi was terribly difficult for Fleur. The next week, she lost the use of her laptop for several days because of a virus. While it was in the shop, she was unable to watch her DVDs of *The West Wing* and fell into a deep funk. One morning, she decided to take a hot bath to forget her troubles and foolishly decided to bring a ceramic brazier into bathroom with her to keep warm. Luckily, her maid was in the house that morning and came to check on her. Fleur had passed out from the high concentration of carbon monoxide that built up in the closed space and nearly died. Despite the close call, Fleur survived her brief adventure in Malawi and made it back to Arkansas in one piece. As far as I know, she hasn't made any trips outside the United States since.

As the year progressed, I found some of my biggest challenges came from dealing with the University's bureaucracy. My students had warned me that the grades I was giving them were too high. "Nonsense!" I said, "Anyone who gets an A from me earned it." "They won't let you give us As," they insisted. I didn't understand what they were talking about until we got to the strange ritual of "reading the grades." Representatives from each Department within the Humanities met to read the grades that had been assigned to each student. No context was given, just a list of grades. Apparently, I had given too many As and Bs. The other lecturers told me I'd just have to lower every student's grade by fifteen points. I refused. "Well, we can't have this many As. Your grades will be rejected when we meet at the University level." They could see I hated the idea of lowering my students' grades, but they insisted. We finally agreed that I would lower each grade by three points. That reduced a few As to Bs and Bs to Cs. I felt horrible about it. I met up with Rex later who had a similar experience with grades in his section. "It's a shame," he agreed. "The lecturers think it makes the university look good to fail students, but it doesn't. A high failure rate doesn't say much for the lecturers' abilities to an international audience."

After we finished reading the grades by section, we spent another several days reading through grades for the entire University. The sheer absurdity made me feel like I was trapped in a Monty Python skit. At one point, the Principal noticed I was giving a young man in my archaeology class an A, while several other lecturers were giving him very low grades. I said I had no idea how he performed in other classes, but he always showed up on time and did very well on assignments. A male lecturer then said that made no sense. "That boy is always rude to me. I would never give him an A," he said. I was already annoyed by the whole process, so I said, "I don't grade on personality. If he's rude, did you ask him why or just fail him?" The Principal decided to prevent any further disagreement by allowing both our grades to stand. I learned from the process, though, that Malawians thought a student who was capable of an A in one subject should excel in all classes, while those who got a C or lower could never rise above mediocrity in any subject. While I did my best to preserve my students' grades, some slipped. I dreaded giving them the bad news, but they were very gracious about the whole process. They knew better than I did what would happen.

One of my last acts at the University was to participate in the televised graduation ceremony. We lecturers gathered in a campus room to select a black robe and cap before heading to the Great Hall. I remember walking past the President's vehicle, which was equipped with a large machine gun on the back. Most of us expats elected to walk together. After we had taken our seats on the stage, I realized the government officials were seated a couple of rows in front of us. About twenty minutes into the ceremony, I noticed an elegantly dressed woman stand up to make a brief exit. She knocked over several chairs on the way, and I got the distinct impression she was trying to attract attention for the cameras. Then, despite the heat of the day, I felt a cold chill run down my spine. The elegantly dressed woman was none other than Patricia Kaliati.

My year in Malawi ended much as it began: with minor riots and political conflict. President Mutharika's political opponents were refusing to pass the budget, and the economic effects were far-reaching. Lecturers were worried they wouldn't get paid, as were police officers. On the way back from a day trip with Rex and Judy, an officer pulled us over and threatened to beat Rex. I was scared, but Rex remained calm. "All my papers are in order," he said. "You're not going to beat anyone." The cop gave a nervous laugh and decided to walk back to his car. "He was just hoping for a bribe," Rex said. "I wouldn't give him the satisfaction." I would have, but that's just me.

Of course, I'm leaving out many wonderful friends and experiences, but that's enough reminiscing for one chapter. I returned to Kansas City at the end of year, again without a solid plan, but I knew I wasn't finished travelling. I decided to get TEFL certification and spend some time in Moscow teaching business English. While I was there, I applied for a fellowship in Library Science through the University of Missouri-Columbia. When it was awarded, I came back to Kansas City and worked in Special Collections at UMKC Libraries for a couple of years, translating documents and transcribing old interviews with local Holocaust survivors. The work was interesting, and it gave me time to get my act together long enough to prepare my PhD thesis for publication by Archaeopress.[6] The finished product included a few pictures of the wild monkeys I had encountered in Malawi. That year, I returned to Ireland for quick visit with Donncha, the friend who had sent me the initial advertisement. He was relieved to see me alive and well, and I was relieved to be back in Dublin, if only for a couple of weeks. It felt like home, and there's no place like home.

[6]   Greenlaw 2011.

7

Lecturers and Their Side Gigs

ESELA MUNTHALI

The Lecturer

ZAMBIA, 1995: my family and I have just arrived in Zambia, and my twin Emmela and I are enrolled into the American Embassy School of Lusaka (AESL).

The question "Why did I get into Classics?" has been posed to me in several ways, and I have answered in many ways—but for this book, I will give just one word, or rather a name: Hatshepsut.

AESL Middle School Social Studies class, 1996: Egyptology. I was fascinated by a woman as a leader in a time that was dominated by men. Zambia is where my love of the ancient world and (not knowing it then as I do now) my fascination with women in the ancient world began. The foundations of Rome and the Roman Empire were read into my life in Grade Six in Zambia. This was followed by Egyptology in Grade Seven. These two years spent in Zambia planted a classical seed that grew in me into a great love of the ancient world. The history of a woman leading in a man's world—let alone the wonder that is Egypt—sparked my love for ancient studies, my love of women in the ancient world. Now, as in 1996, this is the discipline in the Classics that thrills me the most.

From Zambia came Kamuzu Academy, the "Eton of Africa," where my love for the ancient world grew. Latin and Greek languages and classical civilization were implanted deeper than ever before. I learnt that our society, religion, literature, government, and politics are closely linked, and even some aspects got their origins from the ancient Greeks. My passion for the ancient world thrived and expanded. Their religion, literature, and way of life were remarkable, fascinating—yet at the same time so relatable to the twentieth century I was living in.

Kamuzu Academy was six years of great learning. It was my safe place, where I got to understand the languages and learn the culture, and where my love for Greek literature and myths grew. Great classical learning—the years that formed who I am today. But although I had such a love for Classics, what I really wanted to do in high school was Law. I loved the thrill of the courtroom—all that I saw on television, that is. This changed after I got into college and worked extra hard in my first year to qualify for Law: I gained the marks required, and yet I was not accepted.

My love for Greek theatre and poetry was further enlightened at Chancellor College by the late Mr. Ted Jenner. Ted taught lyric poetry and Greek literature in a way that made me want to discover more. One lyric poet whom I studied was Sappho, whose poetry showed me again, just like Hatshepsut, that women played a great role in passing down the history of the ancient world—in Sappho's case, the Greek world.

My legal career had died aborning, but in my third year of college, I was approached to teach Classics, a course I was doing well in, especially classical literature. The third year of college ended, then the fourth—and I was hired as a Staff Associate. My career in Classics had begun. At the same time, however, a second passion lay dormant at the back of my mind: my passion for the pastry arts.

The Classical Baker

In 2015, seven years after I started my academic career, the classical baker was born. I have had a passion for baking and cooking since I can remember. This comes from the time spent in the kitchen with my mother and the women in my family—my sister and aunts, amongst others. I remember my mother telling me about my grandfather, who was a cook and baker in the 1950s in Zambia. My mother was born there, and I believe there is in my blood both her and my grandfather's talent and love for baking. Along with my home training in the culinary arts, I learned more about food and baking from my Home Economics teacher at Kamuzu Academy, the late Mrs. Dorothy Munyuma.[1] I took Home Economics from Form One to Form Five. My O-Level practical exam showed me that I was better at baking than cooking. My cake turned out perfect. My fish, on the other hand, burned. I mean, who burns fish? Baking and Classics fused together as my two passions in life.

---

[1]   Mrs. Munyuma was the first Malawian to teach at Kamuzu Academy, employed as Head of Home Economics from 25 November 1994. She retired in 2016 and died in Mulanje District on 23 January 2020. I wish to thank Mr. Dowell Nyondo, the Librarian at Kamuzu Academy, for informing me of these dates.

Maipai Treats, my cake-shop in Zomba, was birthed from passion and homage. It was homage to my late mother, who planted the baking seed in me. Along with my sister, Esnatt Jr., and a friend of ours, I opened the café/bakery, where people could get whole cakes made to order or cake slices for home consumption and in-shop eating. I had long wanted to open a small café, not only for myself but mostly in honor of my mother, Esnatt Sr., who died of cancer in 2007. I remember conversations about this with my sisters. The difference was that I wanted to name my café Viwisi's Treats (my mother's middle name was Viwisi), but as Maipai began with a partnership with a friend, we called our shop MaiPai Treats. This name is from the Portuguese words "Mai" for mother and "Pai" for father. Translated, it is "Mom and Dad's Treats." We lost our mother, and my friend lost her father some years before we opened. Our parents had been our biggest fans and gave us the confidence we needed to do whatever we set our minds to. Thus, we wanted to pay homage to them and their support. Maipai Treats, then, came into being as a legacy. It was opened as such, and not necessarily as a business that would immediately provide income, for we knew that profits could only be realized much later. Maipai Treats was an investment we were starting for ourselves and our children. In 2015, I became an Assistant Lecturer with a side gig. The interesting thing, however, is that I was not the only one. Although I might have been the only one who had a café, there were others who baked cakes and sold them from their homes. One colleague had their cake business for longer than I had been at Chancellor College. The café was a side gig indeed—and there were times when money was made, and I used it to help with a bill payment here or there—but in the long run, I cannot say that I profited in a substantial way financially. On the other hand, baking is therapeutic, and I can indeed say that I profited psychologically and socially. The ability to please someone's taste buds with a creation of your own is an awesome feeling.

I probably baked over 3,000 cakes in the five years since we opened until 2020. Although Maipai Treats made cakes for any and all occasions, they were mostly for birthdays. We made about three wedding cakes in our five years, over eighty birthday cakes, and around ten congratulatory and anniversary cakes. These numbers are approximate. We baked and decorated sculpted cakes: in our first year, we sculpted a Lightning McQueen cake for a ten-year-old boy. Maipai baked tiered cakes, animal cakes, floral cakes, etc ... the list goes on. I loved the intricacies of piping a cake. I also liked it when a customer would challenge our skills and ask us to bake and decorate a cake that we had never done before. My most favorite was a Jack and the Beanstalk themed cake, and, next to that, a Treasure Island cake. If the business had continued, I am sure we would have excelled in our design skills. My skills were in the piping of the cakes; my twin sister Emmela, who joined the business years later, is the sculptor and the more artistic one.

Maipai Treats was a business that had four partners, but I, as the culinary head, was very particular about who did what. I had staff to help me in the kitchen and who could cook, but I fired two because they did not cut it—hygiene was not their strong suit. In my kitchen, hygiene is non-negotiable, which is why I preferred to bake and cook the food and cakes myself. My twin sister and my younger sister were the only two people apart from myself whom I could trust to bake a cake for an order. I wanted our customers to have the best we could offer. I would not want a customer to not like something we made, and would prefer that if they did not like it, it was a cake I had made rather than one made by a staff member. I can improve from that criticism—and I would not get angry at the staff member. I would get frustrated when rules and recipes were not followed to the letter, especially after all the time I have spent cooking and baking. The desire to be perfect is my major weakness! Although I know I am not the only one.

My almost perfect side gig was a passion and a long-term goal. Cafés are not very common in Malawi; or at least, in 2015, they were not. In the past five years, Zomba and Malawi have seen more cafés and cake-shops/bakeries open. We are getting more entrepreneurs than office workers—or a great mixture of both. After five years of entrepreneurship, I cannot say that we have made an obscene amount of money in profit, or even a mediocre amount. Maipai has been a side gig—but not one that pays extra, like the side gigs of many of my colleagues at Chancellor College; there are many businesses and extra-curricular jobs that lecturers have. From my more than ten years at Chancellor College, and from chats with many colleagues, I have narrowed the majority of businesses to four primary categories: real estate, lodges/bed and breakfast accommodation, consultancies and companies, and transportation/car-rental businesses.

The Side Gig

The question one should ask is, "Why side gigs?" That is, why should a college professor or lecturer need or want a side gig? The answer is that we are from a third world country where we live hand to mouth.

It is difficult for one to make savings from just a university salary. Moreover, salaries at the University of Malawi are low by international standards.[2] In the Republic of South Africa, the estimate that za.indeed.com gives for professorial salaries (derived from job advertisements and from information from university employees and users of the website) is, as of January 2021, R992,374 *per annum*,[3]

---

[2]   This is a generalization and has been accurate over time.
[3]   Indeed n.d.

which would amount to $67,383 USD at the exchange rate applicable at the time of finalizing this essay. This pay level would apply only at the full Professor grade, and more junior academic staff earn amounts around R530,000 ($31,600 USD) and upwards.[4] In the University of Malawi by contrast, the highest professorial salary as of 1 July 2019—still applicable at the time of finalizing this—is K35,208,639 ($43,230 USD),[5] while the entry point for PhD-qualified staff is K18,810,234 ($23,095 USD).[6]

Pay levels for academic staff in comparable Southern African Development Community (SADC) countries are hard to ascertain, and data gathered from the internet may be outdated or lack credibility altogether. In Tanzania, *Salaryexplorer* puts college professors in eighth place on its 2020 list of best-paying careers in Tanzania, with a range in monthly pay from TZS1,080,000 to 3,540,000 ($466 to $1,527 USD, or $5,592 to $18,324 USD *per annum*).[7] This would point to worse conditions than those experienced in Malawi at present. In Zimbabwe, not for the first time, currency collapse has created a catastrophic situation: in September 2019, *NewsDay* reported that the monthly salaries for lecturers at the University of Zimbabwe were increasing to between $2,790 RTGS and $4,827 RTGS, and monthly salaries for professors to $6,606 RTGS.[8] But the "official" exchange rate is not always what one can actually get for an American dollar: at the time of finalizing this in August 2021, an American dollar buys 84.6 Zimbabwean RTGS dollars according to tradingeconomics.com,[9] whereas xe.com reports that 1 USD = 361.900 ZWD.[10]

In Malawi, there are civil servants who feel that college lecturers are paid more than other public employees, which is true—however, college lecturers are more inclined to look to the international academic labor market for comparisons. A bachelor's degree holder at Chancellor College at either the academic or administrative level earns close to K1 million per month—with more than K700,000 ($859) left after tax. [Unless otherwise noted, currency conversions are to US dollars.] This is not the case in the government or civil service. Degree holders in the civil service enter at a PO (Professional Officer) level, where they receive around K180,000 a month. Other degree holders who have been in the service longer and are at the higher level P7 (Professional Officer at grade 7) receive around K280,000. The amount increases the higher one rises in the civil service. I have a friend who is at the P5 level and receives over K600,000 net

---

[4]   *Glassdoor* 2021.
[5]   The comparable figure for the United States, mean full time salary for a full professor in a public institution across all AAUP categories except IV, was $132,199: American Association of University Professors 2021, Survey Report Table 1 on p. 26.
[6]   University of Malawi revised salary scale for academic staff from 1 July 2019.
[7]   *Salaryexplorer* 2021.
[8]   *NewsDay* 2019.
[9]   *Trading Economics* n.d.
[10] XE currency converter 2021.

salary; this friend of mine has a master's degree. Further education in the civil service can help towards earning higher pay, but not as much as a promotion in rank. As a bachelor's degree holder, I was earning more money than this friend of mine in the civil service. PhD holders at Chancellor College earn over K1.5 million per month (as compared to K1 million per month for a bachelor's degree holder), less the deductions made from salary. For a Senior Lecturer, the monthly pay falls just short of K2 million ($2,455). The largest deduction is thirty per cent for pay-as-you-earn tax (PAYE), and there are further deductions for medical insurance and, in some cases, for housing.

Chancellor College is part of UNIMA (the University of Malawi), a public institution—Malawi's oldest university, established immediately after independence. However, at the finalization of this chapter in August 2021, Chancellor College had delinked from the other colleges federal University. On 4 May 2021, Chancellor College officially became known as UNIMA, or the University of Malawi. Since the advent of multiparty politics in the 1990s, private universities have been allowed, and a good many have come into existence. I have investigated the pay structure after PAYE per month for colleagues in private universities, and there I notice a difference when compared with UNIMA. At the Catholic University of Malawi (CUNIMA),[11] for example, a private university established in 2004, a person at the lowest level of academic staff, who holds a bachelor's degree, as an Assistant Lecturer (which was my level at Chancellor College) earned in 2020 K618,000 ($840) per month before tax. I earned over K700,000— and that was after tax. This K618,000 is broken down in this way: K385,000 is the base salary, and then there is a housing allowance of K155,000 and a professional allowance of K78,000. A holder of a master's degree, who can be employed at the full Lecturer level, earns K812,000 per month ($997), and again this is before tax. Chancellor College pays academic staff much more than the Catholic University.

This difference exists because these private universities do not receive government subvention and rely solely on fees paid by students. Increasing tuition fees would be hard because many students are struggling to pay the fees as is. My cousin, who graduated from CUNIMA in 2019, told me that the tuition was K415,000 per academic year for normal courses, such as Social Work, the course she graduated from; but for courses like Nursing, the tuition cost K600,000. One must bear in mind that this is just tuition and does not include accommodation or food. For the average Malawian, this is a substantial amount of money.[12]

[11] Catholic University of Malawi 2021.
[12] Malawi is a low-income economy as classified by the World Bank (World Bank 2021a). GDP per capita in Malawi stands at four per cent of the world's average (*Trading Economics* 2021b) and is stated by the World Bank for 2020 at $625 (World Bank 2021b). The K600,000 ($736) annual

With figures such as these, one can genuinely feel sorry for civil servants, who get half the salaries of their counterparts in Statutory Corporations, such as the University of Malawi. These same lecturers, however, also feel how the civil servants feel when they compare their salary to academic colleagues outside Malawi. Again, imagine private university lecturers when they compare their salary to those of their counterparts in UNIMA. It is no surprise, then, that lecturers at Chancellor College, as well as others—and civil servants—look for opportunities to make extra money.

The salary I received at Chancellor College was significantly more than my friends in the government were paid, and yet I could not make it last the whole month. Most people in Malawi live paycheck to paycheck. It becomes difficult or impossible to save. Most families rely on two incomes. Yet when you add in children and their basic necessities, it is difficult making ends meet on a Chancellor College salary. If a husband and wife are both working, life is easier. If they have a side gig, furthermore, it gives lecturers leeway, and allows them to save a little extra, to build their own homes or send their kids to a reputable school.

Most parents, myself included, want to give our children more than we had, and a good education is an important element in this kind of aspiration, as is escaping the poverty of our parents and guardians. In my own case, I was blessed to have gone to the best school in Malawi. My parents and family made great sacrifices for me. And this is what I and many colleagues at Chancellor College want for our children: a better education and better opportunities in life than we had. Thus, the academic ladder, and how quick you can climb it, is very important. The higher you climb academically, the more money you get— whether the climb is measured in terms of higher degrees, more publications, or advancement to promoted grades.

The higher the degree and status, the more earning-power an academic has. A virtuous circle may follow: more recognition, hence more consultancies and, in the end, more money. This extra income then allows for investment in business opportunities that can allow one to save money or have more money— more disposable income. During the ten years when I was on the staff at Chancellor College, my observation was that most of the staff who gained some extra money from an increase in status—as either PhD-holders or Professors— used the money to invest in different side gigs or businesses. This brings me to the four categories of business mentioned above: real estate, lodges/bed and breakfast accommodation, consultancies and companies, and transportation/ car-rental businesses.

---

tuition for a nursing student at CUNIMA, then, should be seen in the context of GDP per capita of $625.

Esela Munthali

Real Estate

UNIMA has houses that are given to staff once applicants have met the criteria stipulated. At Chancellor College, the rental rates for college housing range from as low as K15,000 per month for Clerical, Technical, and Secretarial staff (CTS) to as high as K55,000 per month for Academic and Administrative staff. Semi-detached houses cost K25,000 a month. My house, rented in the commercial sector, costs K160,000 ($196) a month. I could have saved a substantial amount of money over the past decade if I had a college house, which is why many College staff apply for houses—but there are not enough houses to meet the demand. With the strict criteria for obtaining a house, it is mostly senior staff who get the houses—and yet they are the ones who could most probably afford commercial-sector rentals. To be awarded a college house, one must get the highest points in the point system. The basic criteria for points are academic seniority, as well as the length of service at the College (up to ten years). The other criterion is special considerations (i.e. whether one is a chaplain or warden). The applicant with the highest points gets the house. These were the criteria for most of the time I was on the staff—they come from the Chancellor College 2011 Academic and Administrative Staff Housing Policy.

However, a draft policy on housing, which, at the time of finalizing this chapter, was still awaiting ratification, is in circulation. This policy also allows for points based on the family situation: one point for a lawful wife or husband and one point for each child—up to four children. Seniority is still a criterion: the higher you are, the more points. A Professor gets twelve seniority-points, whereas an Assistant Lecturer, as I was, gets only two points. Length of service attracts one point for each year served, but only up to six years from the date of starting work for those who commenced in the Lecturer grade; those originally appointed in the Staff Associate/Assistant Lecturer grade may claim more than six points for length of service. The last criterion is that of special considerations, as above. I know for a fact that, over time, many have tried to get changes made to these point systems. As one can see, they favor Professors and senior colleagues. If I were now still at Chancellor College as an Assistant Lecturer, I would have gotten three points for the family situation, two for seniority, and eleven for length of service: a total of sixteen points. This, however, is not a score that would get me a house, especially considering how much a Professor would get for all the categories. Length of service for a Professor who started as a Staff Associate in the 1980s or 90s is far more than all my points combined. Under these circumstances, one can understand why some senior colleagues live in college houses, while renting out their own homes that they have built.

Some rent out their houses commercially to house other families, and others to house businesses and companies. At commercial rates, houses for families can cost as little as forty to fifty thousand kwacha a month, or range as high as K300,000. This kind of supplement is a great financial help. I have been told two colleagues who have built houses, and rent them out for over $2,000 (K1.63 million) a month to Non-Governmental Organizations. Once you are an investor in real estate, you have reached Sapitwa, as we would say. This is the highest peak on Mount Mulanje—the tallest mountain in Malawi. And when your house has for its tenant a company, or an NGO that pays in dollars (a better currency than kwacha), you have reached Sapitwa indeed. This is where most people aim to be. Getting an NGO to rent your house is very lucrative, while others can pay as high as $2,500 to rent a house for an office space.

I, myself, in another "side gig" venture, purchased a home in the Chikanda area of Zomba near the campus, together with some friends, for the same purpose as many other colleagues: student lodging. There are many lecturers, as well as support staff, who benefit from this business. Student housing is scarce, and demand is very high. Students are charged from as little as K10,000 per month to as much as K25,000; this all depends on whether a single room is rented, students are sharing a room, or there are several beds squeezed into a living-room. Depending on how big your house is, and how many beds you can fit in it, this can earn someone approximately K50,000 to K125,000 a month, or even more.

Apart from lecturers, secretaries and other technical and clerical staff also have side hustles. They, too, may have real estate. I know of a secretary who has several hostels for students in Chikanda, as well as a former cleaner who has the same and has even told me that she is expanding and building more. The demand for private-sector housing for students began in late 2008/early 2009, when there was an influx of what were then called parallel students, or those who were learning parallel with other students but had not gained admission through the previously-established selection procedure. This group of students was larger in number and not entitled to on-campus accommodation. Thus, many lecturers and other staff, and even Zomba residents, started the hostel business for students. I know of at least three academic colleagues who own student hostels in Chikanda.

The building of such hostels has increased in the past five to seven years. Many houses and hostels in Chikanda have been built for the sole purpose of housing Chancellor College students. It is a lucrative business. A fellow parent, with whom I am acquainted, told me that he too had a hostel that houses Chancellor College students—and that he was building another. This was about two years ago. As you drive through Chikanda today, there is a noticeable difference from four years ago: the Chikanda road coming from Chancellor College, leading to Mponda Bwino market in CheMpunga, has been tarred all the way to New Road, which has made travelling between Chancellor College and Chikanda much easier. It has increased business for taxi drivers and has made travel on the road better for those who are building in Chikanda. This is how much Chikanda has developed over the past few years: a very high-density area necessitated a tarred road for easy access for students and lecturers, as well as Zomba residents and business-owners. This allows students to breathe a little easier and enjoy studies and college life. Where students would take longer to get to class on rocky and dirt roads, they now take less than five minutes on the tarred road.

Lodges/B&Bs

If we can see such supplemented incomes in the housing and NGO accommodations, imagine the numbers possible with a lodge or bed and breakfast with facilities for conferences, trainings, or workshops. These side gigs have the potential to earn money not only from the actual accommodation itself, but from fees for such events and even catering revenue. Rooms at a lodge can cost from as low as K20,000 to as high as K80,000 per night for bed and breakfast. A lodge at full capacity would generate a substantial amount of money. These, in my opinion, are the side gigs of side gigs!

NGOs and companies that have projects in Zomba use these lodges as venues for meetings, trainings, and conferences, as well as lodging for their employees. Once again, there are many at Chancellor College who have such side gigs. On Chirunga Road alone—the road leading down from Zomba Zero to Chancellor College—there are two such businesses. Altogether I know of five colleagues who have lodges and accommodation spaces. I am sure the total is larger, as others have properties like this in other districts. I was told of one colleague who opened a lodge in Liwonde, thirty-seven kilometers from Zomba, in Machinga district—but from what I was told, this enterprise was not long-lived.

There are about four lodges and guesthouses within Zomba that have stood the test of time or that predict future success. These lodges belong to Chancellor College staff, as well as former or retired staff. One thing is for sure: the majority of these proprietors began their bed and breakfast side gigs while under the employment of the University of Malawi. More than five of the lodges mentioned above are run by retirees of the College, while the other three are run by staff who are still employed by the University. These lodges are funded by retirement money, or by consultancy money. Many of the people who own these lodges are either at the PhD or the professorial level: as described above, these levels can garner a substantial amount of money. A friend described to me how a Lecturer with a PhD and the right skill-set can earn up to $400 (K326,000) a day as a consultant, and I can only imagine how much a Professor would earn. This becomes seed-money for other businesses, as the College salary is not substantial enough for this kind of investment.

Consultancies/Companies

In 2019, I attended a humanities workshop on publishing. One Professor was candid enough to mention that publishing has its perks: publications can lead to consultancies, and consultancies lead to money. Most of the time, this money is in dollars and does not come from the University but from a particular company, NGO, or UN (United Nations) agency. This Professor mentioned that he built his house thanks to authored publications. Thus, it can be surmised that the more publications one has, the more one's academic status grows, thereby procuring more income.

College employees make more money the higher they advance, and, thus, the more they earn as a consultant. There are two primary ways of consulting: on an individual basis or as a group. As individuals, the higher the position one has, the more money one can earn. With complete anonymity as local consultants, Malawians within UN agencies can earn fees from as little as $250 (K204,000) up to $400 (K326,000) per day. In 2018, I got a taste of the consultancy life, in the form of a speaking engagement, for which I received over K500,000 as my honorarium, which is $679.16. Despite the fact that I only have a bachelor's degree, I was able to earn that amount for just ten minutes of speaking—imagine what is earned by seasoned academics who have been speaking for years! The fees for consultants from the College may be as high as $1,500 (K1.2 million), depending on the consultancy and the organization—figures that my friend and I discovered when we were researching starting our own consultancy company. Furthermore, these amounts can increase when a consultancy firm has won a big project: there is one major consultancy in town whose bids are higher than their counterparts, ranging from as much as $100,000 to $200,000. This figure is for both their operational costs as well as their own fees as proprietors of these consultancies, so one can only imagine the profit margins which are possible in this market.

Academic centers within faculties can also be considered a form of consultancy. These centers conduct funded research on different aspects within their discipline, and their activities generate income for the faculties as well as the College. They operate in the same market as the private consultancy firms, which allows staff to view this work as an extension of their ordinary College jobs. Apart from these different levels of consultancies, several colleagues—due to extensive research in their fields—have also been seconded to different government, private sector, or UN agencies.

It seems that an academic of any standing can secure various consultancies and publication deals. From my days at Chancellor College, I have come to realize that the real motive of many junior academics in becoming senior academics is acquiring these opportunities for more money, as is desired by most. While the academic salary in Malawi is insufficient, other opportunities may make the academic career worthwhile. My informal understanding is that, because of their many projects and linkages, colleagues at the College of Medicine in Blantyre earn more than Chancellor College lecturers do. And yet, at Chancellor College, when an academic is at the senior level, they may be approached to work on projects, while, at the same time, academics with this level of expertise can easily obtain grants for specific research. Others are called to consult on systems and policies within the government. This kind of work can be looked at as more of an extension of the job in academia than a matter of actual side gigs or businesses.

Transportation/Car Rentals

Car rental companies, by contrast, are, in every sense of the word, businesses and truly can be called "side gigs." Three staff members that I know of have car rental enterprises. Two of these are lucrative because they are used by different NGOs within Zomba for different projects. The third has just started, and this one has lower rates for car rentals than the other two. This is another side gig that can earn College employees a substantial amount, as the cost for renting one of the third friend's cars can start from as low as K16,000 to 18,000 ($20 to $22) a day, depending upon the size, the distance to be traveled, etc. Other suppliers might charge K30,000 to 40,000 ($37 to $49) a day.

In 2018, one of the more lucrative rental companies, owned by one lecturer on campus, was charging between K35,000 and 45,000 ($48 to $61) a day without a driver for Toyota Twin Cab vehicles. A driver would add some K5,000 ($7) a day to the cost. In 2020, a smaller car would probably have cost between K20,000 and 25,000 ($27 to $34) per day. The car rental company I just recently used also charged extra for a driver: their fees might be as low as K2,500 ($3.50) or as high as K15,000 ($20) a day, depending on whether the driver was required for ten or more days—the higher amounts are charged if the driver must travel overnight. One should bear in mind that these costs do not include fuel. Car rentals are a self-sufficient business, in the sense that the owner does not need to be there:

one can just hire a manager. Thus, profits can indeed be made in this type of transportation business.

Unionism

When I first started at Chancellor College, I was approached to see if I wanted to be involved in unionism. Chancellor College has two unions: the UWTU (University of Malawi Workers Trade Union) and CCASU (Chancellor College Academic Staff Union). As one can decipher from the name, one is for College support staff, and the other for academic staff. I took some time to decide whether I wanted to be a member or not, although I ultimately, and I believe rightly, decided to join. Our union played a great role in increasing the salary of university employees—from K80,000 net when I first began lecturing in 2008 to about K700,000 in 2019, which led me to conclude that unionism triumphed during this period. Although it is necessary to bear in mind the devaluation of the kwacha and other economic challenges, at the same time, whenever there is a problem over salaries and other important issues, such as political intimidation, the union has prevailed.

In February 2012, political intimidation came in the form of the police interrogation of an academic staff member—an incident that gave birth to the eight-month fight for academic freedom at Chancellor College, which we knew we and our students were entitled to, and which was breached. This breach occurred when a Professor in Political Science was accused of having planted the seed of violence among his students when he taught an example from the Arab Spring riots. This was the moment when I fully and wholeheartedly joined the union.

Why? Because I was afraid that maybe one day, I could be next, and I saw the benefit of protecting and safeguarding our academic freedom, especially because I was teaching the origins of democracy, oligarchy and tyranny, and aristocracy. These political matters were covered in the first-year course of the Classics Department: CLA111 *Greek Politics and Society*. The second semester course was CLA121 *Roman Politics and Society*. A classicist will know that one can only truly educate students about the ancient Greeks by delving deep into the complexities of political systems and how they came into place. I teach my students to compare the foundations of democracy to the democracy of Malawi today. The question I ask every year I teach this course is, "Are Malawian democracy and Greek democracy similar?" The only way I can test whether my students have understood the foundations of democracy (the transition and progression from kingship in the Bronze Age, passing through aristocracy, oligarchy, tyranny, then finally to democracy) is by critical analysis of the Greeks and Malawi today. Owing to this pedagogical imperative, I felt a strong call to join

Figure 10. CCASU members unveil new academic freedom banner for display
at Chirunga Road entrance to Chancellor College, February 2018.
Photograph by Paul McKechnie.

the union—although I was very scared at first. I even became Vice-Treasurer in 2013, and, although the positions within the Committee have one-year terms, my Treasurer and I ended up holding office on and off until 2019. That is to say that we were signatories on the CCASU account through those years, and I remember still signing cheques even when I was no longer an official Vice-Treasurer.

From fear grew courage. The union was a brotherhood and created camaraderie and commitment to our common goal and good. After the long struggle for academic freedom came battles for higher salaries, and, in 2017, against salary disparity when it was discovered that College of Medicine lecturers, by virtue of the fact that some are medical doctors, were being paid more than non-medically-qualified colleagues in the same grade—a disparity of about K100,000 ($1,360) a month. This was a battle that was fought and won in 2018.

Before this, there was a salary increment battle, which saw my monthly salary after tax rise from around K400,000, which I had been paid for a number of years, to about K600,000. Unionism changed this. As lecturers we have the right to complain about what we view as meagre salaries. Within a stretch of five years, our salaries have increased by about K300,000 per month. This change shows the effectiveness of the union and unionism. The value of the dollar to the kwacha was, as of 31 January 2008, $1 USD to K140.48, meaning that my 2008 monthly salary was $569. In 2019, the dollar to the kwacha was $1 to K735, putting my salary of K700,000 at $952.38. Our effective union activity brought about this increase.

It is equally important to note that that unionism helped me and my CCASU colleagues to have a collective voice—one that has allowed us to be recognized nationally. This, in turn, shed light on what Chancellor College lecturers cared about professionally as well as individually, and was a platform for other opportunities, such as those in the political and administrative arena, and invitations as guest speakers, and general recognition, among others. Furthermore, the academic freedom movement put Chancellor College on a greater academic map: it gave us a voice, and it gave me a voice. This voice, and the struggle, indirectly, led CCASU members to opportunities that we might not have known we had otherwise.

Analysis

I feel the main question that needs to be answered to close this chapter is: "Can side gigs coexist with the principal academic work?" This question can be answered in two ways. The first answer is, "Yes, it can." This coexistence comes when one realizes that there are some side gigs that come about because of the academic world. By virtue of being an academic, one will publish papers or articles in learned journals, or will write book-chapters and full books—because this is what is expected. "Publish or perish" is not as strictly followed at Chancellor College as in some places, but one still must publish in order to progress in academia. The greater the number of publications, the higher the status and the salary of the academic in question. This, in the end, will lead to more grants or projects for the Department or College as a whole—and more money for individuals.

Then again, can we concretely call consultancies and publications side gigs? Or are they integral to academic work? Do they become "side gigs" only when one is taken away from one's core job?

The second answer is that there are cases in which coexistence is, in reality, impossible. When there is evidence that the primary job is compromised, then it becomes impossible to look at consultancies and publications as anything else but a toxic kind of side gigs. I remember my third year of College when some juniors told me of a lecturer who left for a month during the semester to consult/lecture in another country. The lecturer left his students and did not teach them for a month, but still expected them to know the content in their end-of-semester exam. This is not the only story I have been told by other students in my years at the College. As a student, you experience and hear of lecturers leaving without proper procedure for a consultancy or a project elsewhere and not making up the missed classes. This is unprofessional, or something even worse. This is when these extended academic achievements become toxic side gigs. In these cases, by leaving their main job to make extra money, lecturers have turned the side gig into the main gig.

This, in a way, answers the question of why staff members still stay at Chancellor College even when they have a clearly profitable side gig, whether that is a business, consultancy, or public speaking engagements. In hardly any discipline would staff members actually quit their Chancellor College job for another, but, in the end, they make their students and colleagues suffer because there are gaps. There is such a lack of professionalism, in some cases, that even Heads of Departments do not call their subordinates out on the lack of class attendance. A few years back, some of my first-year students told me of one of their lecturers who did not attend class from the beginning of the semester, and only started coming towards the end. This, I later found out from colleagues, was their *modus operandi*, which puts the departments and students in a situation where their academic excellence, if ever there was any, is compromised. One cannot come and cram three months of work into one month. This, in fact, is how you get half-, or in this case, quarter-baked students.

These half-baked students will go on to be half-baked leaders in their communities. The main complaint from potential employers is that contemporary graduates do not know how to write reports, let alone have the confidence to give an oral one. This is where the Malawian academy, and the African academy more generally, cannot survive if we allow unprofessionalism to prevail. It is terribly harmful when a lecturer prioritizes their side gig above their main and core job of teaching. In these circumstances, side gigs cannot coexist with the core job.

The name of the College or the University is also attached to whatever side gig. If someone is making more money consulting, and they miss their classes and tutorials more often than they actually go to class, they still do not leave the College. The Chancellor College name, now UNIMA, is what allows them to obtain those gigs in the first place. Their level and status at the College is what pushes them above others when it comes to bids for certain projects and such. Most staff members, as I see it, use the College name and their positions to further their goals and wishes. Who can blame them? With the Malawian economy and the College salary structure, one can understand. And yet, too often this potentially beneficial symbiosis turns into an abusive form of exploitation.

From when the College first opened, if a lecturer got a masters or PhD opportunity, they would cease to receive what was called the "chalk allowance."

Until the mid-'90s, lecturers' salaries had divisions, housing, and so on, and one such part of the salary was the chalk allowance, which was given to those who were teaching. If one left to pursue more education, they ceased receiving this and the housing allowance, along with a decrease in their salary. This proved difficult, however, especially in cases where a staff member had a family who still needed a home in Zomba. Therefore, staff campaigned for and secured a fairer deal.

Lecturers have been fighting for increased salary since long before I came to Chancellor College as a student. Lecturers are used to an unending struggle for sufficient pay, and, within that context, side gigs will always be the norm, a constant. However, their prevalence had led and continues to lead to instances of discarded professionalism—and, furthermore, the academic career seems to have become more about money and less about the impact one has by imparting knowledge. The impulse to earn the most money possible is what drives the many entrepreneurs who are, in effect, moonlighting as professors and lecturers—while, if one places any value on education, it should be the other way round.

I am unable, therefore, to conclude on an optimistic note. Side gigs will always be there, even though, in too many cases, professionalism suffers, and money is chosen in the end. How this extra income is achieved seems to be, in my observation, of no consequence either to the lecturers or the authorities. Why would this be? It comes about because even the authorities have the same side gigs, as their salary is a hand-to-mouth salary. Even highly-placed academics need the extra income, although this was still more the case in the '90s and early 2000s than it is now. Thus, one can understand why these side gigs exist. When your salary is K1,000,000 ($1,228) and your child's tuition is the same amount a term, what would you do? What if you had more than one child? If the cost of living is high, and your monthly salary was not making ends meet, what would you do? Can your core job and side gig co-exist with good outcomes for the University and students?

I have been obliged to answer this question with both a yes and a no. In the past, yes, they could co-exist, especially in the case of a gig that also promoted the College. In Malawi, as it is today, it is very hard for them to co-exist—because side gigs are compromising the effectiveness of the University and the quality of the students who are being produced. If employees of the College are not teaching to the capacity they are hired and paid to teach, then their students will end up half-baked. Five to seven years ago, these other businesses to supplement income made sense, and they were better contained, but, nowadays, lecturers are often taking advantage; of course, this is not the case with all lecturers or all employees who have side gigs. There is such an influx of side gigs in some cases, however, that the main job suffers. Professionalism is out the window. This has been my experience. It is difficult to juggle, however, and I would not want to compromise my students' future, or the future of the African academy, just to make extra money. Yet, at the same time, with the way the economy in Malawi is, can you blame lecturers for trying hard to make ends meet?

8

Chancellor College Classics
An Oresteian Retrospective

M. D. Usher

IN PIER PAULO Pasolini's film *Notes for an African Oresteia*, there is a scene where Orestes, cast as a university student from Dar es Salaam, looks out onto a long, straight, solitary road stretching as far into the savannah as the eye can see. The camera pans to crossroads, each of which are equally long, straight, and desolate. Viewers are invited to ask themselves, "Where to turn? Where does it all lead? What will be the outcome?"[1] Orestes is being pursued by the Furies—hounded and hunted by ghosts of his mother—as he makes his way from Delphi to Athens at the behest of Apollo. At Athens, Orestes will stand trial for matricide before the first-ever human tribunal. The scene is dramatic, but it is not dramatized as such by Pasolini. Like the rest of the film, it consists rather of camera footage only, accompanied by a frenetic score composed by Gato Barbieri and, dubbed over, Pasolini's own editorializing. This is not a feature film. It's notes for a film—an audio-visual essay—and the notes are the thing.[2]

Pasolini's powerful thought-experiment to transpose the *Oresteia* of Aeschylus to sub-Saharan Africa circa 1970 is what impelled me to travel to Malawi. My own road was more circuitous, far less dangerous, and the ghosts less haunting. But the "trial" I faced in Zomba, the colonial capital—call it Malawi's

---

[1] Aeschylus, too, goes out of his way to emphasize the travails of Orestes's journey (cf. *Eumenides* 75–79, 235–241, 248–251, 276–285, 451–452).

[2] Pasolini intended to include his "Notes for an African *Oresteia*" (*Appunti per un'Orestiade africana*) as part of a trilogy of essayistic films about what he somewhat polemically insisted on calling the "Third World"—*Appunti per un poema sul Terzo Mondo* (*Notes for a Poem on the Third World*, 1968). Pasolini's other filmic notes include *Sopralluoghi in Palestina per Il Vangelo secondo Matteo* (*Location Scouting in Palestine for the Gospel According to Matthew*, 1964); *Appunti per un film sull'India* (*Notes for a Film on India*, 1968) and *Le mura di Sana'a* (*The Walls of Sana'a*, 1971). Italian transcript of "Notes for an African *Oresteia*" (which is overdubbed in English in the North American release by Mystic Fire Video) is collected in Siti and Zabgali 2001.

Athens—was a reckoning of sorts, one that forced me to reconsider priorities and my orientation to my profession and the world. But I am getting ahead of myself. To write the "Oresteian retrospective" about Classics at Chancellor College that I have been asked to offer here—a backstory and update, as it were, to an essay from 2014 about my Malawian sojourns in light of Pasolini's film[3]— I should begin, again, at the beginning.

• • •

In the final year of graduate school, one starts looking for jobs. And so it was that an advertisement came my way in the heady, early days of internet communication via that venerable Classics Listserv managed by Linda Wright at the University of Washington. The year was 1996. I had finished and defended my dissertation at the University of Chicago and was making the most of a year-long fellowship to turn the dissertation into a book and to probe the job market. The ad was for a position as Lecturer at Chancellor College in Zomba. It was forwarded by Linda on behalf of one Henri de Marcellus, whom I presumed to be a French or Belgian expat, or maybe an émigré from the Francophone, Western side of the continent. "Who knew there was a Classics department in Malawi?" was my first thought.

De Marcellus, it turned out, was in fact American, a former Captain in the US Army, with a DPhil in Classics from Oxford. (He is now a Latin teacher at the prestigious Branson School in Ross, California.) Having received a remarkable, truly comprehensive education at Chicago, for which I will be eternally grateful, I had come to think there was more to Classics than textual editions and commentaries, and more geographical horizons for our field than Western Europe. My wife and I also had something of a non-conformist streak: we had birthed our children at home (the youngest born in our one-bedroom graduate-student apartment on the third floor of a Chicago brownstone), were schooling them ourselves (the other two, that is, aged six and eight), and dreamed of one day building a farm and homestead in the country. The notion of re-locating to Malawi did not strike us, on the balance of things, as daunting. In fact, we looked upon the opportunity as an adventure. I applied. They sent me a two-year expat Lecturer's contract (more on the details of which below). We rummaged through our closets and got rid of sweaters and parkas. We inquired about buying an old Land Rover in Lusaka; a propane-powered refrigerator, too, in Harare, to forestall what we were told were the frequent power outages in Zomba. (Brian Burgess, a British colonial-era security officer who stayed on after Independence and settled on a farm on Zomba Plateau, where he kept a dairy herd and horse

---

[3] Usher 2014.

stables, once mused to me, recalling his own classical education in the UK and alluding to the rather insidious former motto of the Nyasaland Protectorate,[4] that bath time in Zomba was often a vespers ritual involving "Lux in Tenebris," so-called after the ubiquitous brand of soap.)

At about the same time as all this was coming together, I discovered Caroline Alexander's memoir in *The New Yorker* about her experiences founding the Classics Department at Chancellor College,[5] as well as her *Granta* essay "Plato Speaks,"[6] a profile of the adulatory culture of cleanliness, surveillance, and pilfering of State coffers under Malawi's *pater patriae*, Dr. Hastings Kamuzu Banda. By a fortunate coincidence, Alexander had been a student of my *Doktormutter* Laura Slatkin at Columbia University, before Slatkin moved to Chicago. We arranged to speak, and I spent an hour or more with Alexander on a pay phone in the Regenstein Library, asking every conceivable question about what to expect. I was put in touch via email also with Moira Chimombo, a British national who had married Malawian poet Steve Chimombo (now deceased) years prior and had raised a family in Zomba. Chimombo spoke joyously of her family "making its own entertainment" in sleepy Zomba town—a prospect that appealed well enough to us as a homeschooling family without a television. The actual terms of the contract were also hard to turn down: I would receive a salary (a pittance in US dollars, but a goodly sum in Malawian kwacha with plenty of buying power on the ground); we would be given an old colonial house to live in, with a gardener, cook, night watchman, and a woman to do the laundry. Our children could attend the Sir Harry Johnston International School free of charge. For a family like ours, that had been riding the poverty train through graduate school on a small annual stipend and a whole lot of frugality, this was like the end of the rainbow.

And yet, I did turn it down. The idea of bringing a newborn to a malarial region that was also susceptible to the usual panoply of tropical diseases was too much for us to countenance. Despite de Marcellus's enticements *per litteras electronicas* to accept—rapturous descriptions of freshly baked bread and exotic fruit, evocations of the majestic landscape, fulsome praise and admiration for Malawians' generous, peaceful, easy-going nature, and the prospects of research relevant to my interests in oral traditions and kinship structures—I, nevertheless, felt a Hesiodic inhibition that it was not the right job for the right time. In the end, I took a different job, but as the months and years wore on, we vowed strangely that we would someday "go back" to Malawi, never having been, so close were we to going in the first place.

---

[4] De Vries 2009.
[5] Alexander 1991.
[6] Alexander 1995.

Ten years after that, our self-inscribed return narrative took shape. While teaching at Willamette University in Salem, Oregon, I happened upon a DVD in the library titled *Notes for an African Orestes, by Pier Paolo Pasolini*, released by Mystic Fire Video (1970). Intrigued, I started watching and discovered immediately that this was a case of mislabeling or mistranslation from the Italian because the film concerned not Euripides' mediocre play of that name, but Aeschylus's *Oresteia* trilogy. This was a welcome, if unexpected, surprise, as I had just read George Thomson's *Aeschylus and Athens: A Study in the Social Origins of Drama* (1941), a book of deep learning and totalizing vision that left quite an impression on me.

Thomson was Classics' first card-carrying Marxist. He combined an evolutionary, dialectical-materialist reading of Greek antiquity with a "Cambridge School," Myth-Ritual approach to Greek tragedy. *Aeschylus and Athens* grew out of Thomson's two-volume text, translation, and commentary on the *Oresteia* from 1938; a heading in the Introduction to the commentary actually bears the same title as the 1941 book. I saw much in common between Thomson and Pasolini. In fact, I soon discovered, with a bit of research, that Pasolini, himself a member of the Italian Communist Party, relied heavily on Thomson's commentary when he undertook a translation of the *Agamemnon* in 1959, for a staged production of the play by Vittorio Gassman for Sicily's *Teatro Popolare*. I learned, too, that *Aeschylus and Athens* had been translated into Italian in 1949[7] and was a direct influence on Gassman and co-director Luciano Lucignani, as can be seen in an exchange of letters that was printed in the program notes to their production. Indeed, Thomson's book was used as a something of a training manual for Left-leaning dramatic troupes in post-War Greece, Great Britain, and Italy.

The extent and nature of Thomson's influence on Pasolini is recounted more fully in my *Arion* essay.[8] Suffice it to say here, by way of retrospective, that it was, above all, Pasolini's treatment of the Chorus that captivated me most. Footage and commentary devoted to depicting or imagining the Chorus comprises the bulk of the film. Pasolini focuses particularly on the material privation of the poor and the plight of the powerless. Farmers, tailors, beggars, barbers, old men, rough-looking youths, kerchiefed women, and children all move through Pasolini's frames as the heroes of his story.[9] The backdrop is European colonial. The socio-economic *mise-en-scène* is what Pasolini repeatedly

---

[7]   Thomson 1949.

[8]   Usher 2014.

[9]   On the folk quality of the film's Chorus: "Ripeto, il carattere del mio film, deve essere profondamente popolare. I protagonisti devono essere questi, ecco qui [camera shots of various persons]: questa donna che raccoglie l'acqua dal pozzo, questo bambinello, questo giovanotto elegante" (Siti and Zabagli 1179). Cf. 1180: "Questa gente colta nel suo daffare quotidiano e nella sua umile vita di ogni giorno, dovrebbe essere la protagonista del mio film l'Orestiade Africana"; and 1185:

describes as "Neo-Capitalist." As footage of the Chorus runs in the foreground, Soviet anthems play in the background like so many fists clasping hammers and sickles thrust into the air. Over these scenes, Pasolini reads passages from Aeschylus, like the second strophe of the first stasimon of the *Agamemnon*, to express his folk Chorus's longings and aspirations. Here is Pasolini's paraphrase:

> God, if that is your name, if you want me to call you by that name, I have weighed everything, and I know only you who can truly free me from the nightmare that lies upon my heart.

Indeed, Aeschylus' maxim πάθει μάθος, "learning through suffering," from that same choral passage (*Agamemnon* 177), is a leitmotif throughout. In the *Oresteia*'s description of the struggle to displace Old World monarchy (the fall of the House of Atreus) with democratic self-determination (Orestes's adjudication by jury at Athens), Pasolini sees hope for a resolution to class conflict and colonial exploitation by the establishment of a new social order. That new order is symbolized by the transformation of the Erinyes—vengeful goddesses from the primordial past who enforce tribal loyalties, terror, and vendetta—into Eumenides: "Kindly Ones" of the present and future who preside over social cohesion, prosperity, trust, and the public good. As Pasolini saw it, newly formed nation-states in Africa provided the ideal social conditions and political prospects to realize Aeschylus's synthesis of the past, present, and future, of the mythic and historical, of the ancestral and contemporary.

By 2010, I was keen to test Pasolini's hypothesis and to assess the validity of his observations, a generation on. With great efficiency and kindness, the Head of Classics at Chancellor College, Steve Nyamilandu, arranged a six-week visit, during which time I would screen the film and teach a seminar on the *Oresteia* to a small group of hand-picked students. (Brian Rak of Hackett Publishing generously provided free copies of Peter Meineck's translation.[10]) In addition to looking forward to experiencing the academic atmosphere at Chancellor (more about which below), I was intent, above all, on opportunities for interaction on the ground with real, living members of Pasolini's Chorus. This latter objective materialized in unexpected ways on my first and on two subsequent visits to Zomba. It would be remiss of me not to describe a few of these briefly here, since they were formative/informative experiences that speak to how, in my view, the poetic and political vision of Aeschylus, novel in 458 BCE, continues to be relevant for today's globalized, pluralistic world, where a twofold truism

---

"Naturalmente, come ho più volte ripetuto, il grande protagonista di questo mio film, di cui questi non sono che appunti, dovrebbe essere il popolo."

[10]   Meineck 1973.

still rings true: the poor you may have with you always, but the consolidation of wealth and power in the hands of a few unjustly disadvantages the many and impedes social progress. Aeschylus describes the problem as a matter for righteous indignation. Here is a sample of his thinking, in Thomson's translation:[11]

> For lo, swift ruin worketh sure judgement on hearts
> With pride puffed up and high presumption,
> On all stored wealth that overpasseth
> The bound of due measure. Far best to live
> Free of want and griefless, rich in the gift of wisdom.

• • •

On my first visit, accompanied by my wife and youngest son, by then fourteen, we befriended a young man who worked as a pantry keeper where we were staying: Christopher Mswang'oma.

We shared several meals together and talked well into the evenings after I got back from the College. Christopher was keenly religious and, while clearly enjoying our company, was also clearly trying to convert us. We learned a lot about Malawi from Christopher. He himself was an AIDS orphan, so his church and the several villages to which he was connected meant everything to him. It seemed everyone we met when we were with him was either a brother, sister, aunt, or uncle. (Some of this, I surmised, probably also had to do with Chewa kinship terms.) Christopher brought us to Namikango village, where he grew up and where his then-girlfriend lived. It was about a five-mile walk from the outskirts of Zomba through leafy paths and byways dotted with plantings of maize, banana, and brickworks. He also brought us to Matiya village, which we reached by *matola* minibus to Jali, followed by a ten-mile journey into the interior on a sandy, mogul-ridden dirt track by bicycle taxi. We were welcomed by the village chief, who gave me a ceremonial local chicken that I proudly carted back (by bike taxi and *matola* minibus) to Zomba. On the minibus, I was wedged between two nursing mothers—one of them nursing twins, one on each breast—holding that chicken on my lap. The whole bus was laughing, knowing exactly what had happened: a *mzungu* ("white person") had spent the day in the village and was gifted a chicken by the chief. Codes of hospitality are universal, and their tokens immediately recognizable, as is their violation (cf. Aeschylus *Agamemnon* 40–103). The cook at our residence prepared the chicken for our supper, which was, from start to finish, about a four-hour affair, since the

---

[11] Aeschylus *Agamemnon* 385–390.

Figure 11. Christopher Mswang'oma in Namikango, August 2010.
Photograph by M. D. Usher.

chicken had to be slaughtered and plucked and much of the cooking in Malawi is done over charcoal, and no one in Malawi is in a rush.

I experienced village life on my second visit too, but this time alone. I was staying at the College guesthouse, where the cook and caretaker, Precious Mereka, and I struck up a friendship. It was early February 2011, and the Arab Spring was in full bloom. The television in the guesthouse got only two channels, one of which was the Iranian English-language cable news station Press TV, which covered the protests non-stop. (The other channel was a faith-healing televangelist's network from South Africa.) Over full English breakfasts in the morning and tea in the afternoons, Mereka and I watched Press TV and conversed about the state of the world (in need of systemic change) and the quality of life in Malawi (difficult, challenging). Mereka insisted on doing the shopping himself after I brought home from the market a bag of unripe mangoes and papayas. I agreed, but was sure to give him at least twice what he needed for the day's supplies and insisted that he keep the change for himself. I suppose that it was out of gratitude for this gesture over a month's time and because we enjoyed one another's company that he invited me to lunch one Sunday at his home in Chikanda, not far from the College. (Actually, it seemed like another five-mile walk through serpentine sideroads that cut through forest and cropland. Mereka will have walked this route to and from work every day.) Mereka's wife Gladys made a delicious lunch consisting of rice, some sautéed greens, a hard-boiled egg, and peri-peri sauce. I had every impression that this was a special dinner prepared for an honored guest. Mereka's daughters, Margaret and Eveline, wore their Sunday's best for my visit, and his two younger boys were dressed in crisply pressed white shirts. Again, I was touched to find the timeless codes of human hospitality inviolate.

The third time I visited Malawi, in 2015, I was on assignment as External Examiner for the Department. This work consisted of reading through student papers that had already been marked by faculty and assessing syllabi and course materials for the College's re-accreditation. I was accompanied this time by my middle son, who had recently graduated from college. When I had finished my assessment work, we decided to take a few days to visit Monkey Bay, on the southern tip of Lake Malawi. Steve suggested that, rather than renting a car, I borrow his 1992 Toyota pickup. I had driven this vehicle before—for an outing we took during our first visit to Liwonde National Park. On that adventure, the truck overheated in exactly the middle of nowhere, though there was a village fairly close by. Two men and about twenty children helped us top up the radiator with water, and we somewhat miraculously made it to our destination. Upon leaving, parked for a few days at a boat jetty, the truck's battery died, and we had to get a jump start from safari guides across the Shire River. For this trip to Monkey Bay, I decided to splurge and pay someone to drive us in Steve's truck. The truck itself, I must say, is a wonder to behold: a patchwork of spare body and mechanical parts that still runs strong—a testament to Steve's own handiwork and ingenuity. Steve's friend, Mervin Mbewe, a motor mechanic and farmer, agreed to drive the three-day trip for fifty dollars. I paid him twice that, so relieved was I to be free of the responsibility and in such good hands. About two hours into our four-hour journey, however, after much pleasant conversation with Mervin about his work and family (and more than a few police checkpoints), Steve's Toyota threw a wheel bearing.

It was 6 p.m., which is about when the sun begins to set in Malawi. Mervin called Steve, who drove up to the breakdown site with a used bearing set he picked up at Zomba market. My son and I hitched a ride for the rest of the way to Monkey Bay, traveling in the bed of another pickup filled with sacks of potatoes, two nursing mothers (yes, again), and some Australian hippies. Meanwhile, Steve and Mervin repaired the Toyota at nine or ten o'clock at night on a desolate stretch of road, their work illuminated only by the headlamps of Steve's car. Steve drove back to Zomba, and Mervin pulled in to Monkey Bay around midnight—remarkably, with a smile on his face—the truck as good as new.

Figure 12. Mervin Mbewe sizing up the damage to Steve Nyamilandu's Toyota Hilux, 2015. Photograph by M. D. Usher.

The resilience and sheer competence of Steve and Mervin, and the disarming hospitality of Christopher and Mereka, are exactly the noble traits, I think, Pasolini sought to magnify and celebrate in his folk Chorus. Many other everyday experiences confirmed this verdict for me, too: an afternoon spent with a team of sawyers, who were hand-sawing boards from an enormous hardwood tree that had been felled near the golf course; and another afternoon spent at church with a student in my seminar, Bernard Mkonkha, who aspired to be ordained an Anglican priest, among others. Bernard had read the *Bacchae* and a good deal of the New Testament in Greek, and wrote an impressive essay on the night watchman in the *Agamemnon*, comparing his anxieties about the situation at Argos with his parents' generation's fears during Banda's reign. And I am somewhat embarrassed to mention the countless hours I spent patronizing the curio stalls, talking to guys named Frank and Happy and Blessings, whose carvings I could not resist and for the quality craftsmanship of which I could not bear to pay anything but the full asking price.

• • •

When I show Pasolini's film to American students, many are troubled by the camera's intrusive gaze: "Here is a white European male," they say, "gallivanting around Tanzania and Uganda filming Black Africans in the streets without necessarily having their permission." It is true that many persons caught on camera appear bashful. Some, indeed, are visibly uncomfortable. Others,

Figure 13. Sawyers at work near Zomba Golf Course, 2015.
Photograph by M. D. Usher.

however, appear to bask in the limelight. Pasolini's aesthetic commitment to Neorealism in film drives this controversial decision to verge on voyeurism and, in a sense, heightens the tension. As Pasolini scholar Luca Caminati describes Pasolini's thinking on the matter, "Ideological disengagement from reality triggered by media, urbanization, loss of traditions: to this Pasolini opposes 'reality,' the agricultural and subproletarian past, primitive religious sentiment, the Third World, not as escape, but rather as a possible political alterity."[12] And, as Caminati puts the same point elsewhere, "Film, Pasolini believed, provided a unique and indispensable instrument in the pursuit of the anti-capitalist Third World struggle. Shouldering his faithful Arriflex camera, Pasolini was fighting *irrealtà*—the 'unreality' of modernity."[13] At one point, in a masterstroke of Neorealism, to depict the fall of Troy, Pasolini splices in actual newsreel footage of Nigeria's brutal Biafran War: we see the jungle floor littered with war dead and victims being dumped into roadside graves. Indeed, the viewer is witness to an actual execution. "For this," Pasolini declares, "I have no words."

What he does say about this video montage, however, clarifies for me what the great Athenian playwrights—Aeschylus perhaps most of all—were doing by setting their theater of contemporary ideas dramatically in a distant mythological time. "Nothing could be farther from the image than the idea we normally

[12] Caminati 2016:131.
[13] Caminati 2018:64.

have of classical Greece," Pasolini says of the Biafran footage. "And yet suffering, death, mourning, tragedy are eternal, an absolute element which can easily link searingly up-to-date scenes with the fantastic images of ancient Greek tragedy." Thomson, for his part, on the very first page of his 1938 edition, published on the brink of WWII, characterizes Aeschylus's own motivation thus, putting his finger thereby, I think, on how the *Oresteia* still speaks across centuries to developing nations like Malawi:[14]

> When the Athenians returned to the smoking wilderness which was all the Persians had left behind them, they rebuilt the city and reconstructed the social order. To that task the plays of Aeschylus were a direct contribution. He wrote plays for the same purpose he had fought at Marathon and Salamis. His aim as an artist was to evoke and organise the collective energy requisite for the task of reconstruction.

In gaining its independence, Malawi is fortunate not to have suffered such violence as what was perpetrated during the Persian or Biafran Wars; nor, on the whole, in sorting out its political reconstruction in the aftermath of Banda's departure. More in harmony with what I saw and experienced first-hand amongst real Malawians who form a chorus of voices yearning for a better life—one grounded in a trustworthy, fair, and functional political economy—are Pasolini's notes for a conclusion: [15]

> The new world is established. The power to decide one's own future is formally at least in the hands of the people. The ancient, primeval divinities [represented by the Erinyes] coexist with the new world of reason and liberty [represented by Athens and Athena]. But how to conclude? Well, the ultimate conclusion doesn't exist. It's suspended. A new nation is born. Its problems are infinite. But problems are not resolved, they ... they must be lived, and life is slow. The proceeding toward the future is without any temporal break. The labor of the people knows no rhetoric and no pause. Its future lies in its eagerness for a future. And its eagerness is also a great patience.

---

[14] Thomson 1938:1.

[15] "Ecco gli ultima appunti per una conclusione. Il nuovo mondo è instaurato. Il potere di decidere il proprio destino, almeno formalmente, è nelle mani del popolo. Le antiche divinità primordiali coesistono con il nuovo mondo della ragione e della libertà. Ma come concludere? Ebbene, la conclusione ultima non c' è, è sospesa. Una nuova nazione è nata, i suoi problem sono infiniti, ma i problemi non si risolvono, si vivono. E la vita è lenta. Il procedere verso il futuro non ha soluzioni di continuità. Il lavoro di un populo non conosce né retorica né indugio. Il suo futuro è nella sua ansia di futuro; e la sua ansia è una grande pazienza" (Siti and Zabagli 2001:1196).

M. D. Usher

· · ·

In the end, then, I achieved my Malawian *nostos* after all, thanks to Pasolini and Thomson. This is perhaps not so surprising since the *Oresteia* is, in a sense, also an *Odyssey*; that is to say, an account of a homecoming—albeit less happy for Agamemnon than for Odysseus, or indeed for Orestes himself. By the time I visited Malawi, Banda had stepped aside, there had been two national elections, and the country was in the throes, not of an old dictatorship, but of a young democracy. Like the Tanzania of Pasolini's film under President Julius Nyerere, Malawi was on the cusp of something new. The field of Classics, however, was seen by many stakeholders as a reactionary bastion of white colonialism. Not only that: given its association with Banda himself, it was decried in some circles as an unwelcome leftover from the *ancien régime*. Indeed, the survival of the Classics into the twenty-first century and its persistent popularity among students in Malawi today are something of a small miracle. The continued interest is explained, I think in part, by the rationale for the founding of the Department in the first place. Alexander may have been the first Lecturer in Classics at Chancellor, but the story does not begin with the formation of the Department in 1985.

In 1979, Banda invited Professor R. M. Ogilvie to visit the country and make recommendations as to the establishment of Classics as a field of study at Chancellor. The choice of a distinguished Latinist from St. Andrews was logical enough, given Malawi's (and formerly Nyasaland colony's) strong ties with Scottish Presbyterian missionaries, beginning with Livingstone. The fact that Scotland was also where Banda had earned his medical degree (Edinburgh) increased the affinity. (As a mature undergraduate in the US, Banda had studied at Bloomington, Indiana, where he was a student of, and a resource for, folklorist Stith Thompson. He later attended the University of Chicago, where he advised on the Chewa language for linguist Edward Sapir, eventually earning his BPhil in History in 1931. Chicago is doubtless also where Banda bolstered his inclination toward the Classics.)

It is instructive to look back at Ogilvie's recommendations from 1979: namely, three faculty in a self-standing department consisting of three Latinists, at least two of whom fully equipped with Greek—one an historian, one a philologist, and one specialist in philosophy and/or the history of ideas. What Ogilvie imagined for Malawi looks a lot like Classics departments in many small liberal arts colleges in the US today, and it seems to me now that this is still an appropriate, workable model for Chancellor College. It is also refreshing to see Ogilvie make the same arguments for Classics in Africa that many of us find ourselves making for the discipline today to Deans and Provosts at our own US/UK/

European institutions. I cannot resist reproducing here the four key points from Ogilvie's white paper, now yellowed and dog-eared in a manila folder in Steve Nyamilandu's desk, plunked out on an actual typewriter. Notably, he begins by saying "I believe there are strong grounds for thinking [the introduction of Classics to the University of Malawi] is a far-sighted and important development. If I were not personally persuaded by its wisdom, I would not have undertaken this assignment." The points themselves are, and I quote:[16]

- Structurally, Latin is a language of great clarity and knowledge of it can help linguistic understanding not only of derivative languages, such as English, French, Spanish, Portuguese, and Italian, but of any language.

- The study of Classics is demanding and requires high standards of accuracy and application. The precision of thought and expression, acquired through studying Classics, can be transferred, as has been seen throughout history, to other fields—administration, law, business, government, and so on. This is an important counterpart in a University to courses of a more immediately practical nature.

- The social, political, and economic aspects of the ancient world, precisely because they have both similarities and dissimilarities with the African scene, are of great educational value as a comparison.

- The modern world has inherited a great deal of philosophical, religious, political, cultural, and artistic legacy from Greece and Rome and it is both of intrinsic interest and of contemporary relevance to be able to go back to the sources of that legacy, and to study them at first hand.

Ogilvie was, like all of us, a person of his time, with blinkers and blind spots, as Paul McKechnie highlights in the introduction to this volume. But what classicist, humanist, or enlightened administrator could dispute the basic soundness of these propositions? Nor is what Ogilvie says, to my thinking, any less true *vis-à-vis* the political climate in Malawi today. Even (and perhaps especially) in a changing, pluralist world, the Classics, of every age and every culture, still speak to the agonies and ecstasies of human experience.

Over the years, however, other realities on the ground left the many expat Lecturers who came to Chancellor College to teach less optimistic about the viability of Classics in Malawi. Recruiting energetic, qualified faculty from abroad (from the US and UK mostly) proved a challenge. Those foreign nationals who did come to Zomba to take up the position faced all sorts of cultural, financial, and bureaucratic challenges, as the Department's annual reports reveal.

---

[16] Ogilvie 1979.

One expat Lecturer/Head of Department in the late 1990s recommended consolidation with the Department of Philosophy (which would have marked a return to the pre-Alexander era), fearing the alternative he felt was looming on the horizon: an impending closure of the Department. Trepidation and disillusionment at that prospect color every sentence in his capitulating, disheartening memo.

Fortunately, Classics still lives on in Zomba,[17] but there are still considerable challenges, recounted ably by colleagues in other chapters of this book. One thing, however, safe to say without exaggeration, is that the success and survival of Classics in Malawi over the past fifteen years or so is due entirely to Steve Nyamilandu's dynamic teaching, his idealistic dedication to the value of a classical education for Malawian students, and his cheerfulness and optimism in the face of adversity.[18] In concluding my own notes here, I can do no better than to quote again Pasolini's retrospective of his experiences in the countries of newly-independent East Africa, which seems to me true also of Chancellor College Classics: "The labor of the people knows no rhetoric and no pause. Its future lies in its eagerness for a future. And its eagerness is also a great patience."

[17] Chancellor College is in the midst of a process of being delinked from the larger University of Malawi system, and future institutional arrangements for Classics were unknown at the time of writing.

[18] I hosted Steve at the University of Vermont for two weeks in October, 2016. My colleagues in Classics (and in the Dean's Office) were amazed by the number of students in Years One to Four that the Department at Chancellor College is able to attract (running into the triple digits).

Coda

Zomba

The First 48 Hours (17–18 March 1998)

AT CHILEKA AIRPORT, we clamber on board our minibus to Zomba driven by Peter _____, who claims to have ferried dignitaries in the Banda era. On the journey, I note a dramatic landscape of escarpments and jagged razorbacks rising out of open plains or isolated clumps of sparse woodland; the horizon is a series of undulating camel humps punctuated by soaring cones. The rural population straddling the highway seems to be constantly on the move or shopping; along both sides of the road stand vast metal containers, cauldrons, and the like, clothes on hastily erected wooden frames and carcasses of meat suspended from trees. Entranced by this landscape, the polar opposite of the gentle, rolling downs I am so used to, I almost regret hearing Professor Hoffmann announce that we have reached the last leg of the journey. A quiet evening at dinner with the Professor and family is followed by a sleepless, jet-lagged night in the otherwise serviceable College guesthouse. My first dawn in southern Africa is capped by a deputation of pied crows stalking the length of the guesthouse roof.

In the morning, the Professor introduces his two raw recruits (Mike Chappell from the UK and myself) to Chancellor College, President Banda's redbrick university showpiece. Architecturally, I find it a fascinating assortment of Greco-Roman echoes: countless garden courtyards (*peristylia*), long, roofed colonnades for peripatetics, and octagonal structures with tiled, conical rooves topped by finials (the Great Hall, the Little Theatre, etc.), somewhat reminiscent of the Arsinoeion of Samothrace, for example. But pride of place amongst all these constantly surprising evocations of the classical past must go to something I discovered a week later: the monumental University Administration building on the slopes of the foothills of Zomba Mountain, overlooking the district we would know later as Chirunga. The Administration building has a tall apse fronting an austere rectangular structure surmounted by a gabled roof;

consequently, it bears more than a passing resemblance to the Constantinian Basilica in Trier.

This incongruous juxtaposition of classical echoes in (mainly) red brick with Malawi's verdant and luxuriant foliage seems to match my presence here as a Lecturer in Greek and Roman history (possibly even a tutor in the languages) at a university in Equatorial Africa. Greek and Roman merchants and mercenaries may never have penetrated this far south into the lands of the "blameless Aithiopes," but the Greeks are here all right in spirit, even well beyond the confines of the campus—in Limbe, I would later note AGORA and ACROPOLIS on someone's signwriting, and Horace too is here at this university, courtesy of President Banda in a dedicatory plaque at the Little Theatre (EXEGI MONUMENTUM AERE PERENNIUS).

• • •

The longer shadows cast by the setting sun emphasize the formal symmetries in the *peristylia* and the colonnades at the College. This evanescent geometry disappears with the constant "quark ... quark" of the pied crows. As the shadows lengthen on my short journey back to the guesthouse (how brief is the dusk this close to the Equator!), lizards with vivid blue tails scurry in and out of drains, little brown frogs leap out of reach of my feet, and fireflies glow on the hedges. Without the invasive street lighting I am so used to, my view of the constellations is untrammelled and spectacular. Orion and his dogs are out hunting, sparkling in the apex of the vault, not fully inverted as in the Southern Hemisphere.

At the guesthouse this evening the four of us—Ian from Canada; Mike from the UK; Bruce, a fellow New Zealander; and myself—are treated to our first display of sheet lightning (what field-days this climate would have offered Roman augurs!). The lightning doubles as the television we do not have. We sit around the dining room table talking about films in a country which does not have a single cinema. Otherwise, the discussion centres on the virtues and vices of our respective malaria prophylactics.

• • •

Rows of eucalyptus on red earth, wattles with large, curved pods, and paper wasps building a nest in a corner of the casement window in my bedroom—I could be in New South Wales, but the bright yellow culms of bamboo are twice the height, and the pied crows are twice as raucous as our magpies. You could almost be viewing the first twenty minutes of a sci-fi movie—you suddenly realise you are in an alien world where nothing ultimately proves to be familiar.

Does water swill around the plughole clockwise, as in the Southern Hemisphere? No, in this vicinity of the Equator, the evidence is confusing and ambiguous.

The neighbourhood of Chirunga Road reverberates with the deep-throated horns of long-range juggernauts on Kamuzu Highway. In the intervening silences, I can hear the "still small voice" of the Mulunguzi River sluicing its way through the boulders it has brought down from the plateau on Zomba Mountain or babbling its way through Chirunga's fields of maize. Jet-black birds with brilliant red breasts or bright yellow shoulder bands flash or flicker overhead (birds I will come to know, respectively, as the red bishop and the yellow-mantled widowbird). Presiding over Chirunga is the escarpment of Zomba Mountain, an exposed rock face which describes, in the heat haze of early afternoon, the features of a sleeping giant or some ancestral patriarch. The effect is uncanny, but entirely fortuitous. This is not President Banda's Mt. Rushmore.

At our second gathering around the dinner table at the guesthouse, the four of us learn that Chancellor College may not open until well after Easter. The College is a good 34,000 kwacha short of the subvention it asked for. Our immediate reaction is the thought of the extra time we will have to prepare our first lectures. And I have more time now to work on my physics problem—the vortices of water and the directions they assume at the drain. I suspect that much depends on the configuration of the bathtub or the basin.

I think I will learn to love this country.

Bibliography

Ancient Texts

Aeschylus. 1998. *Oresteia*. Trans. P. Meineck. Indianapolis.

——. 1938. *Oresteia*. Ed. and trans. G. Thomson. Cambridge.

Aristotle. 1996. *The Politics and the Constitution of Athens*. Trans. S. Everson. Cambridge.

——. 1995. *Politics*. Trans. E. Barker. Oxford.

——. 1981. *Politics*. Trans. T. A. Sinclair and T. J. Saunders. London.

[Demosthenes]. *Speeches*.

Diogenes Laertius. *Lives of the Philosophers*.

Euripides. *Medea*.

Homer. 2015. *Iliad*. Trans. C. Alexander. New York.

Horace. *Epistles*.

——. 2004. *Odes and Epodes*. Ed. and trans. N. Rudd. London.

Plato. 1905–1911. *The Dialogues of Plato*. Trans. B. Jowett. 4 vols. New York.

——. *Republic*.

Plutarch. *Alexander*.

Sophocles. 1982. *The Three Theban Plays*. Trans. R. Fagles. With introduction and notes by B. Knox. New York.

Archives

H. K. Banda Archive. African Studies Collection, Indiana University. Bloomington.

W. E. B. Du Bois Papers (MS 312). Special Collections and University Archives, University of Massachusetts Amherst Libraries. Amherst.

Modern Literature

"Academy is for Classics Pupils." [Malawi] *Daily Times*, 19 August 1983:1.

African Journals Online. "*Journal of Humanities*." https://www.ajol.info/index.php/jh/about.

Agamben, G. 1998. *Homo Sacer: Sovereign Power and Bare Life*. Trans. D. Heller-Roazen. Stanford.

———. 1999. *Potentialities: Collected Essays in Philosophy.* Trans. D. Heller-Roazen. Stanford.

Alexander, C. 1985. "Classical Studies at the University of Malawi." Unpublished report, 26 June 1985. Chancellor College. Zomba.

———. 1991. "An Ideal State." *The New Yorker,* 16 December 1991:53–88.

———. 1995a. "A Classic Dictator." *The Independent,* 8 October 1995. https://www.independent.co.uk/arts-entertainment/a-classic-dictator-1576491.html.

———. 1995b. "Plato Speaks." *Granta* 51:91–108.

Althusser, L. 2008. *On Ideology.* London.

American Association of University Professors. 2021. *Annual Report on the Economic Status of the Profession, 2020-21.* Washington, DC. https://www.aaup.org/file/AAUP_ARES_2020-21.pdf.

Andrews, W. L. 1989. "The Representation of Slavery and the Rise of Afro-American Literary Realism, 1865–1920." In McDowell and Rampersad 1989:62–80.

Appiah, K. A. 1988. "An Evening with Wole Soyinka." *Black American Literature Forum* 22:777–785.

Ayers, D. M. 1986. *English Words from Latin and Greek Elements.* 2nd ed. Tucson.

Badiou, A. 2003. *Saint Paul: The Foundation of Universalism.* Trans. R. Brassier. Stanford.

———. 2012. *Philosophy for Militants.* Trans. B. Bostels. London.

Bailey, C., ed. 1923. *The Legacy of Rome.* Oxford.

Banda, H., and T. Cullen Young, eds. and trans. 1946. *Our African Way of Life.* Cambridge.

Baker, C. 2001. *Revolt of the Ministers: The Malawi Cabinet Crisis 1964-1965.* London.

———. 2008. *Chipembere: The Missing Years.* Zomba.

Baker, S. 2021. "Oriel U-turns on Removing Cecil Rhodes Statue." *Times Higher Education,* 20 May 2021. https://www.timeshighereducation.com/news/oriel-u-turns-removing-cecil-rhodes-statue.

Bakhtin, M. 1984. *Rabelais and his World.* Trans. H. Iswolsky. Bloomington. Orig. pub. 1968.

Banda, A. 2012. *The Life of Rodney Squire Hunter and his Contribution to the Development of Indigenous Leadership of the Church in Malawi.* BA diss., Mzuzu University.

Banda, K. N. 1982. *A Brief History of Education in Malawi.* Blantyre.

Bayart, J-F. 1993. *The State in Africa: The Politics of the Belly.* New York.

Beard, M. 2013. *Confronting the Classics.* London.

Bernal, M. 1987–2006. *Black Athena: The Afroasiatic Roots of Classical Civilization.* 3 vols. New Brunswick.

Biebuyck, D. 1969. *The Mwindo Epic*. Berkeley.

Bogonko, S. N. 1992. *Reflections on Education in East Africa*. Oxford.

Boucher, C. 2012. *When Animals Sing and Spirits Dance. Gule Wamkulu: The Great Dance of the Chewa People of Malawi*. Mua.

Bradley, H. 1923. "Language." In Bailey 1923:351–384.

Breugel, J. W. M. van. 2004. *Chewa Traditional Religion*. Zomba.

Brown, D. 1962. "Dr. Hastings Kamuzu Banda." *Interviews from Hell*. Video, 1:15. https://youtu.be/3PYz3mwLTWo.

Budelmann, F. 2004. "Greek Tragedies in West African Adaptations." *Proceedings of the Cambridge Philological Society* 50:1–28.

Bulman, S. P. D. 1997. "A Checklist of Published Versions of the Sunjata Epic." *History in Africa* 24:71–94.

Carver, R. 1990. *Where Silence Rules: The Suppression of Dissent in Malawi*. Africa Watch Report. New York.

Caminati, L. 2016. "Notes for a Revolution: Pasolini's Postcolonial Essay Films." In *The Essay Film: Dialogue, Politics, Utopia*, ed. E. Papazian and C. Eades, 129–146. New York.

———. 2018. "Filming Decolonization: Pasolini's Geopolitical Afterlife." *Pier Paolo Pasolini, Framed and Unframed: A Thinker for the Twenty-First Century*, ed. L. Peretti and K. T. Raizen, 63–77. London.

Campbell, J. 1949. *The Hero with a Thousand Faces*. Princeton.

Césaire, A. 1983. *The Collected Poetry of Aimé Césaire*. Ed. and trans. C. Eshleman and A. Smith. Berkeley.

Chakanza, J. C. 1998. *Voices of Preachers*. Zomba.

Chandilanga, H. 2007. "Kaliati Accused of Abuse." *Saturday Nation*, 23 June 2007.

Chaudhuri, A. 2016. "The Real Meaning of Rhodes Must Fall." *The Guardian*, 16 March 2016. https://www.theguardian.com/uk-news/2016/mar/16/the-real-meaning-of-rhodes-must-fall.

Chikoko, R. 2018. "Group against Gandhi Statue." *The Nation*, 10 October 2018. https://www.mwnation.com/group-against-gandhi-statue/.

Chimombo, S. 1978. *The Rainmaker: A Play*. Limbe.

Chinard, G. 1929. *Thomas Jefferson, the Apostle of Americanism*. Boston.

Chipembere, M. 2002. *Hero of the Nation. Chipembere of Malawi: An Autobiography*. Ed. R. I. Rotberg. Zomba.

Chipembere, H. B. M. 1970. "Malawi in Crisis." *Ufahumu* 1:1–22.

Chirwa, V. 2007. *Fearless Fighter: An Autobiography*. London.

Chisiza, D. K. 1962. *Africa: What Lies Ahead*. New York.

Chisiza, Z. 2017. "In Search of Theatre for Development in Malawi: A Modern History." *Critical Stages/Scènes Critiques* 15. http://www.critical-stages.org/15/malawi-theatre-history-theatre-for-development/.

Chiume, M. W. K. 1975. *Kwacha: An Autobiography*. Nairobi.

Claassen, J-M. 1999. "Classics for the Next Millennium: African Options." *Classical Outlook* 76: 125–132.

Clark, M. 2012. *Exploring Greek Myth*. Chichester.

Cruise 5. 2018. "Cruise 5 with John Zenas Ungapake Tembo." Video, 59: 57. https://www.youtube.com/watch?v=NDwyTV2TkxQ.

Csapo, E. 2005. *Theories of Mythology*. Oxford.

Currey, J. 2008. *Africa Writes Back: the African Writers Series & the Launch of African Literature*. Athens, OH.

Davis, G. 1997. *Aimé Césaire*. Cambridge.

———. 2007. "'Homecomings without Home': Representations of (Post)colonial Nostos (Homecoming) in the Lyric of Aimé Césaire and Derek Walcott." In Graziosi and Greenwood 2007:191–209.

Dawson, M. 2001. *Black Visions: The Roots of Contemporary African-American Political Ideologies*. Chicago.

De Kuyper, J. 1993. "Classical Studies in Malawi." *Scholia* 2:146–148.

———. 1994. "Letter to Chairman of Chancellor College Computer Committee." Unpublished letter, 7 May 1994. Chancellor College. Zomba.

Deleuze, G., and F. Guattari. 2019. *Anti-Oedipus: : Capitalism and Schizophrenia*. Orig. pub. 1972. London.

Dickinson, E. 1958. *Letters*. Ed. T. H. Johnson. 2 vols. Cambridge, MA.

Djisenu, J. 2007. "Cross-cultural Bonds between Ancient Greece and Africa." In Hardwick and Gillespie 2007:70–85.

Dominik, W., ed. 2002. *Words and Ideas*. Mundelein.

Donge, J. K. van. 1998. "The Mwanza Trial as a Search for a Usable Malawian Past." In Phiri and Ross 1998a: 21–51.

———. 2002. "The Fate of an African 'Chaebol': Malawi's Press Corporation after Democratization." *Journal of Modern African Studies* 40:651–681.

Douglass, F. 2017. *Narrative of the Life of Frederick Douglass, An American Slave. Written by Himself*. Ed., with an introduction by, D. W. Blight. Boston. Orig. pub. 1845.

Dubbey, J. 1994. *Warm Hearts, White Hopes*. Gaborone.

Du Bois, W. E. B. 1903a. *The Souls of Black Folks: Essays and Sketches*. Chicago.

———. 1903b. "The Talented Tenth." *Washington* 1903:33–75.

———. 1933. "The Negro College." *The Crisis* 40:175–77.

———. 2007. *The Autobiography of W. E. B. Du Bois*. Intro. W. Sollors. Oxford. Orig. pub. 1968.

———. 1986. *Writings*. Ed. N. Huggins. New York.

Duff, H. L. 1969. *Nyasaland Under the Colonial Office*. London. Orig. pub. 1903.

Dzimbiri, L. B. 2008. *Industrial Relations in a Developing Society: The Case of Colonial, Independent One-Party and Multiparty Malawi*. Göttingen.

Ellison, R. 1995. *Invisible Man*. New York. Orig. pub. 1952.

Englund, H., ed. 2002a. *A Democracy of Chameleons: Politics and Culture in the New Malawi*. With afterword by J. Mapanje. Blantyre.

———. 2002b. "Introduction. The Culture of Chameleon Politics." In Englund 2002a:11–24.

Everson, S. 1996. *Aristotle: The Politics and the Constitution of Athens*. Cambridge.

Fagles, R. 1982. *Sophocles: The Three Theban Plays*. London.

Fairbanks, E. 2015. "The Birth of Rhodes Must Fall." *The Guardian*, 18 November 2015. https://www.theguardian.com/news/2015/nov/18/why-south-african-students-have-turned-on-their-parents-generation.

Farrell, J. 1999. "Walcott's *Omeros*; The Classical Epic in a Postmodern World." In *Epic Traditions in the Contemporary World: The Poetics of Community*, ed. M. Beissinger, J. Tylus, and S. Wofford, 270–296. Berkeley.

Finnegan, R. 1970. *Oral Literature in Africa*. London.

Forster, P. G. 1994. "Culture, Nationalism, and the Invention of Tradition in Malawi." *Journal of Modern African Studies* 32:477–494.

Frazer, J. G. 1994. *The Golden Bough*. Ed. R. Fraser. Oxford. Orig. pub. 1890.

Freud, S. 1950. *Totem and Taboo*. Trans. J. Strachey. London. Orig. pub. 1913.

———. 2001. *Moses and Monotheism*. Trans. J. Strachey. London. Orig. pub. 1955.

Fugard, A. 1974. *Three Port Elizabeth Plays*. Oxford.

Fugard, A., J. Kani, and W. Ntshona. 1974. *Statements: [three plays]*. London.

Glassdoor. 2021. "University of Johannesburg Lecturer Salaries." https://www.glassdoor.com.au/Salary/University-of-Johannesburg-Lecturer-South-Africa-Salaries-EJI_IE378176.0,26_KO27,35_IL.36,48_IN211.htm.

Goff, B., ed. 2005. *Classics and Colonialism*. London.

———. 2007. "Antigone's Boat: The Colonial and the Postcolonial in *Tègònni: An African Antigone* by Femi Osofisan." In Hardwick and Gillespie 2007:40–53.

———. 2013. *"Your Secret Language": Classics in the British Colonies of West Africa*. London.

Goff, B., and M. Simpson. 2007. *Crossroads in the Black Aegean: Oedipus, Antigone, and Dramas of the African Diaspora*. Oxford.

Goings, K., and E. O'Connor. 2010. "Lessons Learned: The Role of Classics in Black Colleges and Universities." *Journal of Negro Education* 79:521–31.

———. 2011. "Black Athena before Black Athena." In *African Athena: New Agendas*, ed. D. Orrells, G. Bhambra, and T. Roynon, 90–105. Oxford.

Gondwe, E. 2015. "Ngoza na Kasiwa." [Translated into English from Tumbuka.] Trans E. Munthali. Makewana's Daughters. https://makewana.org/2015/06/ngoza-na-kasiwa-english-version/.

Gooding-Williams, R. 2009. *In the Shadow of Du Bois: Afro-Modern Political Thought in America.* Cambridge, MA.

Graziosi, B. 2007. "Homer in Albania: Oral Epic and the Geography of Literature." In Graziosi and Greenwood 2007:120–144.

Graziosi, B., and E. Greenwood, eds. 2007. *Homer in the Twentieth Century: Between World Literature and the Western Canon.* Oxford.

Greenwood, E. 2010. *Afro-Greeks: Dialogues between Anglophone Caribbean Literature and Classics in the Twentieth Century.* Oxford.

———. 2016. "Reception Studies: The Cultural Mobility of Classics." *Daedalus* 145:41–49.

Greenlaw, C. 2011. *The Representation of Monkeys in the Art and Thought of Mediterranean Cultures: A New Perspective on Ancient Primates.* BAR International Series 2192. London.

Guggenheim, D., dir. 2006. *An Inconvenient Truth.* Lawrence Bender Productions and Participant Productions.

Gunning, T. 1990. "Cinema of Attractions: Early Film, Its Spectator and the Avant-Garde." In *Early Cinema: Space, Frame, Narrative*, ed. A. Barker and T. Elsaesser, 56–62. London.

Gwede, W. 2019. "UNIMA Delinking Approved by Parliament." *Nyasa Times*, 16 March 2019. https://www.nyasatimes.com/unima-delinking-approved-by-parliament-poly-will-now-be-malawi-university-of-business-and-applied-sciences/.

———. 2020. "Lilongwe Mahatma Gandhi Statue Unveiled at Indian High Commission." *Nyasa Times*, 2 October 2020. https://www.nyasatimes.com/lilongwe-mahatma-gandhi-statue-unveiled-at-indian-high-commission/.

Hall, E. 2008. *The Return of Ulysses: A Cultural History of Homer's Odyssey.* London.

Hall, E., and H. Stead. 2020. *A People's History of Classics: Class and Greco-Roman Antiquity in Britain and Ireland, 1689 to 1939.* London.

Hamner, R. D., ed. 1993. *Critical Perspectives on Derek Walcott.* Washington, DC.

Hanink, J. 2020. "Not all Classicists." *Times Literary Supplement*, 24 July 2020. https://www.the-tls.co.uk/articles/postclassicisms-postclassicisms-collective-book-review/.

Hanson, V. D., and J. Heath. 1998. *Who Killed Homer?* New York.

Hanson, V. D., J. Heath, and B. S. Thornton. 2001. *Bonfire of the Humanities: Rescuing the Classics in an Impoverished Age.* Wilmington.

Harding, A. 2015. "Cecil Rhodes Monument: A Necessary Anger?" *BBC News*, 11 April 2015. https://www.bbc.com/news/world-africa-32248605.

Hardwick, L. 2004. "Greek Drama and Anti-Colonialism: Decolonizing Classics." In *Dionysus Since 69: Greek Tragedy at the Dawn of the Third Millennium*, ed E. Hall, F. Macintosh, and A. Wrigley, 219–242. Oxford.

Hardwick, L. and C. Gillespie, eds. 2007. *Classics in Post-Colonial Worlds*. Oxford.

Haubold, J. 2013. *Greece and Mesopotamia: Dialogues in Literature*. Cambridge.

Hawkins, T. 2018. "The Veil, the Cave, and the Fire-Bringer." *International Journal of the Classical Tradition* 26:38–53.

Hegel, G. W. F. 1977. *The Phenomenology of Spirit*. Trans. A. V. Miller. London. Orig. pub. 1807.

Higginbotham, E. B. 1993. *Righteous Discontent: The Women's Movement in the Black Baptist Church, 1880-1920*. Cambridge, MA.

Hobsbawm, E. 2007. *Globalisation, Democracy and Terrorism*. London.

Hodder-Williams, R. 1974. "Dr. Banda's Malawi." *Journal of Commonwealth and Comparative Politics* 12:91–114.

Hoffmann, R. J. 1997. "The Department of Classics, Chancellor College: Draft Plan for Restructuring Classics: Towards a Department of Cultural Studies." Unpublished report. Chancellor College. Zomba.

———. 1998. "The Status of Classics within Chancellor College: Memo to Dean of Humanities." Unpublished memo. Chancellor College. Zomba.

Holpuch, A. 2021. "House Votes to Remove Statues of White Supremacists from US Capitol." *The Guardian*, 30 June 2021. https://www.theguardian.com/us-news/2021/jun/30/house-remove-statues-white-supremacists-us-capitol-confederates.

Hughes, A. 1973. "Malawi and South Africa's Co-prosperity Sphere." In *Land-locked Countries of Africa*, ed Z. Červenka, 212–232.Uppsala.

Huizinga, J. 1949. *Homo Ludens: A Study of the Play-Element in Culture*. London.

Indeed. n.d. "Professor Salaries in South Africa." https://za.indeed.com/salaries/professor-Salaries (accessed 9 July 2020).

International Monetary Fund. n.d. "Malawi." https://www.imf.org/en/Countries/MWI (accessed 27 August 2023).

Jenner, E. 2001. "A Short History of the Department of Classics, Chancellor College, University of Malawi." *Scholia* n.s. 10:161–169.

Johnston, S. I. 2008. *Ancient Greek Divination*. Oxford.

Kainja, J. 2019. "Kamuzu Day: Malawi Remembers Ruthless Dictator who Caused a Lot of Pain to Many People." *Nyasa Times*, 14 May 2019. https://www.nyasatimes.com/kamuzu-day-malawi-remembers-ruthless-dictator-who-caused-a-lot-of-pain-to-many-people/.

Kalinga, O. J. M. 2012. *Historical Dictionary of Malawi*. 4th ed. Lanham.

Kambalu, S. 2008. *The Jive Talker: Or, How to Get a British Passport*. London.

Kanyama-Phiri, G. Y. 2016. "Evolution of Bunda College of Agriculture into Lilongwe University of Agriculture and Natural Resources." *RUFORUM Working Document Series* 14:55–75.

Kayambazinthu, E., and F. Moyo. 2002. "Hate Speech in the New Malawi." In Englund 2002a:87–102.

Kerr, D. 1987. "Unmasking the Spirits: Theatre in Malawi." *Drama Review* 31:115–125.

Kerr, D., and J. Mapanje. 2002. "Academic Freedom and the University of Malawi." *African Studies Review* 45:73–91.

Kishindo, P. J. 1998. "Politics of Language in Contemporary Malawi." In Phiri and Ross 1998a:252–280.

Knight, T. 1997. "Classics in Malawi." *Epistula Zimbabweana* 31:6-10.

Lacey, A. T. 1934. *Notes on a Recent Anti-Witchcraft Movement in Nyasaland.* Diploma in Anthropology thesis, University of Cambridge.

Lamba, I. C. 1983. *Primary History. Malawi: An Early History.* Blantyre.

Lambert, M. 2011. *The Classics and South African Identities.* London.

Langworthy, H. 1996. *"Africa for the African": The Life of Joseph Booth.* Zomba.

Lewis, D. L. 1993. *W. E. B. Du Bois—Biography of a Race, 1868-1919.* New York.

Linden, I. 1979. "Chisumphi Theology in the Religion of Central Malawi." In Schoffeleers 1979a:187–188.

Locke, A., ed. 1925. *The New Negro: An Interpretation.* New York.

Luce, J. 1969. *The End of Atlantis: New Light on an Old Legend.* London.

Ludwig, E. 2005. *Napoleon.* Trans. E. Paul and C. Paul. London.

Lwanda, J. L. 1993. *Kamuzu Banda of Malawi: A Study in Promise, Power, and Paralysis. Malawi under Dr Banda 1961 to 1993.* Glasgow.

———. 2002. "Tikutha: The Political Culture of the HIV/AIDS Epidemic in Malawi." In Englund 2002a:151–165.

Makewana's Daughters. n.d. "Home." https://makewana.org/ (accessed 20 August 2020).

Makondesa, P. 2006. *The Church History of Providence Industrial Mission.* Zomba.

Malamud, M. 2016. *African Americans and the Classics: Antiquity, Abolition and Activism.* London.

Malawi Department of Economic Planning and Development. 1988. *Statement of Development Policies, 1987-1996 (DevPol II).* Zomba.

Malawi Historic Pictures. 2017. "Yatuta Chisiza Weapons." https://www.facebook.com/Malawi-historic-pictures-223413367741871 (accessed 27 February 2020).

"Malawi Parliament Approves to Revert to Original Flag." *Nyasa Times*, 28 May 2012. https://www.nyasatimes.com/malawi-parliament-approves-to-revert-to-original-flag/.

Mandela, N. 1994. *Long Walk to Freedom.* London.

Mandini, A. 2017. "Dr. Banda Speech at Dinner Hosted in his Honor by the Queen at Buckingham Palace." Video, 6:06. https://www.youtube.com/watch?v=ZR6d4AE3FUc.

Mapanje, J. 1993. *The Chattering Wagtails of Mikuyu Prison.* Oxford.

———. 2002. "Afterword: The Orality of Dictatorship. In Defence of My Country." In Englund 2002a:178–87.

———. 2011. *And the Crocodiles Are Hungry at Night.* Banbury.

Marcellus, H. de. 1995. "Head of Classics Memo to University Registrar." Unpublished document, dated 29 March 1995. Chancellor College. Zomba.

Marx, K., and F. Engels. 2012. *The Communist Manifesto.* Ed. J. C. Isaac. New Haven. Orig. pub. London, 1848.

Mauss, M. 2001. *A General Theory of Magic.* Trans. R. Brain. London. Orig. pub. 1972.

Mbembe, A. 2001. *On the Postcolony.* Berkeley.

Mbiti, J. S. 1975. *Introduction to African Religion.* London.

McConnell, J. 2013. *Black Odysseys. The Homeric Odyssey in the African Diaspora since 1939.* Oxford.

McCracken, J. 1977. *Politics and Christianity in Malawi, 1875-1940: The Impact of the Livingstonia Mission in the Northern Province.* Zomba. Repr. 2008.

———. 2012. *A History of Malawi (1859-1966).* Woodbridge, UK.

———, ed. 2015. *Voices from the Chilembwe Rising.* Oxford.

———. 2017. "Hastings Kamuzu Banda: The Edinburgh Years." *Society of Malawi Journal* 70:1–18.

McDowell, D. E., and A. Rampersad, eds. 1989. *Slavery and Literary Imagination.* Selected Papers from the English Institute, New Series 13. Baltimore.

McKechnie, P. 1992. "Kamuzu Academy, Mtunthama, Malawi." *Scholia* n.s. 1:142–143.

Meiggs, R. 1982. "Robert Maxwell Ogilvie." *Proceedings of the British Academy* 68:627–636.

Meineck, P., trans. 1973. *Aeschylus. Oresteia.* Indianapolis. Repr. 1998.

Mgawi, K. J. 2005. *Tracing the Footsteps of Dr. Hastings Kamuzu Banda.* Blantyre.

Mkamanga, E. 2000. *Suffering in Silence: Malawi Women's 30-Year Dance with Dr. Banda.* Glasgow.

Mlanjira, D. 2019. "Malawi: Fresh Campaign to Stop Gandhi Statue From Being Erected in Malawi—Vigil at India Embassy." *Nyasa Times*, 12 October 2019. https://allafrica.com/stories/201910120013.html.

Morris, B. 2000. *Animals and Ancestors: An Ethnography.* New York.

Morrow, S., and J. McCracken. 2012. "Two Previously Unknown Letters from Hastings Kamuzu Banda, Written from Edinburgh, 1938, Archived at the University of Cape Town." *History in Africa* 39:337–354.

Moses, W. J. 2008. "Africa and Pan-Africanism in the Thought of Du Bois." In *Cambridge Companion to W. E. B. Du Bois*, ed. S. Zamir, 117-130. Cambridge.

Mtegha, M. 1995. *Independent Commission of Inquiry into the 1983 Mwanza Incident: Chaired by Mr. Justice Michael Mtegha, Appointed May 1994 & Reported 4 January 1995*. Blantyre.

Muluzi, B. 1999. *Democracy with a Price: The History of Malawi since 1900*. Blantyre and Oxford.

Munger, E. S. 1983. *Touched by Africa*. Pasadena.

Mwakasungura, K., and D. Miller. 2016. *Malawi's Lost Years*. Mzuzu.

Mwase, G. S. 1967. *Strike a Blow and Die*. Ed. and intro. R. I. Rotberg. Cambridge, MA.

Namangale, F. 2021. "Court against Gandhi Statue." *The Nation*, 2 May 2021. https://www.mwnation.com/court-against-gandhi-statue/.

Nazombe, A. 1987. "Chimombo's Use of the M'bona Myth in The Rainmaker." *Journal of Humanities* 1:37–53.

NewsDay. 2019. "Varsity Employees Get Salary Hike." *NewsDay*, 5 September 2019. https://www.newsday.co.zw/2019/09/varsity-employees-get-salary-hike.

Nisbet, R. 2007. "Horace: Life and Chronology." In *Cambridge Companion to Horace*, ed. S. Harrison, 7–21. Cambridge.

Nthenda, L. 2020. "Once upon a Time in 1967: University of Malawi in a Crisis." https://historyofmalawi.com/?p=1712. (Accessed 28 May 2020).

Nyamilandu, S. 1999. *Using the Communicative Approach in Latin Reading at Junior Certificate Level in Malawi*. MA thesis, University of Malawi.

———. 2015. *Myth and the Treatment of Non-Human Animals in Classical and African Cultures: A Comparative Study*. MA (MLC) diss., University of South Africa.

———. 2016. *Contextualising Classics Teaching in Malawi: A Comparative Study*. PhD diss., University of St. Andrews.

Ogilvie, R. M. 1964. *Latin and Greek: A History of the Influence of the Classics on English Life from 1600 to 1918*. Hamden, CT.

———. 1979. "Classical Studies in Malawi." Unpublished report. University of St. Andrews, Department of Humanities. St. Andrews.

Olney, J. 1984. "'I Was Born': Slave Narratives, Their Status as Autobiography and as Literature." *Callaloo* 20:46–73.

———. 1989. "The Founding Fathers—Frederick Douglass and Booker T. Washington." In McDowell and Rampersad 1989:1–24.

Ó Máille, P. 1999. *Living Dangerously: A Memoir of Political Change in Malawi*. Glasgow.

Oriel College. 2020. "Statement from the Governing Body of Oriel College." University of Oxford. https://www.oriel.ox.ac.uk/about-college/news-events/news/statement-governing-body-oriel-college.

Orrells, D., G. Bhambra, and T. Roynon, eds. 2011. *African Athena: New Agendas.* Oxford.

Orwell, G. 1949. *Nineteen Eighty-Four.* New York.

Osborne, C. 2007. *Dumb Beasts and Dead Philosophers: Humanity and the Humane in Ancient Philosophy and Literature.* Oxford.

Osofisan, F. 1994. *Tègònni, an African Antigone.* Ibadan.

———. 1999. "Theater and the Rites of 'Post-Negritude' Remembering." *Research in African Literatures* 30:1–11.

Parke, H. W. and D. E. W. Wormell. 1956. *A History of the Delphic Oracle.* Oxford.

Parker, G., ed. 2017. *South Africa, Greece, Rome: Classical Confrontations.* Cambridge.

Pasolini, P. P., dir. 1965. *Sopralluoghi in Palestina per il vangelo secondo Matteo.* [Location hunting in Palestine.] Arco Film.

———, dir. 1968. *Appunti per un film sull'India.* [Notes for a film on India.] RAI Radiotelevisione Italiana.

———, dir. 1970. *Appunti per un'Orestiade Africana.* [Notes for an African Oresteia.] IDI Cinematografica, I Film Dell'Orso, RAI Radiotelevisione Italiana.

———, dir. 1971. *Le muri di Sana'a.* [The Walls of Sana'a.] Rosima Anstalt.

Peretti, L., and K. T. Raizen, eds. 2018. *Pier Paolo Pasolini, Framed and Unframed: A Thinker for the Twenty-First Century.* London.

Pfaller, R. 2017. *Interpassivity: The Aesthetics of Delegated Enjoyment.* Edinburgh.

Phillips, H. 1998. *From Obscurity to Bright Dawn: How Nyasaland became Malawi: An Insider's Account.* London.

Phiri, D. D. 1982. *From Nguni to Ngoni: A History of the Ngoni Exodus from Zululand and Swaziland to Malawi, Tanzania and Zambia.* Lilongwe.

———. 2004. *History of Malawi. From Earliest Times to the Year 1915.* Blantyre.

Phiri, I. A. 1997. *Women, Presbyterianism and Patriarchy: Religious Experience of Chewa Women in Central Malawi.* Zomba.

Phiri, K. M. 1982. "Afro-American Influence in Colonial Malawi, 1891–1945; A Case Study of the Interaction between Africa and Africans of the Diaspora." In *Global Dimensions of the African Diaspora,* ed. J. E. Harris, 250–267. Washington, DC.

———. 1998. "Dr Banda's Cultural Legacy and its Implications for a Democratic Malawi." In Phiri and Ross 1998a:149–167.

Phiri, K.M., and K. R. Ross, eds. 1998a. *Democratization in Malawi: A Stocktaking.* Blantyre.

———.1998b. "Introduction: From Totalitarianism to Democracy in Malawi." In Phiri and Ross 1998a:9–16.

Popper, K. 2005. *The Open Society and Its Enemies. Volume One: The Spell of Plato.* London. Orig. pub. 1945.

Postclassicisms Collective. 2019. *Postclassicisms.* Chicago.

Potts, D. 1985. "Capital Relocation in Africa: The Case of Lilongwe in Malawi." *Geographical Journal* 151:182–196.

Power, J. 2010. *Political Culture and Nationalism in Malawi. Building Kwacha.* Rochester.

Pryor, F. L. 1990. *The Political Economy of Poverty, Equity, and Growth: Malawi and Madagascar.* A World Bank Comparative Study. Oxford.

Puhvel, J. 1987. *Comparative Mythology.* Baltimore.

Ralston, R. D. 1973. "American Episodes in the Making of an African Leader: A Case Study of Alfred B. Xuma (1893–1962)." *International Journal of African Historical Studies* 6:72–93.

Ramsby, T. 2018. "Applying the New Standards for Classical Language Learning to Latin-Teacher Education." *Teaching Classical Languages* 9:118–130.

Rangeley, W. 1952. "Two Nyasaland Rain Shrines." *Nyasaland Journal* 5:31–50.

———. 1953. "Mbona—The Rain Maker." *Nyasaland Journal* 6:8–27.

Rankine, P. D. 2006. *Ulysses in Black: Ralph Ellison, Classicism, and African American Literature.* Madison.

Read, F. E. 1967. *Malawi: Land of Promise.* Blantyre.

Reinhold, M. 1984. *Classica Americana: The Greek and Roman Heritage in the United States.* Detroit.

"Response of the Faculty of Humanities Addressed to Chairman of College Restructuring Committee." 2008. Unpublished paper, 15 December 2008. Chancellor College. Zomba.

Richardson, M. 1998. *George Bataille: Essential Writings.* London.

Ritchie, F. 1909. *First Steps in Latin*, ed. F. C. Staples. New York.

———. 1924. *Second Steps in Latin*, rev. John C. Green, Jr. New York.

Ronnick, M. V. 2004. "Twelve Black Classicists." *Arion* 11:85–102.

Roscoe, A. 2008. *The Columbia Guide to Central African Literature in English.* New York.

Ross, K. R. 2004. "'Worrisome Trends': The Voice of the Churches in Malawi's Third Term Debate." *African Affairs* 103:91–107.

Ross, K. R., and K. Fiedler. 2020. *A Malawi Church History 1860-2020.* Mzuzu.

Rotimi, O. 1971. *The Gods Are Not to Blame.* London.

Rudd, N. 2004. *Horace: Odes and Epodes.* London.

Rushforth, G. McN. 1923. "Architecture and Art." In Bailey 1923:385–428.

Russell, B. 1930. *The Conquest of Happiness.* New York.

Russell, C. A. 2010. *Reckoning with a Violent and Lawless Past: A Study of Race, Violence and Reconciliation in Tennessee.* PhD diss., Vanderbilt University.

Sabin, F. 1931. *The Relation of Latin to Everyday Life.* Chicago.

Salaryexplorer. 2021. "Best Paying Jobs in Tanzania 2020." http://www.salaryexplorer.com/best-paying-jobs.php?loc=214&loctype=1 (Accessed 27 August 2021).

Salomone, R. 2019. "Court Moves beyond the Past in Favouring English." *University World News*, 19 October 2019. https://www.universityworldnews.com/post.php?story=20191017160303180.

Sasnett, M., and I. Sepmeyer. 1967. *Educational Systems of Africa: Interpretations for Use in the Evaluation of Academic Credentials.* Berkeley.

Schoffeleers, J. M., ed. 1979a. *Guardians of the Land.* Gweru.

———. 1979b. "The Chisumphi and Mbona Cults in Malawi: A Comparative History." In Schoffeleers 1979a:146–186.

———. 1980. "The Story of Mbona the Martyr." In *Man, Meaning and History: Essays in Honour of H. G. Schulte Nordholt*, ed. R. Schefold, J. W. Schoorl, and J. Tennekes, 246–267. The Hague.

———. 1999. *In Search of Truth and Justice: Confrontation Between Church and the State in Malawi 1960–1994.* Zomba.

Schoffeleers J. M., and A. A. Roscoe. 1985. *Land of Fire. Oral Literature from Malawi.* Limbe.

Scotland-Malawi Partnership. 2021. "Success! Prof. Kambalu's John Chilembwe Statue to be Placed in Trafalgar Square." News, 5 July 2021. https://www.scotland-malawipartnership.org/news/success-prof-kambalus-john-chilembwe-statue-to-be-placed-in-trafalgar-square.

Segal, R. A. 1987a. *Joseph Campbell: An Introduction.* New York.

———. 1987b. "In Defense of the Comparative Method." *Numen* 48:339–373.

Sevenzo, F. 2000. "Bedtime for Banda." *Transition* 85:4–29.

Shepperson, G. 1998. "Memories of Dr. Banda." *Society of Malawi Journal* 51:74–84.

Shepperson, G., and T. Price. 2000. *Independent African: John Chilembwe and the Nyasaland Rising of 1915.* Zomba. Orig. pub. 1958.

Short, P. 1974. *Banda.* London.

Shumba, M. 1985. "Memo from Dean of Humanities to Vice-Chancellor." Unpublished document. Chancellor College. Zomba.

Simpson, M. 2007. "The Curse of the Canon: Ola Rotimi's *The Gods are Not to Blame*." In Hardwick and Gillespie 2007:86–101.

Siti, W., and F. Zabagli, eds. 2001. *Pier Paolo Pasolini: Per il cinema.* Vol. 1. Milan.

Smith, B. 2001. "Forbidden Images: Rock Paintings and the Nyau Secret Society of Central Malawi and Eastern Zambia." *African Archaeological Review* 18:187–212.

———. 2005. "Makewana." In *Encyclopedia of Religion and Nature*, ed. B. R. Taylor, 1028–1030. London.

Smuts, F. 1963. "A Wider Range of Latin Reading." In *Ex Africa: A Sequel to the Conference on the Teaching of Latin Held at the University College, Salisbury, August, 1962*, ed. M. E. Toubkin and C. R. Whittaker, 74–82. Salisbury.

Snowden, F. M., Jr. 1997. "Misconceptions about African Blacks in the Ancient Mediterranean World: Specialists and Afrocentrists." *Arion* 4: 28–50.

Sorkin, A., exec. prod. 1999-2006. *The West Wing*. 7 seasons, 156 episodes. NBC.

Southern Poverty Law Center. 2019. "Whose Heritage? Public Symbols of the Confederacy." https://www.splcenter.org/20190201/whose-heritage-public-symbols-confederacy.

———. 2021. "SPLC Reports over 160 Confederate Symbols Removed in 2020." https://www.splcenter.org/presscenter/splc-reports-over-160-confederate-symbols-removed-2020.

Soyinka, W. 1973. *The Bacchae of Euripides: A Communion Rite*. London.

Speight, A. 2021. "Friedrich Schlegel." In *Stanford Encyclopedia of* Philosophy, ed. E. N. Zalta. https://plato.stanford.edu/archives/spr2021/entries/schlegel/ (Accessed 1 July 2021).

Stepto, R. B. 1991. *From Behind the Veil: A Study of Afro-American Narrative*. 2nd ed. Urbana.

Stonehouse, J. 1960. *Prohibited Immigrant*. London.

Stroh, W. 1988. "The Importance of Latin Studies for the Present Age: A Lecture." Unpublished pamphlet, dated February 1988. Zomba.

Sundu, Y. 2021. "Chilembwe wins Trafalgar Square Space." *The Nation*, 2 July 2021. https://www.mwnation.com/chilembwe-wins-trafalgar-square-space/.

Swidler, A., and S. Cotts Watkins. 2017. *A Fraught Embrace: The Romance and Reality of AIDS Altruism in Africa*. Princeton.

Thomson, G., ed. and trans. 1938. *The Oresteia of Aeschylus*. 2 vols. Cambridge.

———. 1941. *Aeschylus and Athens: A Study in the Social Origins of Drama*. London.

———. 1949. *Eschilo e Atene*. Turin.

Toner, J. 2002. *Rethinking Roman History*. Cambridge.

Trading Economics. n.d. "Zimbabwean RTGS Dollar." https://tradingeconomics.com/zimbabwe/currency (accessed 27 August 2021).

Trading Economics. n.d. "Malawi GDP per capita." https://tradingeconomics.com/malawi/gdp-per-capita (accessed 27 August 2021).

Tratner, M. 2001. *Deficits and Desires: Economics and Sexuality in Twentieth Century Literature*. Stanford.

UNESCO. n.d. "Gule Wamkulu." Intangible Cultural Heritage. https://ich.unesco.org/en/RL/gule-wamkulu-00142.

United Kingdom Government. 1921. "Report of the Commission to Inquire into the Position of Classics in the Educational System of the United Kingdom." London.

University of Malawi. 2017. "University of Malawi: A Brief History." http://www. unima.mw/about/about-unima-history.

Usher, M. D. 2014. "An African Oresteia: Field Notes on Pasolini's Appunti per un' Orestiade Africana." *Arion* 22:111–149.

Vandiver, E. 2010. *Stand in the Trench, Achilles: Classical Receptions in British Poetry of the Great War*. Oxford.

Vaughan, M. 2000. "Reported Speech and Other Kinds of Testimony." *Journal of Historical Sociology* 13:237–263.

Vries, H. de. 2009. "Malawi." http://www.hubert-herald.nl/Malawi.htm.

Waegeman, M. 1987. *Amulet and Alphabet: Magical Amulets in the First Book of Cyranides*. Amsterdam.

Walcott, D. 1997. *The Bounty*. London.

Wark, M. 2011. *The Beach beneath the Street: The Everyday and the Glorious Times of the Situationists International*. London.

Washington, B. T., ed. 1903. *The Negro Problem: A Series of Articles by Representative American Negroes of To-day. Contributions by Booker T. Washington, W. E. Burghardt Du Bois, Paul Laurence Dunbar, Charles W. Chesnutt, and Others*. New York.

———. 2010. *Up from Slavery*. Intro. I. Reed, afterword R. J. Norrell. New York. Orig. pub. 1901.

West, M. L. 1997. *The East Face of Helicon; West Asiatic Elements in Greek Poetry and Myth*. Oxford.

———. 2007. *Indo-European Poetry and Myth*. Oxford.

Wetmore, K. J. 2002. *The Athenian Sun in an African Sky: Modern African Adaptations of Classical Greek Tragedy*. Jefferson, NC.

White, L. 2001. "'My Dear Osagyefo': Letters between Dr. Banda and Dr. Nkrumah." *Times Literary Supplement*, 17 August 2001, 12–13.

Wikipedia. n.d. "Hastings Banda." https://en.wikipedia.org/wiki/Hastings_Banda#The_Mwanza_Four_incident (accessed 4 April 2023).

Wikipedia. n.d. "Kanyama Chiume." https://en.wikipedia.org/wiki/Kanyama_Chiume (accessed 4 April 2023).

Wikipedia. n.d. "Orton Chirwa." https://en.wikipedia.org/wiki/Orton_Chirwa (accessed 4 April 2023).

World Bank. 2021a. "World Bank Country and Lending Groups." Data. https://datahelpdesk.worldbank.org/knowledgebase/articles/906519-world-bank-country-and-lending-groups (accessed 27 August 2021).

World Bank. 2021b. "GDP per capita (current US$)–Malawi." Data. https://data.worldbank.org/indicator/NY.GDP.PCAP.CD?locations=MW (accessed 27 August 2021).

XE currency converter. 2021. https://www.xe.com/currencyconverter/convert /?Amount=1&From=USD&To=ZWD (accessed 27 August 2021).

Young, R. 2013. "The Postcolonial Comparative." *PMLA/Publications of the Modern Language Association of America* 128:683–689.

Younge, G. 2021. "Why Every Single Statue Should Come Down." *The Guardian*, 1 June 2021. https://www.theguardian.com/artanddesign/2021/jun/01/ gary-younge-why-every-single-statue-should-come-down-rhodes-colston.

Žižek, S. 2012. *Organs without Bodies*. London.

———. 1993. *Tarrying with the Negative: Kant, Hegel, and the Critique of Ideology*. Durham.

———. 1996. *The Indivisible Remainder: On Schelling and Related Matters*. London.

———. 1999. *The Ticklish Subject: The Absent Centre of Political Ontology*. London.

———. 2003. *The Puppet and the Dwarf: The Perverse Core of Christianity*. Cambridge, MA.

———. 2008. *For They Know Not What They Do: Enjoyment as Political Factor*. London. Orig. pub. 1991.

———. 2016. *Disparities*. London.

Zupančič, A. 1917. *What is Sex?* Cambridge, MA.

Index of Names and Places

Index of Names and Places

Younge, Gary, 5
Zambia, 62, 78–79, 219–220
"Zambia" (Masauko Chipembere's
      camp in Fort Johnston District),
      77, 91
Zomba, Malawi, 9–10, 13–15, 19,
      21, 23, 25, 28, 33–34, 52, 77,
      99, 113, 131, 153, 172, 177–178,
      200–201, 204, 206, 208, 215, 220,
      222, 227–228, 230, 235, 238–239,
      241–242, 244, 246, 249, 251, 253;
      Zomba Golf Course, 246; Zomba
      Gymkhana Club, 15; Zomba
      Mountain, 116, 177–178, 209, 253;
      Zomba Zero, 228

282